IMAGE
OF THE
BODY

IMAGE
OF THE
BODY

Aspects of the Nude

MICHAEL GILL

DOUBLEDAY

New York London Toronto Sydney Auckland

PUBLISHED BY DOUBLEDAY

a division of Bantam Doubleday Dell Publishing Group, Inc.
666 Fifth Avenue, New York, New York 10103

DOUBLEDAY and the portrayal of an anchor
with a dolphin are trademarks of Doubleday,
a division of Bantam Doubleday Dell Publishing Group, Inc.

Library of Congress Cataloging-in-Publication Data

Gill, Michael.
Image of the body : aspects of the nude / Michael Gill.—1st ed.
p. cm.
Bibliography: p.

1. Nude in art. 2. Feminine beauty (Aesthetics) 3. Art and society. I. Title.
N7573.G5 1989
704.9'421—dc19 88-26713

ISBN 0-385-26072-5

Printed in the United States of America
November 1989

FIRST EDITION

*To the memory of K
with love and gratitude*

CONTENTS

FOREWORD

My intention in this book is to describe some of the roles the human image has been given since its first appearance, scratched and painted on the walls of caves over twenty thousand years ago. Such a vast subject could only be encompassed in the modest confines of a few hundred pages by being treated selectively. So each chapter takes a different theme, though from the second onward they follow a roughly chronological order.

Nowadays the general public are most aware of the nude as a female pin-up. Bearing that in mind, I have traced in the opening chapter the concept of physical beauty to its origins with the ancient Greeks. I have also in the first and last chapters dealt more directly through my own observation and experience with the act of creativity itself; that mysterious subjective process without which there would be no image of the body whose evolution we can follow through human history.

The second chapter, "Energy and Fertility," returns us to that history and to the earliest representations that man made of his kind. "Men Like Gods" describes how in the first great civilization of Egypt the human image replaced the animal as the object of prime interest and worship; with this fundamental change came new responsibilities and a shift in status between male and female. As society grew more complex it was able to devote more time to the pursuit of enjoyment; "The Perfection of Pleasure" looks at the sensuous art of Greece, India, and Japan and traces its relationship to the ritual performances of religion and the theater.

The suffering body was given a new meaning in Christian iconography. The Church grew despite the persecution of a grossly material and dissolute society, that of Imperial Rome; this fiery baptism affected the Western attitude to the human image for a thousand years. The Renaissance brought a triumphant return of physical beauty to painting and sculpture, and an increased recognition of creative skills gave the artist additional stature and influence—though at a price.

While the conventions established in the Renaissance dominated Western art for several centuries, some artists of genius were able to create unique perceptions that added to our comprehension of the human condition. Then during the Romantic Movement, in the early nineteenth century, the body was made a vehicle for extreme feeling and social protest. This brought the artist into conflict with accepted values; was he expressing true emotions or simply seeking to scandalize polite society: was it "Pathos or Pornography?"? In the first half of the twentieth century the split between individual freedom and state authority was accentuated. The image of the body reflected the convulsions of a violent time, as artists dismantled all the carefully wrought traditions of four hundred years.

A world undergoing ever-more rapid change produces an art where the body is seen under many metamorphoses. Just as humanity has weathered world wars and social upheaval, so the human image has survived the assault of abstract art and veering fashions and has blossomed into some strange new forms.

In following this wayward progress I have always chosen my route by looking first at the visual evidence. So I have written almost entirely about things I have personally seen, images that have excited and moved me, and that seem to me symptomatic of major shifts in human understanding and sensibility. I have selected those examples that seem decisive in establishing a style, or as having unique significance in recording the emergence of a particular feeling or attitude. Thus there are many scenes of war that include naked men, from Roman sarcophagi to the vast neoclassical canvases of revolutionary France at the beginning of the nineteenth century. But I have chosen only one: the earliest battle of which we have written records from both sides. In its vainglorious emphasis on heroic action, its welter of dying enemies and misrepresentation of the actual events, the huge stone relief of the battle of Kadesh in 1294 B.C. can stand for all man's later efforts to make propaganda out of the muddled slaughter of war.

This means that there are some masterpieces and a host of secondary works which are not here. Especially is this true of the female nude in the last three hundred years. She has been a constant theme and inspiration for generations of artists, but these decorative hordes of reclining bodies do not bring a new concept to humanity's contemplation of itself, once the subject had been established in the sixteenth century, until we reach the ironic questioning of the whole genre in Manet's *Olympia* in the mid-nineteenth century.

Equally, though my brief is to look at the various manifestations of the naked body, I have interpreted this widely and included parts of the body and their symbolic representation and occasionally partially clothed or draped figures where it suited my purpose. The earliest image in the book is only a fragment: the hand of the cave painter imprinted deep underground in the sacred mountain of El Castillo in northern Spain. This gesture, which seems both a signature and a greeting, has been repeated on the engraved plaque on the *Pioneer 10* spacecraft, the first to travel out of our solar system.

Like the spaceship, man is traveling he knows not where at ever-accelerating speed. Our belief in the outcome of the human journey will be influenced by the worth we put on man's past achievements. That includes our evaluation of the images that he has made of himself and his kind. Fragments shored up against the ravages of time, they speak to us still with the reassuring voice of that humanity that we sense in the hand of the cave painter, stretched out to us across the centuries.

IMAGE
OF THE
BODY

1

IDEAL BEAUTY

"God created man in his *own* image, in the image of God created he him; male and female created he them. And God blessed them, and God said unto them, Be fruitful, and multiply, and replenish the earth, and subdue it . . . And they were both naked, the man and his wife, and were not ashamed."[1]

Jew and Christian must rejoice that they are cast in the form of the creator of the universe. They are not alone in believing their bodies to be the yardstick of perfection. For over two thousand years European artists have portrayed naked men and women as the epitome of beauty, power, and energy. The nude was taken as the vehicle for expressing the most profound emotions: love, sorrow, anger, ecstasy. The study of the naked figure, with all its intricacies, was long considered essential for an artist's training. It is still an important discipline at most art schools. The body has been supposed the measure of ideal form. Its proportions are said to be the basis of classical architecture.

Increased awareness of other cultures has led us to question the validity of these assumptions. Yet we continue to talk as though a standard of ideal proportion exists. We speak of someone's neck being too short or his arms too long. We think we can recognize beauty when we see it. We expect others to agree with our judgments. Generally they do. Hence the wide acclaim for a Garbo or a Princess Diana. Is this more than fashion? Is there such a thing as an enduring appreciation of certain proportions built into the human psyche?

Such considerations are far from academic. They presented themselves acutely in considering the very first image of this book—the

1. Mapplethorpe, Lisa Lyon, *1983.*

cover. What picture of the body should stand representative for all those portrayed within? Should it be the first: the hand of the cave painter [20]? Or the last: the semi-abstract energy of Matisse's cutout [301]? Should it be male or female or both? Sifting through the alternatives led to the conclusion that any choice from the past would carry with it associations that could be misleading. Thus a reproduction of a Michelangelo or a Rodin would suggest a study of the body in traditional Western terms. Equally, a reproduction from another culture would connote ethnic or sociological preoccupations that are only part of the story.

As the book was being written in the 1980s, it had to be relevant to contemporary readers, which suggested it should be a modern work, in a medium uniquely accessible to the modern age: photography. Photography is the way we all record those shapes that please us; our lovers, our children. The photographic pin-up is the convention through which most people, who never go to an art gallery, are acquainted with representations of the nude. Ephemeral and often vulgar, it is the continuing manifestation of art's long preoccupation with the female form. As such it has been viewed with antagonism—not without cause— by the women's movement.

I did not want a pin-up on the cover, nor a montage of family snaps. It had to be an image that connected various themes, as I hoped the book would do. Perhaps it should be a commissioned photograph? By involving a distinguished photographer and observing him at work, I might gain insight into some of the contemporary problems of portraying the body. Perhaps I should also learn more of the mysterious process of creativity itself. And grapple more closely with the question of ideal beauty. So it proved. I was also to be confronted with the unexpected: the continuing power of the naked form; its ability to arouse fear and discomfort and other emotions that many would prefer to suppress.

"I suppose the men couldn't have cocks," said Robert Mapplethorpe.

His New York studio was large and bare, with shiny wooden floor and a wall of windows blinded against the clamor of Twenty-third Street below. Lamps of different circumferences were set into the ceiling in irregular blisters. There was one modern painting, several small bronzes of pierrots or satyrs in theatrical poses, and between, an island fenced against space, four black leather settees facing each other. Mapplethorpe was also in black: black shirt, black jacket; dark, moody face. Over his shoulder peered a black and white photograph of a naked man leaning across a fence. The top bar obscured his genitals.

"He might be one to do it," said Mapplethorpe. "His body's perfect. But the others, all naked—they must have great rapport. Perhaps they should be dancers."

I had suggested that the cover should show three figures. My argument was as follows: I did not want a book about the body in general to have one gender only represented on the cover. Nor did it seem right to have one man, one woman. That would suggest too specifically a sexual relationship. A trio implied movement, unresolved tensions, the pursuit of contrapuntal harmonies. Less complete than a couple, three figures could be linked in a circle of complementary gestures. A circle gave no point of rest, no suggested solution.

One of the earliest representations of the human body showed three figures: a goddess supported by two leopards [57]. Dating from approximately 6000 B.C., it was found in the excavations of Çatal Hüyük in Anatolia: a powerful image from the beginnings of urban life. I had never seen the original, but even in photographs I was drawn to the pose, not only because of its age and authority, but because of the central position it gave to the female. I began to make tentative doodles, replacing the leopards with male figures. One of my problems was that, while still by no means certain about the composition, I had to enlist the interest of the photographer Robert Mapplethorpe, whom I hoped was going to take it.

He glanced over my sketches critically, and asked a crucial question: "Must they have heads?" Our faces reveal our individuality. The body alone would better suggest the universality of the theme. In Mapple-thorpe's studio was a large photograph he had taken of the body-builder Lisa Lyon [1]. The picture cut her off at the neck, leaving her splendid weight-lifter's body as noble and confident as a Greek marble goddess of victory. This was triumphant woman in general without the identification of Lyon's toughly independent twentieth-century face [2]. But if we were to follow the same convention of cropping the heads in our photograph, it followed that the models would all be at the same level. I would have to abandon my original idea of a pyramidal group.

I remembered that there was a famous sculpture of three female figures without heads. Returning to my home in London, I found a reproduction of it [3]. *The Three Graces* had the confident amplitude of late Hellenistic-early Roman times, their hips swaying to an antique melody. Kenneth Clark had suggested in his book *The Nude* that their complicated pose might be originally derived from a row of dancers in a classical frieze. He thought them one of the last beautiful inventions of antique art, but he admitted their origin was obscure. Such a compelling image seemed worth more investigation.

In classical and Renaissance art the Graces were beautiful naked girls. Seneca explained they were always three and interlaced their hands because of the triple rhythm of generosity, which consists of giving (on one side), accepting (on the other), and returning (on the

2. Mapplethorpe, Lisa Lyon, *1983.*

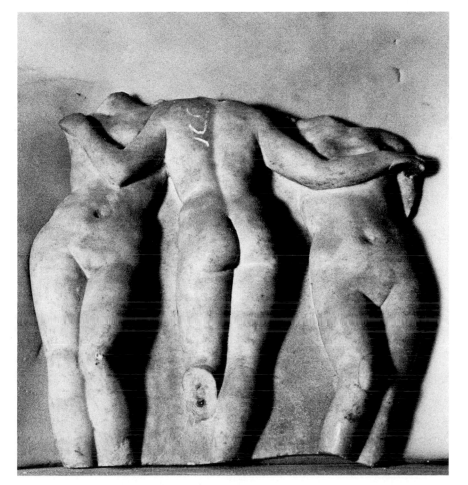

3. Graeco-Roman, The Three Graces, *ca. first century.*

third). This reminded me of the complex pattern of gift-giving in the South Seas where each year the young men sail around the islands. In their outrigger canoes they carry the splendid green stone ax blades which are their culture's most treasured possession. Making such a gift bestows honor on the giver, but custom ensures that similar gifts will reach his community. The ax blades have only a conventional value like a gold bar, but their true worth is to cement this scattered society in a ritual that launches the young out of their island isolation.

The gift-carriers are always men. Strangely enough, the Renaissance glosses on the meaning of the Graces usually referred to *men* acting graciously and bountifully though the illustration was of the three goddesses. Perhaps by participating in the act of generosity, Homeric man took on some of the tender virtues of gracious woman, and so could be appropriately signified by the feminine Graces.

I was pleased to find this ancient rationale for choosing three figures to express my theme. It seemed appropriate that they should be gift-bringers. But I did not think it right for my book that they should all be women.

I recalled a Rodin sculpture that has three men whose hands come together in a unifying gesture, possibly representing comradeship. Then I remembered they are pointing the way down into *The Gates of Hell* [4]. Originally their hands had held a band on which was engraved Dante's doom-filled words: *"Lasciate ogni speranza, voi ch'entrate!"* (Abandon hope, all ye who enter here!) It was some consolation to find that the man on the left had been first sculpted by Rodin as a single figure called successively, Primeval Man, then Creation, then Adam. He was in fact modeled from a fairground strongman, named Cailloux, who could lift one hundred kilos with his jaws. This almost seemed a sign, as this was exactly the sort of person whose modern equivalent in New York Robert Mapplethorpe would be likely to photograph. I also felt unreasonably reassured by the figure having been called Creation. It further convinced me that I was right to have male figures as well as female in the triad. Working toward something you only half understand, you are likely to grasp at such irrational straws.

My reasoning may seem to proceed in an excessively tentative and haphazard manner but in my experience that is how acts of creation often evolve. A rational examination of the alternatives rapidly gives way to flashes of intuition, often drawing on the work of past artists.

Experience makes one either accept or reject these insights. Professionalism relates not to the insights but to the depth of previous practice from which one can judge their worth.

The photograph could not follow the same simple contrapuntal pattern of the traditional female Graces. The compositional requirements of the camera demanded that the figures should be much closer together than they would be in life. The standard lens greatly accentuates the recessive distance between objects. The same thing occurs with that other two-dimensional image, the moving picture. Two people talking have to be practically in each other's laps not to appear a vast gulf apart.

"They must feel at ease with each other," Mapplethorpe repeated.

4. *Rodin,* The Three Shades, *1881.*

At this second meeting, we were to choose the models. Facing us was a line of large card-mounted photographs propped against the wall. Each of a separate naked figure, men and women, they looked uncomfortably as if lined up for execution. Nowadays nakedness always implies inspection. If the stripping is for one other person, it invests us with power, the power of sex. If it is in front of many, it makes us the victim. Police regimes often demand that the prisoner be naked when questioned. Clothes are an assumption of status, in which we can rest passively. They assert our authority without the flesh within needing to flicker a muscle. Deprived of clothes, the body is waiting for action: for love or torment, for ritual purification or physical prowess. Only in art can the body be frozen: an end in itself.

"What do you think of her?" asked Mapplethorpe. "She's half-Chinese, but that wouldn't matter. We shan't be seeing her face."

Her proportions looked more Greek than oriental: a body as ageless as Parian marble.

"Good: she's probably about twenty-six. You see the man at the end. He has a great body; so expressive."

I recognized the figure I had seen leaning over the gate on my previous visit.

"Isn't he a bit old?"

"I was afraid you might say that. He is older. He's just very rewarding to work with. But I guess we need classical perfection. How about the guy next to him?"

The black man in the photograph had a back that would have inspired Michelangelo. An ardent recorder of male beauty, Michelangelo was at the same time a devout Christian who saw the human form as the mirror of the soul, a reflection of the divine spark.

The nude was a key symbol for the Renaissance and for the earlier pagan cultures whose standards helped to formulate our own. In ancient Greece it was the ultimate visual expression of the society's values. The austere frontality of the marble young men who walk toward us out of the archaic past [5] reminds us of the rectilinear grandeur of the temples in which they worshiped. Columns, frieze, and cornice echo the harmonies of thighs, torso, and shoulders. Their confident grace survives the sophistication of decorated bronze, which the Greeks were to develop to a degree of realism we would find disturbing if carried out in sculpture today.

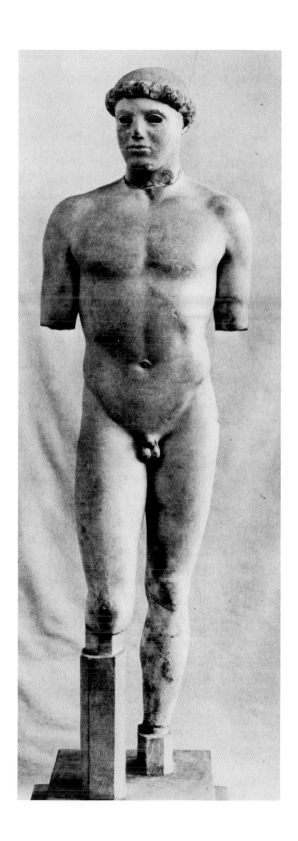

5. *Greek,* Standing Youth (The Kritios Boy), *ca. 480 B.C.*

A few years ago, in 1972, two statues of warriors of the fifth century B.C. were rescued from the sea off Riace in the south of Italy. A bronze hand was seen sticking out of the sand of the seabed. The shoal, which perhaps had wrecked the trireme bringing the figures from Greece, helped to preserve them through the centuries. Restored, they were first put on display in Florence, where I saw them. No sculpture from distant times has kept so well the almost unnervingly naturalistic detail that the ancients favored [6]. Bronze eyelashes, hooding eyes of inset limestone and ivory with tinted glass pupils; copper inlaid on lips and nipples; silver on the teeth. Every curl of beard and luxuriant hair, the veins on wrist and ankle convincingly displayed.

6. Greek, Warriors, *ca. 460 B.C.*

Despite their tapering legs, leanly muscular bodies, and uncircumcised genitals, the profusion of hair and eyelashes gave them a decadent, almost oriental appearance. Perhaps they seemed so exotic because so few classical bronzes long survived. The Roman author Pliny tells us there were more than 6,000 bronze figures in Greece in his day. Now there are less than a dozen and none as well preserved as these two. Slightly over life size, they were placed separately on two five-foot-high plinths so that the great crowds, jostling around them in absorbed silence, could view them from all sides.

Similar awe and curiosity must have emanated from the mob who elbowed Michelangelo as he watched the expressive anguish of the

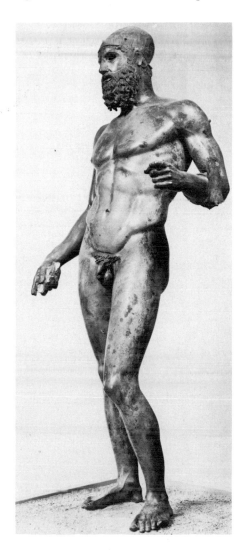

Laocoön group [7] being dug out of the earth nearly five hundred years ago.

It was Wednesday, January 14, 1506, in a vineyard on the outskirts of Rome. News that something remarkable was being revealed in a long-covered-over cellar spread rapidly. "Within a few hours, Michelangelo was on the spot."[2] He was able to identify the hardly damaged find immediately from classical descriptions. Pliny had called it "a work of art to be preferred above all else in painting and sculpture." Just as the warriors of Riace belie the sober monochrome we have come to associate with classical marble, the contorted posture of the Laocoön shows the range of emotion that Greek sculpture learned to encompass. Shock, fear, and pain twist the features of the priest of Troy and his sons as they wrestle ineffectively with the sea serpents sent by Apollo to destroy them. We are more likely to associate such violent expressionism with Japan than with Greece. Equally, the exotic warriors remind us of the inlaid temple figures of Indonesia. Yet both agonized priest and calm soldier preserve the broad torso with its repeated rhythms of swelling chest, horizontal diaphragm, and terminal downward curve of abdomen from hips to sex that is one of the most characteristic signatures of Greek art. Like the embossed patterns of a turtle shell, they are repeated so regularly that they even became the basis for the design of body armor, the classical breastplate.

For the Greeks such uniformity expressed that confidence in the body that can encompass sport and war, love and death, the awesome authority of a god [8]. This wide strider was found in the sea, as the warriors were. He may in fact represent Poseidon. Whether the thrown-back right arm held trident or thunderbolt, the figure needs no weapon to assert his power. The straddle of the legs, the gesture of the arms, and, above all, the strength of the barrel-like body confirm the arrogance of masculine command. This is the embodiment of the Greece of hard pitiless light giving ferocious clarity to the stony hills, glittering on the spray that lashes the rock-strewn seas.

An influential modern critic, Adrian Stokes, stirred both by the old Mediterranean heritage and modern psychoanalytic theory, thought the nude was the unique achievement of the Greek way of life. He suggested

7 Hagesandros, Polydoros, and Athanodoros of Rhodes, Laocöon and His Sons, *ca. 175–150 B.C.*

8. Greek, Poseidon (or Zeus?), *ca. 460 B.C.*

that we recognize our own bodies as the physical manifestation of our character. Seen each day, they give reassurance of the continuation of our drives, traits, and feelings. "The human body thus conceived is a promise of sanity."[3] So far we might agree. Stokes goes on to suppose that the nude represents the potential wholeness of an individual. "I propose that the respect thus founded for the general body is the seal upon our respect for other human beings as such."[4] When like the Good Samaritan we make a gesture of benevolence toward a stranger, we are implicitly recognizing the precious naked whole-object that his parents knew. The artist painting a nude model is in one sense involved in an act of reconciliation; revealing the relationship of parts to the whole.

Classic art involves a harmony between all the elements. Nothing in excess meant disciplining every gesture and emotion to the service of the total effect. We still acknowledge the power of such control in psychic terms when we speak approvingly of someone having a well-balanced personality. Yet, in art as in life such a pursuit of orchestrated perfection can seem bland, even dull. We look above all else in our art for vitality. Living in a world of fragmented values it does not seem odd to us that much modern art is ugly, disturbing, bifurcated. That is the way life is, and above all we want our creations to be truthful and innovative. Today we do not ask for an art that *reconciles* opposites as the Greeks did. Rather, we want it to go to extremes, to highlight uniqueness, to be daring and provocative. We approve of it when it expresses not classical certainty but ambiguity, appropriate to the television age when it is often difficult to tell the good from the bad in the daily stream of conflicting news stories.

All these qualities apply to the photographs of Robert Mapplethorpe. They are both calculating and intense; cold and intimate; abstract and erotic; cruel and witty; classical and pornographic; clinical yet human. A disturbing mixture of opposites gives piquancy to many of his studies of Lisa Lyon [9]. Punitive arm or nourishing breast: one appears to contradict the other. Modern society seems built on such contradictions. Other societies may have been in conflict; but ours is more self-aware than those before. When all things are at odds, we are pressed to look for the motives. Does this photograph represent a brave woman successfully venturing into what had been entirely male territory without losing her traditional feminine charms, or does it represent the latest twist in the age-old female complicity with male exploitation?

One of Mapplethorpe's strengths resided in the questions his work generates (he died, aged forty-two, while this book was in proof). He did not flinch from pushing his art into previously taboo areas with intimate portraits of black studs, and seedy images of sadomasochistic males. Even the most directly sensuous of his pictures are not as simple as they seem [10]. This clever and witty juxtaposition of black and white, light and shadow, pendulous and rigid verticals, also carries a powerful shock to conventional sensibility. Mapplethorpe would say he

9. Mapplethorpe, Lisa Lyon, *1983.*

10. Mapplethorpe, Untitled, *1981.*

took the commonplace of grubby male porn imagery and turned it into a formal study. The artistry restrains the prurient element by distancing the spectator from the event through a coolly calculating eye. Yet Mapplethorpe could not explore something he did not relate to. "I zero in on the part that I consider the perfect part in that particular model."[5] An artist of his time, living in the most savagely divisive city, New York, he could not but reflect its often manically egoistic obsessions.

A fragmented society inevitably fragments the body into areas of specialist interest. Back home I asked my wife if she felt fragmented. Yes, she thought, after consideration, she did. What form did this fragmentation take? Well, looking in the mirror after a bath, her head signified her true, appraising self, while her body was something other, an object of desire. She added that this might be because, as a woman, she had been led to regard herself like that. This split between reason and emotion could only be healed by action, according to my late professor of moral philosophy, John Macmurray. His practical existentialism, I remembered, had stressed that while reason might will an action, an emotional drive was needed to carry it out. The real world of integrated values was therefore always in a state of becoming. It was demonstrated by doing; it did not exist as a static perfection. Where did that leave art?

The artist, said Macmurray, expresses the nature of the objective world as apprehended in emotion. What will make his contribution valuable or significant is the way in which his emotions refer to the world. If his feelings are merely subjective reactions, his work will be bad.[6] I felt fairly uncertain what value I would allocate our cover photograph when arriving on a wet December morning at Mapplethorpe's studio on the day we were to take the picture. Did our concept correspond adequately to the objective world? I wanted a picture that would be both contemporary and classical; perhaps this was too ambitious a brief. Mapplethorpe, who was looking preoccupied and blotchy, did not respond wholeheartedly to my question as to whether he believed there was such a thing as ideal beauty. I persisted. Did the models who were coming that day fulfill his idea of classical beauty?

"I think so; basically. Yes, they do."

Shortly afterward they began to arrive. First Lydia, trim in blue jeans, muffler, and jersey. She was slighter, perhaps about five foot six, than the photograph of her body had led me to expect. Pretty and candid, she had a reassuringly warm personality. Tyler, the next to arrive, seemed equally easy. Handsome, with a lot of wavy hair and frank blue eyes, he had that innate gentleness that is sometimes perceived in young, native-born Californians. Though they had never met before, the two chatted together with the enviable social ease of the New World. I, old and from the Old Country, felt very much the odd one out.

My unease increased when they went away and changed into gray flannel robes. The taciturn assistant started to set up the lights in the studio end of the studio. "Where's Ken? He's never late," someone said. Then Ken arrived: big and black, shaven bald pate, pale gray track suit, and brilliant red T-shirt. What seemed a long period of waiting followed.

Someone put soft jazz on the record player. There was an air of expectancy with the rattle of the aluminum tripods being shoved around.

The assistant hoped no one was wearing anything elastic. No one was. Under their gray robes, their bare legs curled up on the black sofas, they appeared to wearing nothing at all. Was it this potential nakedness that seemed to make them larger than when clothed?

"I like drinking," explained Lydia, "but one drink makes me flush all over. It's a capillary reaction peculiar to the Chinese. We actually have a corpuscular difference."

Mapplethorpe had already taken each of the models aside separately for a brief chat. The lit end of the studio was dressed with a wide cone of black paper and black drapes. Facing it, on a low tripod about twenty feet away, was the camera, a Hasselblad. The models took their places and removed their gowns. There were giggles and shivers at the cold. Ken asked if he could keep his socks on. He could not. Then a window was found to be ajar.

"Who left that open?" said Mapplethorpe. "Can you get another stove in there?"

"It's all right," said Ken. "We'll soon warm up under the lights."

He was right. His body was soon running with sweat. A dark coffee color, completely hairless, his every curve and feature was larger and more pronounced than you would expect and yet in perfect proportion with all the rest. He made the lightly tanned Tyler, actually almost as tall and physically in fine shape, look youthfully slender.

Positioned between them, Lydia seemed small and vulnerably soft with a skin the color of a ripe peach. Yet it was the men who were initially least at ease as they shifted about to Mapplethorpe's instructions.

The first problem was Lydia's height. As we had agreed that the figures should be headless, it was essential that their shoulders should be roughly in alignment.

"We could put her on a block," said the assistant.

"I'd rather try her on tiptoes for this full-length view. The others can stand flat-footed with one leg forward. Could you get on your toes, Lydia?"

She could, with a certain amount of wobbling and giggling.

"Right, now put your hands behind your head, Lydia. And hold it like that. Tyler and Ken, clasp your front hands together. No, lower; straighten your arms, stretch them downward as far as you can."

Robert took a Polaroid.

"We're going to have to light her right leg." While this was being done, he showed the Polaroid to the models and discussed it with them. The main problem was the positioning of the hands. Fingers and thumbs on shoulders in the traditional linked pose of the Three Graces broke the symmetry of the bodies.

Mapplethorpe began to take pictures. As momentum increased, his voice rose.

"Ken, move the whole operation to the left. . . . Watch your fingers. . . . Left foot in more, Tyler. . . . Put your lips together, Lydia. We may see your mouth. . . . Arch your back, Ken. . . ."

"They need a break," whispered the assistant.

"I want to finish this film." Mapplethorpe went on shooting.

"Lydia can't stand on her toes much longer."

Mapplethorpe continued until he had completed the roll.

"Okay, relax everybody. Now what's next?"

What we had taken was a highly formalized pose. I was interested in seeing if the figures could be related more rhythmically. I had come across a reproduction of a fresco of *The Three Graces* by Correggio in Parma [11]. Though essentially static, representing the three as statues on top of an arch, it conveyed an extraordinary sense of movement. This came through the intertwining of the arms, the contrapposto of the legs, and the sideways flow of the hair. Perhaps under the influence of the newly discovered Laocoön statue, Correggio had transformed a conventional pose into a dynamic action. It was easy to imagine his

figures whirling around and around and advancing backward and forward in a dance as complex as a Highland "eightsome."

When we tried to adapt these postures to our living models we were unsuccessful. Mapplethorpe felt the conception was too fluid to work as a photograph. "Really sculpture and painting don't describe what the body does when frozen into position for a photo." Did that mean a photograph could not portray the extraordinary postures achieved by Rodin in some of his small groups? Mapplethorpe felt there were only a limited number of poses available for the camera. No doubt a different method of working, photographing dancers at rehearsal for instance, would give a wider variation of human movement, but Mapplethorpe's strength lay in formal perfection.

He went back to getting a much tighter version of the original composition. This would cut just below the knee and would show no background between the models. The three bodies, no doubt quite warm now, had to be pressed together. Robert kept exhorting them to get closer. It was a hard pose to hold.

"Hurry up, Robert," laughed Lydia, "I've got two quivering men standing here."

11. Correggio, The Three Graces, *ca. 1518.*

12. Mapplethorpe, Polaroid, 1985.

In noticing the cheerful faces in front of the camera, I was suddenly aware of the obvious: they represented the three main races of mankind [12], the African, the Oriental, the Indo-European. That would not be clear in the cover photograph where those faces would be lost. But that distribution of Ken's, Lydia's, and Tyler's ancestry was purely fortuitous. What was relevant was our models' athleticism, their preoccupation with perfecting their bodies.

More than any other society until modern times, the Greeks were concerned with improving the physique of their young men and their performance as athletes. Obesity was scorned; good looks praised in poems and public eulogies. This led to a cult of youth with superficial similarities to our own. Only superficial, for in the Greek world of small competitive states prowess redounded not so much to the individual as to the glory of the city to which he belonged. Festivals, such as the

Games at Olympia, were much more than sporting activity; they were events that brought together these often warring principalities. Held every four years for a thousand years, the Olympic Games were occasions for national rededication, as much religious as athletic. Priestly processions, mass sacrifices, and individual acts of worship preceded the events. The contestants ran, wrestled, boxed, and threw the discus naked. Originally they had worn some sort of loin wrap, but as early as 720 B.C. this was discarded. They trained naked, they gave their oath of dedication to the spirit of the Games naked; naked they paraded and were publicly anointed, naked they presented themselves for the crowning laurels of victory [13]. The sight of oiled and bronzed young men throwing themselves into every exertion, in a state of spiritual and partisan ecstasy, was witnessed only by men. Women were not allowed

13. Greek, A Winner Gets His Ribbons, *ca. 500–475 B.C.*

to participate. Girls had their own event nearby. They ran in a brief tunic which left one shoulder bare.

Greek philosophy taught that all manifestations of goodness, truth, and beauty were ultimately aspects of the universal good. The highest goal was to mingle spiritual, mental, and physical values harmoniously. Hence the admiration for beauty of body, the visible sign of this harmony. Such admiration was a moral as well as an aesthetic experience. Of course it might have a physical outlet. (Homosexual love was an acceptable part of society.) More important for art, it created an idea of perfection that, waxing and waning with fashion, has remarkably survived more than two thousand years.

In *The Symposium* Plato supposes that beauty is a good that all men strive to grasp. "Those whose creative instinct is physical have recourse to women, and show their love in this way, believing that by begetting children they can secure for themselves an immortal and blessed memory hereafter forever; but there are some whose creative desire is of the soul, and who long to beget spiritually, not physically, the progeny which it is the nature of the soul to create and bring to birth."[7] Among these are artists. But even here, the first impetus in the pursuit of the ideal form of beauty is provided by the physical beauty of real individuals. I was reminded of this, when in the days following the photographic session, I was stirred by the memory of Lydia's glowing golden skin. "No nude, however abstract, should fail to arouse in the spectator some vestige of erotic feeling," wrote that most fastidious critic Kenneth Clark; "If it does not do so, it is bad art and false morals. The desire to grasp and be united with another human body is so fundamental a part of our nature, that our judgement of what is known as 'pure form' is inevitably influenced by it."[8] If the spectator's judgment is influenced, at second hand, by the erotic content in the art, what about the artist dealing directly with the source?

The relationship of artist and model is an essential ingredient in the mysterious potion of creativity. Often it has been the ultimate stimulus that led to the making of the art object. Nor is that action always so one-sided as the apparently passive act of posing would suggest. In classical times the importance of the model's beauty as the source of the artist's inspiration was well recognized.

Thus Phryne, the model for the sculptor Praxiteles, was nearly as renowned in contemporary Athenian society as the artist himself. The story goes that she was put on trial on a serious charge. In order to persuade the jury of her virtue, her counsel drew apart her clothes. The court was struck dumb by the sight of such perfection and she was acquitted. Beauty was a god-given gift, and must be part and parcel of an inner nobility of soul. As the outward sign of moral value, a perfect living physique enhanced a community as much as its expression in bronze or marble.

In modern times the body arouses no such clear-cut veneration. The link between artist and model, like those other partnerships, of marriage, business, or entertainment, demonstrates a gamut of responses. "I have been involved sometimes with people I've photographed," said Mapplethorpe. "But it's not necessary to go to bed with every model. You can be in love with the form, not the rest." More common, I would guess, is the experience of another cool recorder of beautiful bodies, Edward Weston. Usually he slept with his models; sometimes having affairs with seven or eight at the same time. "Why this tide of women?" he wrote in apparent surprise in his diary, the Daybooks.[9]

From the artist's point of view an involvement with his model gave an added intensity to the created object. For the model the intimacy brought a trust that would be likely to make her more responsive to the intention of the artist. In any case a creative collaboration has often been compared to a love affair in its demand for a close communion of purpose.

Charis Wilson was twenty and Edward Weston forty-eight when he first photographed her: "I hadn't realized that I was to be such an active participant that my mind would be totally swept up . . . During photographic sessions, Edward made a model totally aware of herself. It was beyond exhibitionism or narcissism" [14]. Another subject wrote to him, "What you do awakes in me so strong a response that I must in all joy tell you your photographs are as definite an experience to the spirit as a whiplash to the body."[10]

No one has explored more nuances of emotion in the relationship than Pablo Picasso. His feelings for the women he painted and lived with are the predominant theme of his work. In his prime he could be like an antique god [15], reclining with the youthful beauty who is his inspiration. They gaze in mutual admiration at the classical torso he has just sculpted. In the marvelous etchings of the sculptor's studio there seems a tranquil balance between his magisterial power and her tender regard. Yet no artist has so continually ravaged the female image in painting, drawing, and sculpture [16]. Such ferocious and ingenious attacks, deforming and mutilating the bodies he had physically caressed into humiliating, disgusting, comical, and often fearsome distortions, must have been powered by intensely ambivalent feelings toward the sex which continued to preoccupy his work until his death. In a drawing of his ninety-first year [17], the familiar piercing eyes of so many of his self-portraits gaze out of a face made more skull-like by the smeared blotches of ink which disfigure it. Alongside him the reclining nude still writhes enticingly. Picasso has twisted her body to concentrate attention on the erotic zones. However mangled and maimed, his figures never lose their provocative sexuality, increasing the outrage his pictures have often aroused.

By debauching such a well-loved object as the female body Picasso was making a direct assault on the whole conception of ideal beauty. "The beauties of the Parthenon, Venuses, Nymphs, Narcissuses, are so many lies," he said in an interview in 1935. "Art is not the application of a canon of beauty but what the instinct and the brain can conceive beyond any canon."[11] He was a spearhead of the general impetus that

15. *Picasso, The Sculptor and His Model, 1933.*

16. Picasso, Nude in an Armchair, *1929. Opposite page*

17. Picasso, Reclining Nude and Head of Man, *1972.*

liberated modern art from the academic disciplines of the past. Almost all the significant artists of the twentieth century contributed to this process, but Picasso, by his creative brilliance, drew the most attention. Nothing disturbed the conservative general public so much as the violent departure from the accepted proportions of the body. They had reason for their unease, because Picasso was out to debunk the entire traditional way of looking at the nude which popular taste had unconsciously assimilated over the centuries. At his first major exhibition after the liberation of Paris in 1944, some of his pictures were forcibly taken down and people demanded their money back.

During the height of his fame in the 1940s and '50s Picasso was widely believed to be a clever charlatan who was earning vast amounts of money by taking in the gullible connoisseurs with work that a child could do better. Popular opinion persisted in approving the decorous pictures of the nude that still graced chocolate boxes and provincial galleries. By and large, the pin-up photograph, which was the only image of the body readily available to the non-gallery-going majority, also expressed the poses and physical proportions that had been formulated in Greece and reasserted by the artists of the Renaissance.

Even in the 1980s the power of the Greek inheritance could be seen in the enormous popularity of two events which regularly brought in a television audience of many hundreds of millions around the world: the Olympic Games and the annual Miss World beauty competition. They uphold the classical veneration for athletic prowess and youthful bodies; contests between naked young women for the prize of beauty are probably as ancient in origin as the contests between naked young men at the Games.

Athletes and beauty contestants no longer appear naked, though the prescribed amount of clothing has continually decreased through the century. The 1960s brought a certain increase in visual freedom in representations of the body, but only within limits. It is impossible for Judaeo-Christian societies to regard naked beauty as an unqualified good as the Greeks did. Its exhibition is hedged in conventions, and they are more stringent when applied to the male than the female. Thus a larger-than-life painting [18] of an American male model, Paul Rosano, would seem to qualify for the Greek criterion of looks except for his hirsute appearance and the fact that he was painted by a woman. Sylvia Sleigh has rendered each curlicue of his luxuriant body hair with Pre-Raphaelite intensity. Perhaps it was this, and the uncomfortable directness of his gaze, that caused a judge to attempt to ban the picture from a New York exhibition in the mid-seventies.

"Someone was heard to declare: 'You can see his front and you can see his back, and he's got an Afro.' Especially as a woman had painted it, they found this very indecent."[12] A student asked the artist what she thought when she painted the male genitals. "I said it's like painting a flower which moves a lot; it is quite a problem."[13]

Sleigh has painted a number of portraits of both men and women in the nude, deliberately ringing the changes on what had tended to be, until recently, a masculine preserve. "I wanted to paint men as I thought women should have been painted, that is as persons of intelligence and affection, reflecting respect, not to say love, showing all the variety of skin tones, and complexions, and form. By being unclothed the paintings are sensual if you like, but there is also a sort of freedom, like feeling the wind in your hair, or bathing in the nude."[14]

Thus Sleigh's purpose in painting the opposite sex was to celebrate it in a gentle and humanistic manner; quite the contrary to the intention of Picasso, many of whose paintings of women were meant as a violent

18. Sleigh, Double Image: Paul Rosano, *1974.*

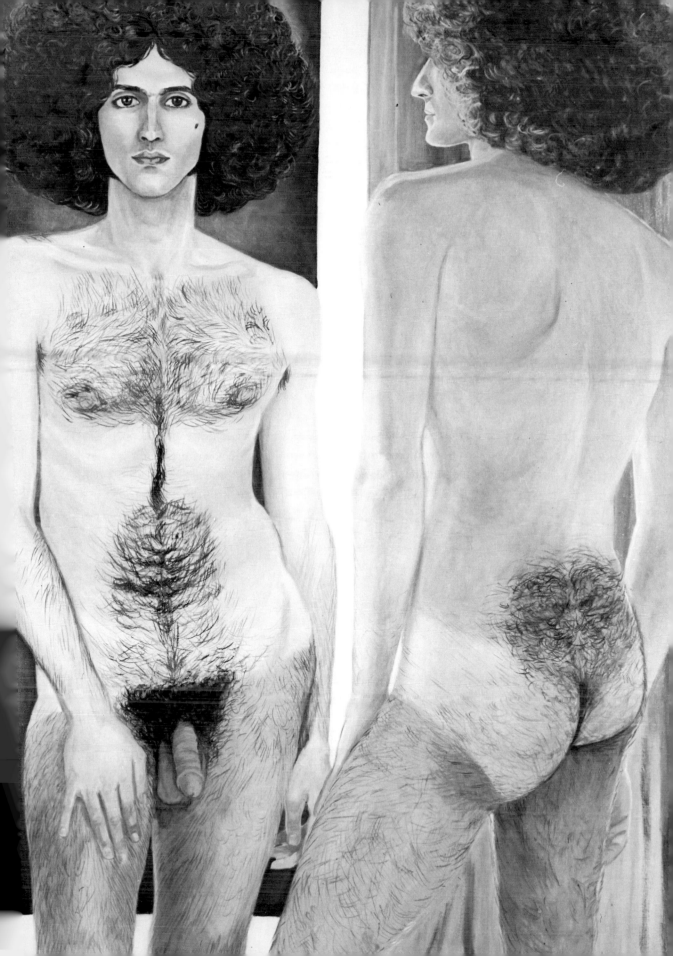

attack on the traditional veneration of female beauty and ideal form. Broadly, Sleigh was rational and working within accepted conventions of art, Picasso was antirational and iconoclastic: yet both attitudes aroused strong opposition from the conventional public. The morning innocence of the body that runs so zestfully through classical art is hard for us to recapture. Even the Greeks were at pains to achieve it, with their habit of depilating all body hair so as not to impede the smooth lines of the figure. This custom led to the convention in Western European art of shading out the female pubic hair; a convention that continued in painting up to the beginning of the century and in photography for general reproduction until much later. Even today it still affects attitudes toward pictures that are to be on wide public display.

The contacts of Mapplethorpe's photographs looked splendid. He had already selected one, which came from the first pose. "I chose it because the guys' feet are in perfect alignment." The figures might have been carved out of marble. "You see the dark patch below their hands. They're not completely covering her pubic hair. Do you think that matters?" On the contrary, I thought it made the picture less slick and coy.

It was a strong image; very controlled, but, because of that central frontal figure, bursting with energy. It no longer reminded me of *The Three Graces,* but of something else: a stone relief four thousand years old [19]. Carved on the throne of a King of Ancient Egypt, it signified the unity of the two lands of the Upper and Lower Nile. On the left is the hawk-god Horus, the son of Isis and Osiris, the god of the Delta. Facing him is his eternal opponent, the warrior Seth, a god of the south, of equatorial Africa. These powerful warring deities meet to bind together the two kingdoms: an act which, in reality, guaranteed the prosperity of the united land and forged the world's first great civilization. Between them, running south to north, was the Nile, whose fertilizing flow was the ultimate source of the nation's well-being.

Representatives of north and south: I could see Indo-European Tyler and Negro Ken in those roles. I also liked the idea of the woman as the symbol of the civilizing fertility of the river. It was salutary also to have a reminder that the heritage of humanity was more than Greece and Rome, overwhelming though that heritage has been for Western art. In a wider context, athletes, gymnasts, devotees of bodily perfection,

19. *Egypt, Middle Kingdom,* Unity of the Two Lands, *ca. 2000 B.C.*

still pay tribute to standards first systematized in the classical era. The cult of beauty has been—and remains through the cosmetic and show business worlds—a powerful element in international culture. But the story of man's interpretation of the human form goes much further back, into the dawn of organized society, when the cave denizens were first groping toward an expression of religious feeling and seeking to control the mysteries of their own fertility.

2

ENERGY AND FERTILITY

A wind from the sea blew all the time we were in the Louisiades. At night the wind rustled the palm leaves of the roof like the scampering of a myriad of rodents. Before dawn it often rose to near gale force. The giant black spiders that crouched among the palm fronds tossed from side to side on their fragile nets. Through the interstices of the bamboo walls, skeins of fine sand lifted in a golden veil, filling the crannies of our sleeping bags with a gritty dust.

The light grew with theatrical speed; the wind hushed, bringing the murmur of the sea on the coral reef suddenly close. In that momentary lull at sunrise we heard a strange, almost mechanical sound. It was like the clapping of a giant hand. Five times it was repeated and echoed, from far down the beach.

This remote island in the Coral Sea had only been converted to Christianity by Australian missionaries at the end of the 1940s. Now a Catholic priest visited the village once a year and held a service in the old Long Hut. But the spirits of ancestors were still present. There were other spirits in the lagoon, on the coral reefs, and in the forest. They needed to be acknowledged and propitiated.

The islanders' somewhat tenuous link with the new religion had given them Christian names beside their Melanesian ones. In a house on stilts next to ours lived a young woman, Julia, with her eight-month-old baby. Like the two or three other nursing mothers in the village, she got up just before dawn. Leaving her child asleep, she climbed down the steep ladder to the beach, and walked out into the gray, warm sea. She had no need to pause to undress. Her only clothing was a crisp grass skirt that stretched from her waist to her knees. Like the other village women she wore it at all times, climbing the palm trees for coconuts, collecting cooking water from the deep grottoes in the

20. Paleolithic, left hand of a cave painter, ca. 15,000 B.C.

center of the island, or swimming and fishing from the coral reef. Now it billowed around her as she pushed out against the early morning swell. When the water was above her waist she stopped.

Holding her breasts in her hands, she squeezed thin spurts of milk into the sea. She was giving the sustenance of life back to the element on which all life depends. Taking a deep breath, she dived down into the deepest part of the lagoon. She drank the clear salt water at the bottom of the sea. She came up gasping for air and shaking the water from her thick curly hair. Water ran down the golden skin of her shoulders and scattered in glittering drops from her breasts. She took half a coconut shell that had been strung to her waist and slapped it rhythmically, five times, on the surface of the sea, each time drinking the dregs it gathered.

Only then did she turn and walk slowly, her skirt heavy with moisture, back to the beach. In her house the baby was still asleep, lying on a red cotton scarf that was perhaps the only Western article that Julia possessed. A gourd of fresh water was boiling on the little fire of coconut fragments. Julia sipped from it, washing down the traces of salt from her mouth. That was the last act of the daily ritual. Gently she lifted the stirring baby and rocked her to wakeful hunger against her breast. The tender patterns of maternal care, older even than the Stone Age values by which Julia still largely lived, reasserted their universal demands.

Julia could give no explanation for her complex actions. They had been handed down, generation to generation, from a past beyond the reach of verbal memory. Yet it would have been unthinkable for Julia not to carry them out. They were part of the reoccurring acts which gave structure to her life, supporting its fragile, transient surface on a series of fulfilled expectations. So she was related to the vaster powers of water, reefs, woods, sky, sun, and stars, which surrounded her. Through acts of giving and receiving, she was linked to the animals, the birds, and the fishes, and the vegetables and fruit on which her well-being depended. And beyond them, and sometimes in them, were the spirits that could assist or hinder. Her life moved through patterns as formal as the graceful dances that embodied many of them. By them she was able to rejoice in the gift of birth, to acknowledge the events of the passing seasons, to be reconciled to the pains of death and bereavement. Such is the nature of ritual.

I am reminded of Julia and her ways of thinking and reacting—so different from our own—when I consider the earliest representations of humanity, the cave paintings. Ritual, we feel, must have been the cause of these powerful and enigmatic creations. We can only guess at their specific meaning. They are so very old and our knowledge of them is very new. Nowadays we expect any child's primer on art to begin with a reproduction of one of the bulls of Altamira or the horses of Lascaux. Yet this first and longest period of human creativity was totally unknown until just over a hundred years ago.

It was in 1868 that a local hunter, following his dog into a patch of scrub on a shallow hillside in northern Spain, stumbled on a previously unnoticed cave entrance. This area of green and rolling hills has many caves, and the cave at Altamira might have been an unremarked discovery if the hunter had not mentioned it to his landlord. Don Marcelino de Sautuola had an amateur interest in prehistory, which was fanned by visiting the Paris World Exhibition in 1878. There he saw recent archaeological discoveries of worked flint and decorated bone. He returned to Altamira with the resolution to explore it in the vague hope of finding some undisturbed traces of ancient man.

The cave consists of a series of interlocking chambers made up of louring blocks of massive limestone. One day in November 1879 Sautuola had his attention drawn from the rubble on the floor by his small daughter. "Look, Daddy, oxen," she called out, pointing at the ceiling.[1] There by the light of the carbide lamp he saw a series of bulging red and black forms.

A child had revealed the supreme achievement of the childhood of art. That was part of the trouble. When Sautuola wrote a detailed paper about his discoveries, including a first sketch of them [21], it was greeted with scorn and derision. The very sophistication of the paintings, so unlike representations of animals in later ethnic art, the grandeur of conception and scale—many of the bulls are six feet in length—all seemed to point to a hoax. Moreover the budding science of prehistory was centered in Paris and few of the skeptics bothered to take the journey to provincial Spain. For over twenty years Altamira was ridiculed or ignored. It was not until long after the death of Sautuola that the finding of similar paintings in caverns in France forced scholarly opinion to recognize the Cave of the Bulls as among the supreme works of man: "The Sistine Chapel of Prehistoric Art."

21. Sautuola, drawing
of Altamira cave
painting, 1880.

The discoveries have continued. By now, in the late 1980s, over a hundred decorated caves have been charted. Richest in northern Spain and southern France, sites where painted and carved objects have been found stretch in a wide arc as far as the Urals. Carbon dating suggests activity over an immense period, some twenty thousand years. Think of groups of hunter-gatherers subsisting in societies little changed for *four times as long* as the period from the first pyramid to our own day. We are closer in time to the last generations of cave painters than they are to their first predecessors.

The cave paintings are our first direct message from the past. The trouble is that more than half the message has been lost. The symbols on the walls were almost certainly just the backdrop to the ritual that took place within these dark depths. We cannot say what the rituals were, but the imagery makes clear that here, at the beginning of human culture, art, magic, religion, and sex are closely interlocked, as they have been ever since.

Of course, man's prehistory as a walking mammal goes back millions of years. Simple tools of bone and flint have been dated to over a million years ago. Yet, significantly, skulls with a cranial capacity similar to modern man have only been found to go back in Europe about forty thousand years. This is within ten thousand years of the earliest known cave paintings.

So we might say that half man's adult existence (that is, as a creature potentially as intelligent as ourselves) has been influenced by what went on in those caves. The paintings have been seen as sympathetic magic, evoking man's hopes for success in the hunt; tribal fetishes; images of cosmic anxiety; representations of the human desire for adornment and decoration; symbols for sexual fertility. Cave painting is like the Rorschach ink blot test: it draws out the inner prejudices of the beholder. All interpretation must be subjective when we are dealing with eras long before the invention of written language and when so little of the ancillary evidence survives.

Visiting the caves quickly convinces the observer of one thing: these are not the doodles of an idle moment in the hunter's life. Nor are they meant to brighten up his cavernous home. Excavations reveal that many of the caves were occupied for hundreds of centuries, but only within the area near the entrance, where light penetrated. Almost invariably the paintings began beyond the familiar twilight, in the realm of absolute darkness. Consider for a moment what this means in specific terms.

One of the most splendid sites is high up on a mountainside in the Castillo range in northern Spain. The cave is a narrowish entrance beneath a rock overhang at the back of a broad ledge. Below the ledge the hillside drops very sharply revealing a wide expanse of wooded pasture land, the valley of the River Pas. Clearly it would be a perfect place to observe the meandering movement of game herds far below. No wonder generations of hunters lived here; El Castillo was a human dwelling place far longer than London or Rome. Not always undisturbed; archaeologists have found cracked bones that suggest raids by marauding hyenas. Nevertheless the overhang of rock provided shelter and a site for the kitchen.

To enter the cave itself would require light. We have found sufficient traces to know what it was likely to be: a hollowed-out stone containing burning animal fat. Once through the cave mouth, the ground falls sharply away into the bowels of the earth. Great rock falls make the descent treacherous and difficult. To climb down into the black depths must have called for courage of the highest order. After about a hundred yards, the entrance gallery opens out into a vast chamber half a mile across. The clutter of giant boulders and mountainous piles of fallen debris turn the area into an underground labyrinth. Even today the thought of getting lost among the maze of narrow undulating pathways makes the skin crawl. On every side menacing shapes loom and jut. There are huge joined columns of stalactites and stalagmites that when struck give out the boom of a giant's drum. Penetrating these awesome deeps sharpens awareness of the natural ferocity that hemmed in our ancestors. The harshness of their daily lives outside must have schooled them to withstand the dangers underground.

It was down here, in the heart of the mountain, that they chose to make their sanctuaries, as always, using the contours of the rocks to accentuate the form of the animal portrayed, a sort of natural relief that greatly adds to the weight of the imagery. This subtle evocation of the three-dimensional can never be captured adequately in still photography, any more than the wonder of the awesome setting. It is perhaps the most conclusive demonstration of their power as artists that they had the imagination to see in the random bulges of stone the potential for a living form they were then able to realize with such economy and vitality.

The cave painter has left us few self-portraits. But here in the depths of El Castillo, he has put the earliest configuration of his presence, the image of his hand [20]. This is where our long pursuit of the body in art begins, in this confrontation with the hand of the first artist, in the bowels of the earth. The hand is held palm toward us in the universal sign of peace and welcome. It is the symbol that was chosen as the gesture of man engraved on a plaque on the *Pioneer 10* spacecraft [22], the first messenger mankind sent into interstellar space. The first artist greets us from across a different void: many thousands of years of time. Appropriately, he has given us most often, as here, a ghost image; not a print of the hand itself, but its negative. Probably it was made in the way Australian aborigines still leave their palm prints on the sacred rocks of central Australia. Moist pigment is placed in a dollop at the end of a rolled leaf. One palm is placed against the rock,

22. Plaque on the Pioneer 10 *spacecraft, 1972.*

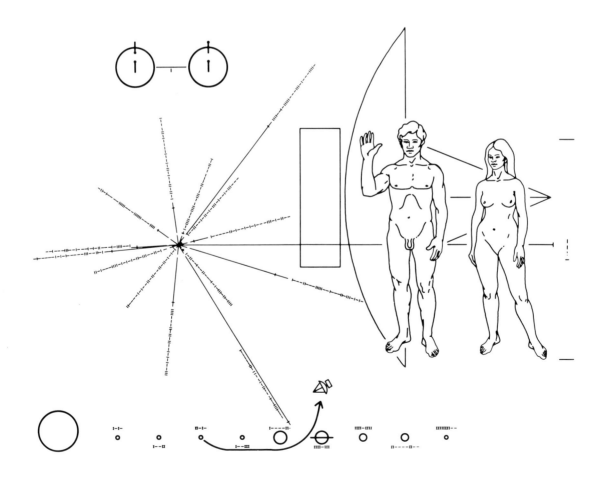

and holding the leaf like a funnel in his other hand, the aborigine blows the pigment through it in a wide scatter over the hand and around it. When the hand is removed its shadow remains. Characteristically explosive outer edges to the paint suggest the prehistoric artist worked in a similar manner.

Why he did so we do not know. Several hundred of these handprints have been found across a wide range of locations. Some have been given an estimated dating as far back as 27,000 B.C. Sometimes the prints are of smaller hands, perhaps women, and certainly sometimes children. I placed my own hand near the print in El Castillo. The hand from the distant past was as large, the fingers sensitively long. The print seemed to suggest that there was nothing brutish about these ancestors, except the harsh circumstances of their lives. Perhaps the handprint should be read as the first appearance of a signature, an assertion of self-identity among all the potent animal shapes.

But there is a deeper significance to its appearance as a forerunner of the portrayal of the whole man. On the cortex of the human brain a disproportionately large area is given up to the motor activity of the hand, particularly the thumb and forefinger, and the tongue. The two are linked, the development of gesture going along with that of speech. We know that it is the prehensile sensitivity of our ancestors that gave us tools, and the development of language that allowed us to command past and future. It was these activities that led to the enlargement of our mental capacities and increased our actual brain cells. Probably it was the physical presence of the hand that has allowed us, and not the whale (with a significantly larger brain size), to dominate the planet. How apposite that it should be our remotest visible ancestors who first commemorated this unique gift.

The handprint dates from the early days of cave art. Two other abstracted aspects of humanity are present from the beginning, the symbols for female and male sexuality, the vulva and the phallus. This too seems to signal a characteristic of profound significance to human development. An abundance of nonseasonal sexual energy is a prime difference between man and most other species. James Drever, my professor of psychology at Edinburgh University, maintained that if he had to define a single unique characteristic to account for man's dominance, it would be "random restlessness." A restlessness ultimately motivated by a highly developed but nonspecific sexual drive.

This must be coupled with the curious fact that the human female has no innate mechanism to signal her fertility. The Tree of Knowledge did not include the information to allow Adam and Eve to know at what times they were to labor to create the human race. Hence, perhaps, the need to be at it six days out of seven. Certainly it is a major preoccupation of the early painters. Virtually every cave contains sexual signs, often in groups or clusters.

The female sex is often represented in paint or engraving as a triangle with a line drawn down to one point [23]; sometimes as lozenges or oblongs. The symbolism of the male organ is equally varied. Sometimes it is a straight line or a dot; sometimes a feathered shaft like an arrow; sometimes, especially on carved deer horns, more or less representational, though often in conjunction with semiabstract patterns which probably had a cult significance [24]. Less usually, accidents of

23. Paleolithic, vulva incised on stone, ca. 27,000 B.C.

rock form have created a natural erection, which has been associated with the appropriate carving or relief of a human figure, or just embellished and polished. Such is the extraordinary stalagmite, nearly three feet tall and smoothed by contact, which stands at the entrance to a cave sanctuary at Pech-Merle in the Lot region of France [25].

Paleolithic artists regularly put male symbols at cave entrances, an association which appears to have survived into classical times. The herm, a rectangular pillar with human head and masculine attributes, was often used in the Graeco-Roman world to mark the boundaries between property, or the termination of a street [26]. Later still, in the Middle Ages, phallic symbols sometimes appear at the entrance to houses, even above the doors of churches. The twin pillars, which form a sturdy portal to so many Victorian terrace houses in London, must be a late echo of this tradition. Such sentinels to good fortune would seem to have distant affinities with their more stolid and somewhat older country cousins, the standing stones, which look out over the Celtic west in sociable circles, line up at attention in long avenues in Brittany, and occasionally rise to the impressive heights of the vast trilithons of Stonehenge.

As with so much of the debris that has come down to us from the

24. Paleolithic, double phallus on branched head of a pierced staff, ca. 12,000 B.C.

25. Phallic stalagmite.

remote past, we have no idea of the purpose that lay behind the raising of these stone monuments, scattered quite thickly over Western Europe. They are often associated with the midsummer solstice in complex alignments that show considerable knowledge of solar astronomy. It seems that these sentinel-like reminders of the masculine demonstrations at the cave entrances are not a talisman of human procreation only, but an invocation at the boundary of the fertilizing combination of sun and earth. Hunters, we may feel, entered the concealing dark of the caves to worship; the later crop-raisers who put up the standing stones needed

26. Greek, herm, ca.
520 B.C.

the nurturing power of sunlight for survival. Yet the image of fertility remained the same: ultimately based on the human male's erection. The purpose of such rather obvious speculations is to remind us of the teasing echoes that the cave imagery constantly arouses. Like a half-remembered tune these vivid forms suggest they might be the key to a universal melody if we could piece them together.

To take one more example of a theme that has continued to have resonance into the modern world: the prehistoric image is an engraving scratched on a reindeer antler [27]. It shows salmon leaping between the legs of reindeer, which are presumably crossing a stream. It could be construed as a characteristically energetic portrayal of the animal world, but the fish are unmistakably pointing to the sexual organs of the deer. Near the antlers are some curious diamond-shaped lozenges (known from other examples to represent the vulva). Similar lozenges and fish occur together thousands of years later in Mesopotamian cylinder seals and later still in Chinese bricks of the Han dynasty.[2] What gives such symbols the energy to travel so far?

We are familiar with the early Christian adoption of the fish sign as a symbol for Christ in the Roman catacombs. In one of his longer poems Dylan Thomas desanctified the image and took it back to its

27. Plaster cast of carved reindeer antler, rolled out to show both sides, ca. 12,000 B.C.

ancient sexual meaning. His fisherman sings of the triumph of his trade and equally of his erotic prowess with his woman, who was both bait and hook, victim and tease.

> *Whales in the wake like capes and Alps*
> *Quaked the sick sea and shouted deep,*
> *Deep the great bushed bait with raining lips*
> *Slipped the fins of those humpbacked tons*
> *And fled their love in a weaving dip.*[3]

Here the whale is a symbol for the phallus; "the great bushed bait" is the female who draws on the male and then eludes him at the vital moment. Ambiguity of identity; a recent interpretation of cave art[4] has suggested that all the teeming host of animals are there as representations of the human male and female. Thus horses, bears, ibex, and felines are masculine, bison and oxen are female. By far the most comprehensive study attempted in the postwar years, it was carried out by a leading authority on man's prehistory, André Leroi-Gourhan. The director of the Musée de l'Homme in Paris, he headed a team that analyzed in detail the content of sixty-six of the hundred or so caves known to contain Paleolithic remains. Previous speculation had centered on the images themselves. Leroi-Gourhan related them to their spatial position in the caves. He also notated all the dots, lines, circles, and oblongs that covered the walls in an apparently haphazard fashion. They had largely been ignored as idle graffiti. Comparative analysis showed that the seemingly random groupings of signs that surrounded many of the animals could not be arbitrary. Moreover, their frequent juxtaposition with the sexual areas of the painted animals gave another clue to their purpose. "When each set of signs was analysed separately, it leaped to the eye that the ovals, triangles and quadrangular signs were all more or less abstract variations on the vulvas which appear among the earliest works of prehistoric art. As for the dots and strokes it was obvious that they are male signs."[5]

Leroi-Gourhan also proposed that in the hunting scenes the signs for arrows and spears were masculine and the wounded animals feminine. "In other words, it is highly probable that Paleolithic men were expressing something like 'spear is to penis' as 'wound is to vulva.' "[6] This seems to the layman an unattractively sweeping generalization, bearing in mind the range and freshness of observation in the caves. In fact, since first advancing it in the 1960s, Leroi-Gourhan has somewhat modified his definition, while maintaining his most important point: that cave art has a metaphysical function and is not to be read, like a natural history film on television, as a narrative portrayal of animal life.

Much of the most impressive evidence comes from Leroi-Gourhan's statistical analysis of the actual content of the caves. He was able to impose, for the first time, order on the apparent buzzing confusion of individual incident and reveal a consistent pattern. The cave paintings were made to a plan, as carefully adhered to as the orientation of a medieval cathedral. Horses and bovines dominate; less commonly represented species (such as felines, reindeer, and wild boar) are grouped around them as their satellites. Their position, bearing in mind the physical differences between caves, also generally follows the same spatial order. Male signs and animals representing masculinity occur at the entrance (just as in the tympanum over the main doorway of medieval cathedrals either God the Father or Christ in Majesty dominates). In the central areas there are both male and female symbols (in the medieval cathedral there are side chapels to the Virgin Mary and female saints and martyrs as well as masculine ones). Finally, only male symbols occupy the backs of the caves (over the altar in the medieval cathedral there are only representations of God the Father, Son, and Holy Ghost). Moreover, the animal species illustrated could not have been chosen at random; many local fauna are never represented (those predatory hyenas at El Castillo are not to be seen there or anywhere else, along with most of the smaller species that must have been a staple in the cave larder); and for twenty thousand years the selection hardly changed.

Nor are all caves chosen for decoration. In the Castillo range twenty-six caves have been found containing traces of occupation by prehistoric peoples. Only four have paintings in them. All are in the same mountain. Seen from afar it has a striking, instantly recognizable shape, quite unlike any of its neighbors. It looks like a perfect woman's breast, as uniform in its slopes as a pyramid. (The pyramid was the first structure man built when he mastered construction in stone. In it he placed a

man-made cavern, the shrine of the Pharaoh.) It does not seem too fanciful to regard El Castillo as a sacred mountain. And the general conclusion seems inevitable: the caves were not haphazard art collections, but shrines for ritual of a highly specific kind.

But ritual for what purpose? If we look at the evidence from the caves themselves certain conclusions are forced upon us. Even if it were true that all the work is for a symbolic purpose, man and woman, the physical beings themselves, come off very poorly. Almost all the energy, the loving vitality, goes into the animals. Man is never portrayed with the plastic realism with which a bison is shown licking itself [28]. Usually the human figures are featureless or represented, in the case of men, with a snouty mask [29]. Perhaps this is a memory of our disreputable and failed uncle, Neanderthal Man. Heavy-jawed and beetle-browed, modern man's closest relative, he may still have been around in the early days of the cave painters. We can imagine him

28. *Paleolithic, carving of bison, ca. 12,000 B.C.*

29. *Paleolithic, man with snout face, incised on stone, ca. 12,000 B.C.*

cadging scraps at the midden and frightening children out wood-gathering, the original bogeyman.

But perhaps these figures are literally wearing the masks of animals, so metaphorically taking on their power. Crouching in his cave-eyrie, early man must have been continually aware of how puny he was compared with the teeming animal kingdom all around. He must have wished for the speed of the horse, the majestic weaponry of the male reindeer, the ferocity and sexual vitality of the tiger. By aping their behavior he may have hoped to acquire their attributes, just as the gorilla goes through the actions of being in a rage, thumping his chest, baring his teeth and so on, in order to get into a rage. The most powerful male figure in all prehistoric art [30 and 31] suggests some such posturing ritual. As Leroi-Gourhan describes him: "his horns and ears are those

30. *Paleolithic, antlered man, ca. 12,000 B.C.*

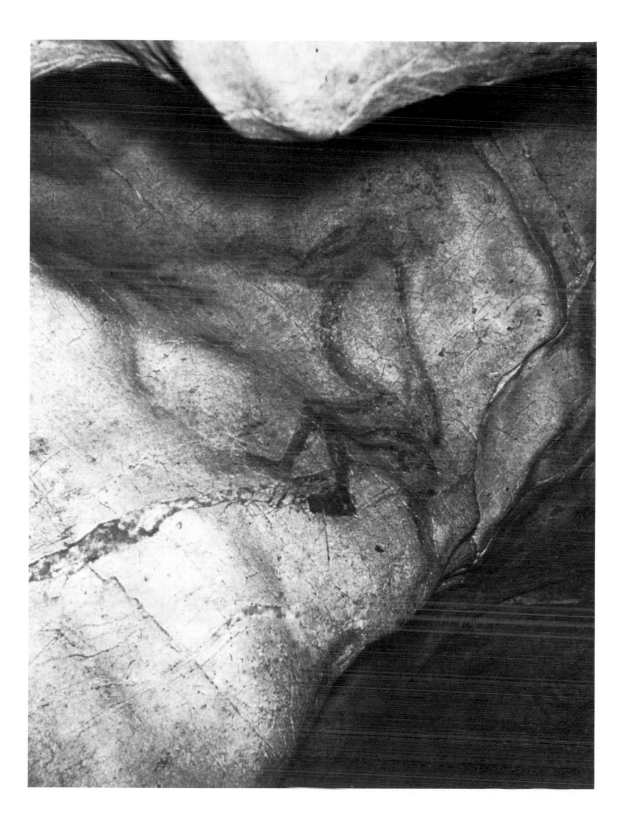

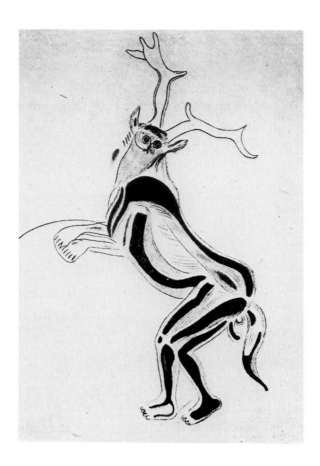

31. Abbé Breuil, drawing of the antlered man.

of a reindeer, his body is that of a man, his tail that of a horse, and his penis, though human, is placed where a feline's would be."[7]

Yet he remains distinctly human, reminiscent of the dancers who still today perform the sacred fire ceremony of the Mescalero Apaches in southern New Mexico. Clanking shapes, made vast by horns and masks, they pace slowly around the leaping flames. Their bent-kneed shuffle, the bearlike twisting and bending of their bodies and waving arms, is mirrored in the scratched human outlines in the prehistoric caves. Around these impressive elders, rhythmically stamping and singing a high birdlike chant, narcotically repeated, scurry and caper small figures with dog-muzzled faces. Young boys, they represent irreverent sexuality. Such limp-wristed prancing, squirrel-like in its perky curiosity, is also present in cave art. In their dancing, the erstwhile hunters are able to assimilate characteristics of many animals while maintaining the unity of a human presence. Perhaps this is also relevant in considering early man's relationship to the natural world.

To be able to imitate the outward behavior of animals would be to participate in their power. Those who could do so skillfully would gain status. Thus the shaman may have been born. Not yet a priest, for there seem to have been no gods to propitiate and no signs of a universal cosmology, a shambling ambiguous figure, part conjuror of spirits, part trickster, the shaman has had a long history among the hunting people of the northern hemisphere. We find him in Finland with the Lapps; in Asia; among the Eskimos and Indians of North America. Did he first appear with the cave people, and with them follow the northward retreat of the reindeer as the melting of the snows warmed the climate of southern Europe? An eighteenth-century engraving of a shaman from the Tungus tribe of Siberia [32] might be the clone of the prehistoric antlered man.

He must have been a fearful presence metamorphosing from his familiar fireside appearance into his other animal self in the shadowy depths underground. We can sense some of the superstitious terror he would have generated from our gullible reaction to horror movies. Perhaps vampires and werewolves retain their power to chill because of the long influence of the shaman on the lives of our ancestors.

What is incontrovertible is that most animals throughout the long history of cave painting are shown in profile, whereas a number of

32. A shaman of the Tungus tribe, 1705.

33. Paleolithic, masklike head, ca. 12,000 B.C.

human, or quasi-human, heads are full-face [33]. It is difficult to be entirely sure of their humanity as they are often so crudely scratched in the stone. What they almost invariably possess are eyes and, like the antlered man, a gimlet stare.

These are the only faces that look directly at us from our remote past. They are still disturbing today: they would have been much more so when flickeringly revealed by torchlight to the accompaniment of ritual chant and ceremony. The ritual of the sacred fire dance commemorates for the Apaches the passage of their young from puberty to adulthood. Many early societies have similar ceremonies. Was this the sort of act that was performed in the caves? The evidence is too fragmentary for us to do more than guess. Footprints congealed in the mud of some caverns tell us that children were often present. One continuous line of such youthful prints shows the weight most heavily on the heels, suggesting that the person was walking backward; perhaps a necessary part of some ritual: perhaps not. Whatever the meaning, we are reminded how often in primitive art the spirits rivet us with their eyes. Two examples, chosen at random, from Africa [34] and medieval Lincolnshire [35], so different in other ways, have in common with the so-called "ghosts" in the caves this frightening gaze.

The topography of the caves themselves produces two overriding

34. African, Janus figure, nineteenth century.

impressions. One is awe. To be picking your way through the boulders of an immense cavern, nearly a mile in extent, vaster than any man-made hall today, to the accompaniment of the thunderous symphony of a subterranean torrent, as you are in the recently discovered Tito Bustillo Cave in Asturias—or on your knees, squeezing into a tiny alcove decorated with the outline drawings of horses and reindeer no more than a handspan in size having just edged past a black abyss said to be a hundred meters deep in the little Buxo Cave high in the

35. The Lincoln Imp, thirteenth century.

mountains of Cantabria—whatever the scale, entering the caves makes you acutely conscious of the enveloping, abiding power of nature.

A power that is alien to man; yet it has immediately recognizable affinities with us. For the second impression is how surprisingly pervasive is the sexual resonance of the underworld. It is not just the damp and wrinkled walls of the main tunnel that suggest you are penetrating mother earth. Below ground animistic shapes abound. Fronds of stalactites are like the delicate inner tissue of the body. Inevitably the individual column jutting out of the earth or hanging pendulous with a drop of moisture on its tip seems a giant phallus. Just as the many natural inlets and slitlike fissures, the bulging and humping rock formations, recall both genders. Here, it might seem, we are only parasites in the entrails of a monstrous bisexual deity.

On her island in the Coral Sea, Julia believed she needed the intervention of ancestors to preserve her from the willfulness of the spirits who infest all natural things. (Of course it is unscientific to draw a direct analogy between a prehistoric society and a contemporary one, however much the latter remains untouched by modern conventions. Nevertheless, there are patterns of thought, unlike our own, which people like Julia still possess. We might consider them when pondering the reasons why early man should have chosen such fearsome sanctuaries as the caves.) Julia, living close to nature, was in a continual dialogue with it. This involved her in actions she did not question but could not explain, like giving her milk to the sea. Giving and receiving are essential to survival in all societies. Sometimes such acts take a symbolic form. Perhaps taking the young ritually into the alien but sex-laden bowels of the earth was a way of hoping to ensure their fertility. In that ambiguous space the familiar forms of the animals might be the intermediaries between early man and the voracious whims of all those natural forces which were beyond his understanding. Significantly, it seems to me, the animals are often painted on low protruding walls or, as at Altamira, on a ceiling then only some four feet above the floor of the cave. The novitiate would best absorb such shapes, flickering and pulsing in the unsteady light of torches, by lying directly beneath them.

Animals at play simulate the patterns of hunting and courtship of their own kind. Paleolithic man could do better than that; he could imagine himself in the role of other animals. He could dress up, and, it seems, play on instruments to imitate animal sounds or evoke their presence. With imagination came the ability to see things in more than one way. Imagination can make us start at shadows, and conjure in our minds the presence of dangers that perhaps are not really there. Julia sometimes saw a cluster of trees near her village as three spirits sitting together. When this happened she would not continue on the path that passed under the trees, though it was the easiest way across the island. Imagination can make it difficult to tell a hawk from a handsaw, and adds to the complexity of life.

Imagination also allows wish fulfillment. We can play in our minds with ideas which we hope will come true. There are a number of small figures of women that have survived from quite early in the period of the cave artists. One found in Haute-Garonne in France is carved from mammoth ivory [36]. It is less than six inches long, has no features and

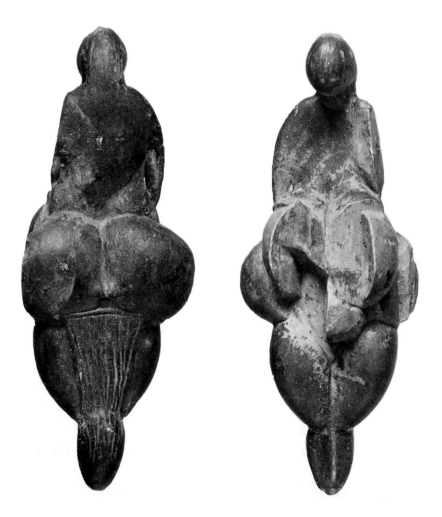

*36. Paleolithic, female
statuette, ca. 22,000 B.C.*

37. Picasso, Head of a Woman, *1931.*

no legs. Breasts, stomach, buttocks, and hips hang in a pendulous cluster like overripe grapes. Inevitably it suggests fertility, but the inclined head has made some see it as a figure of resignation and sorrow. An influential interpreter of primitive and modern art, Herbert Read, thought it was an amulet, a good-luck charm to be held in the hand. Its length and general appearance suggest it could represent the phallus as well as a pregnant female.

Dual sexuality has continued to be strong magic. In the 1930s, Picasso made a bronze head of a woman which played on the metaphors of male and female [37]. The face "is reduced to two features, the nose

rounded and powerful, which thrusts forward and is simultaneously heavy and buoyant; and below it, the mouth, soft, open, and very deeply modelled . . . The nose and the mouth are metaphors for the male and female sexual organs; the rounded forms for buttocks and thighs."[8] The little prehistoric figure is open to a similar reading, with its slender shaft rising from a bulbous mass and ending in a pronounced, slightly drooping, glans. In which case it might well have been a talisman to be grasped by women anxious for a child, but not in the hand.

There is no ambiguity in another of these figurines, the so-called Venus of Willendorf [38]. Since its discovery in Austria in 1908 it has become the most famous early image of the human race. Stocky, with vast thighs and thin arms resting on heavy breasts, it partakes of the strength of natural things: firm fruit, gnarled oak. Though clearly a cult object it has greater individuality than most primitive fetishes. Perhaps this comes from the slant of the head, with its detailed patterning, reminiscent of a modern Afro hairstyle, or even in the bend of the knees. This tiny stone carving has the strength of a clan matriarch, surveying the world from her own domain. Found in the north, it brings to mind the confident maturity of some Mother Courage of the kitchen midden. We have to progress many thousands of years closer to our own time to find a male equivalent. After the final retreat of the ice the long continuum of hunting and gathering underwent changes. The cave paintings came to an end. Rock shelters continued to be adorned here and there, and a number of vivid hunting scenes have been found in eastern Spain. Dating from approximately 7000 B.C., they have an instantly recognized, aggressive vitality. This is man the hunter, glorying in his prowess [39].

Perhaps it is not too far-fetched to see in these early images the enduring contrast of male and female: the woman, ovoid, contained, sufficient unto herself with her potential for fertility and child-bearing; man, a symbol of energy, leaping outward, brandishing the weapons which extend his innate aggression and will eventually ejaculate him to the moon. The symbiosis of predatory male and fertile female seems so fundamental that the prehistoric images are like a forecast of the physiology of the moment of human conception. Modern technology has allowed us to observe on microfilm the behavior of the ova "large and static, revolving slowly under a frilly hat," in contrast to the

38. Paleolithic, female statuette, ca. 20,000 B.C.

39. Mesolithic, rock painting of hunters and ibex, ca. 7000 B.C.

energetically swimming spermatozoa, an aggressive, but accident-prone, little pin-man. While the ova awaits her destiny placidly, the hordes of spermatozoa have to swim the equivalent of six kilometers, helping each other over fast-running shallows, navigating frond obstacles, and struggling to survive in the acid waters by which the female seeks to rid herself of unwanted marauders. And in the end, when the successful remnant cluster around the ova, what leads to one breaking through rather than the others seems as wayward and mysterious as the spell of romantic attraction itself.

In so-called primitive art, that of tribal societies in Africa, Oceania, and New Guinea, the predominant theme is fertility. Sexual energy, and its potential for renewal, has constantly been evoked, either by image or in ritual, to elicit success in hunting, in husbandry, and in war—as well as in the propagation of the species. A prehistoric rock engraving found in a cave in the Atlas Mountains of North Africa gives a direct illustration of this [40]. A hunter, poised to shoot an ostrichlike bird, is linked to a woman standing behind him by a symbolic thread connecting his penis to her vagina. The picture is an act of sympathetic magic. The hunter is able to thrust his phallus into the woman: by the same token he hopes his arrow will penetrate the prey. In recent times hunting expeditions by various African tribes were preceded by acts of ritual intercourse. By releasing sexual energy the hunter sought to participate in, and gain from, divine energy. During the Mau-Mau troubles in Kenya in the 1950s, initiates performed ritual masturbation for a similar purpose.

We look to such examples to give us a possible yardstick in our speculation on the meaning of European cave art. Another ancient

40. Paleolithic, African rock engraving linking sexuality with hunting.

engraving in the North African mountains shows an animal-headed man having intercourse with a woman wearing elaborate and precise ornaments [41]. She is holding her legs apart with her hands. The man also has a short tail, reminiscent of the horned figure in the cave in France [30]. Evidence from other parts of Africa suggests that this is an act of ritual defloration. It was common for priests wearing the masks and skins of an animal sacred to the tribe to have the duty of deflowering virgins. Thus the animal's potency was communicated to

41. African, rock engraving of ritual intercourse.

the daughters of the tribe. And they were ritually united to the animal which was their people's protective totem.

42. *Giorgione,* Venus, *ca. 1500.*

Lacking other evidence, we are inclined to interpret the cave paintings in the light of our knowledge of these more recent societies. Yet a few images survive from Paleolithic culture that confound our expectations. In a small cavern at La Magdelaine in the Tarn region of southwest France are two reliefs of women that are unique in prehistoric art. Facing each other across the narrow cave, their outlines follow the natural contours of the rock. Lightly molded and attenuated by time, they were not noticed until 1952. The subtlety of modeling would be sufficient to rouse interest, but the pose—each figure reclines full length—is hardly seen again until the Renaissance. Kenneth Clark maintains[9] that the reclining figure of a nude woman was not the subject of any famous work of art in antiquity, although sometimes to be found in the corners of Bacchic sarcophagi. (There are also a few examples in the Ancient East.) Yet here, some fifteen thousand years earlier, is the mirror image of Giorgione's *Venus* [42], the forerunner of all the reclining nudes of Western art.

Even in reproduction the prehistoric figures have a quite remarkable elegance of form. It was the deeply cut sexual triangle on the woman on the left-hand wall that caught the eye of a visiting archaeologist [43]. That and the featureless faces are the only details that other cave

43. Paleolithic, reclining female figure, ca. 12,000 B.C.

44. *Michelangelo,*
Captive, *ca. 1520.*

reliefs might lead us to expect. The woman leans back, pillowed on the stone, her left hand beneath her head, her right resting on her hip. Her legs are bent and the right, thrown upward, appears to recede in perspective—though this of course might be due only to the exigence of the rock. The pose inevitably, and not too fancifully, recalls the arched torso of one of Michelangelo's most famous creations, the first of the unfinished figures known as *The Captives* [44]. The male body, like the prehistoric female, has not been completely released from the stone, and seems to be still slumbering within it.

The woman on the opposite wall rests her head on her bent right arm [45]. The long relaxed line of her body (her right leg is stretched full length) follows a natural contour of the rocks. As one of the principal scholars of prehistoric art, S. Giedion, points out, a technique

45. Paleolithic, reclining female figure, ca. 12,000 B.C.

developed to depict animals—catching the essence of their form in a single line of a rock formation—is here applied to the human figure.[10] In an extraordinary feat of observed realism, the flaccid breasts droop naturally across the line of the figure toward the earth.

The sophistication of style suggests there must have been a tradition of work that is entirely lost to us. We are reminded that painting on skins, or on the bark of trees, carving in wood, drawing in charcoal, all the many ephemeral ways primitive man must have left his mark on his environment will have long crumbled to dust. What we are left with can only be a tiny fraction of the repertoire of styles and media in which he could express himself. Imagine if all that survived from our society were castings in iron; what a curious impression that would give to future generations.

The two reclining women of La Magdelaine are without precedent in the meager canon of human figures that we know from the Ice Ages. Nor have they left us any direct descendants. The relaxation of their pose puts them apart from the upright hieratic stance of the fertility figures. Yet even here it is the sexual parts which are most clearly delineated and which first draw the attention. And nearby is the large outline of a horse, representing, if Leroi-Gourhan is right, the male. Sexual reciprocity seems one of the characteristics of cave art.

Undoubtedly sexual in content, and very different in mood and treatment, is an even earlier carving of a woman. It is generally recognized as the first masterpiece of the human image. It was carved on a fallen outcrop of stone on a terrace halfway up the slope of a hillside above a small river, the Beune, in the Dordogne. A jutting overhang of limestone made Laussel an exceptionally sheltered dwelling site. The deposits suggest that generations of hunter-gatherers lived here. A number of figures have been carved on the rocks in a natural sanctuary near the end of the terrace.

The largest of these is the image known since its discovery in 1912 as the Venus of Laussel [46]. Like the reclining figures at La Magdelaine, it follows the curve of the stone. Like them, the face is without features. But the body is far more deeply incised. The maternal swell of the breasts and stomach are accentuated, but not to the grotesque proportions of the fertility figurines. The head is turned to one side and regards the bison horn held out in the right hand. This is carved almost in the round. The left hand rests on the bulge of the stomach, pointing to the

46. Paleolithic, woman holding a horn, ca. 20,000 B.C.

vulva. So the hands draw attention to the areas of maximum interest; the horn of plenty and the fertile mound.

The figure has such monumental assurance that it is a shock to discover that it is less than two feet tall. It encompasses many themes that later artists have labored over. Perhaps no other image has ever expressed so profoundly the dual mystery of male and female sexuality. The recognition of its undoubted sovereignty has even percolated to the exponents of modern art. It has been compared with the series of paintings of women carried out by the abstract expressionist Willem de Kooning in the 1950s [47]. He himself has acknowledged the debt. "The Women had to do with the female painted through all the ages, all those idols, and maybe I was stuck to a certain extent; I couldn't go

47. De Kooning,
Woman III, 1951–52.

on [with pure abstraction]."[11] De Kooning's women are powerful, predatory creatures, as likely to slap as embrace. Despite their wide thighs and universal pretensions, they seem to arise from the ambivalence of the artist, his specific needs and problems, rather than the demands of the subject.

We do not know the incentives of the unknown artist at Laussel. Were there patron-shamans whose requirements would be as precise as those of the curators of the great modern museums and their clientele, on whom ultimately an artist like de Kooning must rely? We do know from comparing their work, that ancient man had one strong benefit: he lacked modern man's paralyzing self-consciousness. However powerful the creative energy that the contemporary artist can liberate, there remains in his work an element of creative play. He must tease himself with doubt. What's it all about, really? Whereas, after all the centuries, the Venus of Laussel still conveys a powerful reverence for life. Because of this it seems an infinitely greater work of art than de Kooning's jokey floozies; but, of course, this is just as much a critique of their cultures as of the artists.

In any direct comparison between a major primitive work and an acknowledged modern masterpiece, the primitive has weighty advantages. Its purpose is to express a belief, and hence it carries an infinitely greater emotional charge, even when we do not know directly the nature of the belief. The purpose of the modern work may be to amuse, or to shock, or to please, but it can do so only from the point of view of the artist. It does not have the weight of a whole culture behind it. Why then should we make the comparison when the aims are so different? Much modern art has invited us to do so, by pillaging the art of earlier societies for fresh idioms and a revival of energy. But such piracy inevitably suffers from the law of decreasing returns. It is not based on the beliefs that motivated the original artists, but simply borrows the stylistic tricks, the rough-hewn forms, by which those beliefs were expressed. In the hands of a nonbeliever, they rapidly become clichés.

Yet we must be careful not to imply a commensurate approval of a whole society, just because its art has a conviction and an energy that ours has not. To return to the Paleolithic caves, we have little knowledge of how the hunter-gatherers organized themselves, how they looked and spoke and decorated their hair. We have no idea what sorts of clothes they wore. (It is unlikely they went naked in an area where the ice began only a few days' travel away.) They have left us far more lively images of animals than of themselves. For a period of over twenty thousand years less than two hundred representations of men and women survive and none of children. There are fewer of women than men, but the women are significantly more powerful as works of art. Whereas the women usually appear nakedly as themselves, that is, in their maternal function, the men are more often masked and given the trappings of animals, that is, of an assumed external authority. That should surely give us food for thought.

In my childhood in the twenties and thirties, it was still common to portray the life of prehistoric man as nasty, brutish, and short. The shocks and pains of relentless change have made us abandon such crude notions. Every gain brings its concomitant loss. The cave painters must have had the confidence that goes with an immensely enduring society. Abundance of game would make their life much easier (and more dangerous) than that of, for instance, the Australian aborigine who were living until recently a somewhat similar existence in a drier climate with far fewer animals to hunt. The first generations of men with a brain power equal to our own, the cave painters had the gift of space and none of the destructive alternatives which nag less developed people now. Even today, isolated communities like Julia's still manifest a sense of order which seems appropriate to their experience. The advantages are so obvious we must not forget the accompanying evils: a relatively brief life, the inability to alleviate suffering, boredom. For us that last would be the ultimate *coup de grâce*.

Art, they say, reflects the values of its time. In Paleolithic culture, we must assume, man saw himself as secondary to the animals upon whom he depended for sustenance. From them he took his metaphors for energy and potency and beauty. It would be many thousands of years before man paced with such lively grace through his own art and that would be in the early days of the first great civilization on the Nile.

3

MEN LIKE GODS

The world remembers Egypt for its mummies, pyramids, temples. No other society has been so obsessed with preparations for eternity. The Egyptian, laboring on the green strip beside the Nile which is the habitable part of his country, had the contrast between life and nonlife constantly before him. At his feet were the fields made fertile by the waters of the great river; on the horizon was the desert, somber, immense, arid. It was on the edge of the desert that Pharaohs built their vast individual memorials, the pyramids. Around them were placed the tombs of favored court officials, lesser mounds in the aeons of sand.

Yet, paradoxically, these monuments to mortality have preserved more vitality than all the other early relics of man. The Egyptian wanted to take the good things of this life with him into the grave. He wanted the objects he had known on earth to be ready for his use in the afterworld. He wanted to be reminded of his wife and family and servants and the existence he had enjoyed on the banks of the Nile. So his tomb had space for furniture and food and the inner walls were covered with a record of daily life in his time. The result is the first great evocation of the human body in art.

It was an intensely visual civilization. Even its writing consisted of pictures, often as beautifully carved as the surrounding scenes. And through its images of the body (often naked or scantily draped, especially in the early formative centuries) we can observe the first development of concepts that we are still grappling with today. Profound changes have taken place since the time when the Paleolithic artists created their fertility figures. The functions of men and women are much more clearly defined and compartmentalized; and the art suggests a shift in the relative status of the sexes. No longer is the female the most important image; it is the male ruler, the Pharaoh, who walks tallest.

18. Archaic Period,
Palette of Narmer
(obverse), ca. 3000 B.C.

The whole organization of society, the crystallization of religious beliefs, the appearance of big troublesome ideas such as kingship, war, conquest, empire, self-sacrifice, resurrection, and immortality—all are literally embodied in an art of unparalleled vividness.

Here there are no mysterious presences like the painted animals in the caves, posing questions that we cannot answer. When we pass through the dark entries of the tombs at Sakkara, we are suddenly in the presence of people like ourselves: working, feasting, quarreling, caught in stone relief in the midst of irrepressibly human acts. A man paces quickly through the market glancing around for customers for the trapped birds he carries on a yoke. In just such wooden boxes live ducks and pigeons can be bought in Aswân today. A line of lissome girls carry baskets of produce on their heads as they still do along the banks of the Nile. Vivid detail continually catches the eye. A youth with a stick urges on a line of animals (they are closer in build to the wild ass than to the modern donkey). Knee-deep in the grain they are threshing, one bends his neck to take a nibble, while the boy puts his hand in front of his face to protect it from the flying chaff. In a pose

49. Old Kingdom, cowherder carrying a calf, ca. 2450 B.C.

that has entered significantly into later art, the herdsman carries a young calf across the water while its mother lows anxiously behind [49].

The animals are portrayed with as much sympathy and vitality as the humans—but no more. They are now the servants of man, not the enigmatic symbols of energy of the prehistoric caves. In the intervening millennia, there has been a crucial shift of destiny. The human species

50. Old Kingdom, the steward Memy-Sabu and his wife, ca. 2500 B.C.

no longer skulks at the cavern mouth in remote uplands, the puny adversary of the powerful animal kingdom. Man is on the way to mastering the environment through the seasonal planting of crops. He has conquered time by his invention of writing. Housing, weapons, social organization, have made him undisputed lord of the planet. Already he hunts the king of beasts, the lion, merely for sport. The resulting optimism and confident enjoyment show in the individual portraits. A steward Memy-Sabu puts his hand affectionately on his wife's breast, while her hand is around his waist [50]. They are a homely, comfortably adjusted couple. We have never seen their like before and will rarely do so again. Most ethnic art celebrates religious emotion and is generalized. When in later civilizations we are brought face to face with individuals, they are almost always the great and powerful. Only from the Renaissance onward will we occasionally be confronted with portraits of ordinary people. In Ancient Egypt they abound.

Especially is this true of the very beginnings of ordered society along the Nile, the Old Kingdom, as it is now known. All the reliefs at Sakkara come from this period, more than forty-five hundred years ago. It was the first great civilization and the longest-surviving. Perhaps never again was man to feel such confidence in his powers—and his destiny [51]. Only in moments immediately succeeding a successful revolution—in America, France, Russia—do we catch in the images of modern man that expression of alert yet contented self-esteem. Now, disillusion quickly follows; in Egypt it took centuries to materialize.

Because its wealth was ultimately based on seasonal agriculture and guaranteed by an assured, predictable event, the annual flooding of the Nile which irrigated the valley of the river, Egyptian culture was highly conservative. Self-sustaining, never needing for many centuries to look outside itself for renewal, its art, though growing ever more sophisticated, became rigidly formalized. But in its first two hundred years the Old Kingdom was amazingly adventurous and innovative. More monuments which beggar description are to be found there than anywhere else in the world, said Herodotus.[1]

The stability necessary to create such vast corporate works as the pyramids came from an event around 3000 B.C. of which we still have a visual record. In the Cairo Museum is a gray triangle about two feet high. Made of slate, it was designed as a palette on which to grind the pigment that went to make eye shadow. The reliefs on it purport to commemorate the unification of Upper and Lower Egypt. On one side a King, Narmer, is shown clubbing a kneeling enemy with a stone mace [48]. We know his name because it appears in primitive hieroglyphs in the image of a palace above his head. He thus becomes the first named human being to be visible to us. By the same token he is the first king we can recognize as such; he already has distinguishing headgear (the high white crown of Upper Egypt) and mace, and behind him his attendant carries his sandals and a pot of water to wash his feet. On the reverse side, wearing the red crown of Lower Egypt, he walks in procession preceded by his long-haired priest in leopard skin

51. Old Kingdom, a scribe (possibly Kai, a provincial governor), ca 2500 B.C.

and four standard bearers carrying fetishes [52]. Today on ceremonial occasions the Queen of England is preceded by her chamberlain carrying a tall white wand; at her coronation she has scepter and crown, and is made the Lord's anointed with holy oil; the symbols of office and the alliance of monarchy and clergy have hardly changed through five thousand years from their first appearance on this palette.

52. Archaic Period,
Palette of Narmer
(reverse), ca. 3000 B.C.

Above the kneeling victim of the King on the obverse is an elaborate design including a hawklike bird. Interpreted as hieroglyphs it is said to read: "Pharaoh, the incarnation of the hawk-god, Horus, with his strong right arm leads captive the marsh-dwellers." Below, two naked, fleeing men can be identified by the emblematic buildings at their shoulders as natives of the Nile Delta. On the reverse the King walks out to inspect the bodies of rebels, laid out with bound arms, their decapitated heads neatly placed between their feet. The slaughter is captioned as taking place in the Delta town of Buto. At the bottom of the palette, the King, in the guise of a bull, smashes into another town which has a large temple or palace in it. He tramples on a prostrate enemy, probably a Libyan.

So Narmer is shown punishing internal rebellion and chastizing his neighbors. The first visible named man in history is glorying in war and the slaughter of his fellowmen. But if it is true that he brought about the unification of Egypt—said to be symbolized by the intertwining of the necks of the mythical beasts that form the cosmetic dish in the middle of the palette—if it is true, then Narmer ensured many centuries of prosperity for his descendants. The Old Kingdom, which was the ultimate result of the union, flourished for over five hundred years. Though there were later periods of Egyptian splendor, known to us as the Middle and New Kingdoms, neither lasted so long nor produced as dynamic art.

We have not yet exhausted the significance of the palette, in its way as loaded with meaning as a microchip. On each side at the top, flanking the hieroglyph of the King's name, is the head of a cow-goddess, probably Hathor. She was a symbol of fertility and joy, the goddess who suckled the Pharaoh. And the King is already shown as divine in himself. He is depicted twice the size of his subjects. The propaganda device of gigantic portrayal has been emulated by many rulers since, down to Hitler and Mao. Just as the victorious pose of Narmer with mace upraised is repeated through three thousand years of Egyptian imagery, so all later Pharaohs elect to be divine.

By getting a representative in Heaven, man drew closer to the gods. Until now divinities were totems; the images of animal energy that rallied the individual tribe or clan. The king was the embodiment of hawk and raging bull, but he was also a man. If he was immortal, the other gods must be like him, and be able to assume human form. So on Narmer's palette we see the cow-goddess in mid-transformation from animal to human. In following dynasties she will often lose her broad ears and horns and simply be represented as a beautiful woman [53], but a thousand years later Hathor can still be a cow, suckling the

53. Old Kingdom, the goddess Hathor, ca. 2500 B.C.

54. New Kingdom, Hathor as a cow giving milk to the young Amenhotep II, ca. 1500 B.C.

youthful Amenhotep II [54]. The pliant Egyptian mind wanted to have it both ways, as it has continued to do. But what was certain was that the King had unified Egypt, so all the local clan totems had to be acknowledged and accepted into his rule. In time they nearly all acquired human characteristics. The Pantheon of gods was born, later to be adopted and adapted by the Greeks.

Initially, it was not so much that God walked on earth, but that man stepped up to Heaven and transformed its occupants into his own image. Intoxicated by his newfound power and good fortune he was soon building the mighty stairways to paradise of the pyramids. Mykerinus, the Pharaoh who built as his tomb the last and smallest of the three pyramids at Giza, advances in his temple image with all the bland self-assurance of a United States senator flanked by cheerleaders at a party convention [55]. In fact the ladies are Hathor and a regional goddess who wears the emblem of her district, a jackal, on her head. Their cozy embrace, sensuous curves, and pronounced pubic triangles emphasize their close relationship with the Pharaoh. The sexual underlining is intentional as they have been given the features of

55. Old Kingdom, King Mykerinus between Hathor and local deity, ca. 2500 B.C.

Mykerinus' wife, suggesting that, in his elevated state, congress with the gods is habitual.

To be represented by such an exalted being made the simple fellaheen eager to labor on the Pharaoh's behalf. And it was physical labor and the simplest tools that produced the great monuments of the Old Kingdom. Through them, and the splendid reliefs and statues they contain, we can observe the progress of society's aspirations from the moderate-sized vitality of the Old Kingdom to the grandiose embodiments of the Pharaohs of the New Kingdom. We can also follow the fluctuating fortunes of male and female principles in their hold on the human heart; a struggle that had already begun in the earliest urban societies of which we have found any record.

The achievements that followed the unification of Upper and Lower Egypt are still so strikingly visible that it is easy to see it as a new dawn. But we could equally regard it as the climax of agricultural and social changes that had begun five thousand years earlier. In scattered places in the Middle East the cultivation of wild wheat and barley, the domestication of sheep, goats, dogs, pigs, and cattle, had begun in the eighth millennium B.C. This was the so-called Neolithic revolution. A more sedentary way of life led surprisingly quickly to the growth of quite large settlements, and this in turn to specialization in crafts, the development of pottery and textiles, and to the beginnings of organized trade. How such centers worked socially we do not know. We are still in the—to us—mute ages before written speech. Nor is there much art to illuminate the feelings of these first citizens. It is tempting to imagine them immersed in developing their skills, living for the first time in their own houses (mud-brick was another invention), obsessed with their burgeoning possessions (each house had its own granary store), and anxious to protect their property from thieves.

The largest of these sites to have been excavated, Çatal Hüyük in Anatolia, was built more than three thousand years before the first pyramids. In it the houses had communal walls with other houses, so the settlement grew like a honeycomb. There were no external windows or doors. Entry was through a hole in the flat roof, presumably down a ladder which could be withdrawn for defense. (The sacred Khiva of the Hopi Indians are not dissimilar today.) The many skeletons found with smashed skulls suggests security was necessary. The acquisition of property was to prove a mixed blessing. Almost the only Neolithic

couple to come down to us as sculpture have a calculating, care-worn air [56]. Çatal Hüyük is also the earliest center from which we have recovered the stamped clay seals which preceded money.

A decisive change was taking place in human society; perhaps the greatest until our own day. The long ages when mankind subsisted in small groups, wandering with the game or the seasonal appearance of fruits, were drawing to a close. The Neolithic revolution was to add unforeseen complexities to all relationships, not least those between the sexes. Frederick Engels, writing a hundred years ago, believed that the groups of hunter-gatherers had shared responsibility for the upbringing of children and the only strong link had been the maternal one. The cultivation of the land required the breakup of the hunting pack, scattering it into smaller units over a wide area. (One plot of land could not support all the diversely linked members of the clan.) Once the split into couples became the norm, Engels argued, the male acquired

56. Neolithic, Europe, man and woman, ca. 3600 B.C.

unique responsibility, because he had to shoulder the physically heavier burdens of plowing, reaping, and animal husbandry. He thus gained much greater authority over the children. "The overthrow of mother right was the *world historical defeat of the female sex*. The man took command in the home also; the woman was degraded and reduced to servitude; she became the slave of his lust and a mere instrument for the production of children. This degraded position of the woman . . . has gradually been palliated and glossed over, and sometimes clothed in a milder form; in no sense has it been abolished."[2] This was strong stuff to publish in the paternalistic 1880s. Engels was so against the family—he believed it contained all the contradictions which later extended throughout society—that he dedicated future Communist states to eradicating it. However, none have done so. Like capitalism, the male/female pair, with all its drawbacks, has proved hard to displace. Perhaps it is important to add that Engels, though a devoted lover, was never a father.

Even if we question Engels' assumption that the earliest human societies were matrilineal—it is hard to see how there would ever be conclusive evidence either way—it seems likely the position of women deteriorated. Once cattle were domesticated they became the province of the men and the main source of livelihood. Handling the nearly wild aurochs, large and ferocious and the ancestor of domestic breeds, must have required all the courage and quick wits displayed by the cowboys on the Chisholm Trail, and the Neolithic herdsman had no horse to canter him out of danger. On the other hand the women found *their* old skills usurped when farming replaced foraging. Instead of being able to wander as freely as the men seeking edible plants and fruits, home duties, basket work, pottery, weaving, bound them ever closer to the drudgery of the individual hearth.

Striking evidence of the glamour attached to cattle herding is to be found in the shrines unearthed at Çatal Hüyük. The place was lived in continuously from 6500 to 5700 B.C. There are no temples as we think of them, but some of the dwellings were clearly set aside for cult purposes. They contain many baked clay images of a bulbous fertility goddess, familiar to us from prehistoric art, in association with a bull's head, usually modeled in plaster with real auroch's horns. The most impressive and mysterious of the goddesses is seated on a throne flanked by leopards and is apparently giving birth to a child [57]. She is the

57. Neolithic, Anatolia,
fertility goddess, ca.
6000 B.C.

first throned figure by thousands of years and has the immense authority
of that great gulf of time. In another sculpture the goddess is trampling
on human skulls, the mistress of death as well as life.

The shrines contain other harbingers of mortality; plaster models
of female breasts are built around the actual lower jaws of boar, skulls
of foxes, weasels, and vultures. The vultures also appear in paintings
where they are given the legs of men. When we are told that the
citizens of Çatal Hüyük put the bodies of their deceased out to be eaten
by such scavengers, prior to burying their bones beneath their beds, our
distaste is increased.

There is something grating, savage, and unresolved about these shrines, poised at equidistance from the last energetic flowering of the cave paintings and the serene art of the Old Kingdom tombs. Everywhere there are the giant horns of the aurochs: jutting from benches, raised on brick pillars, rising in tiers on the walls. We feel the male principle in its most aggressive form bursting into the sanctuary of the female deity. Over a doorway through which peer the heads of three ferocious bulls is straddled the plaster figure of a woman nearly four feet high, giving birth—to a bull. In the plaster reliefs it is only the goddess who is granted human shape; the male is represented by his symbols, the bull, the ram, occasionally the stag or wild boar or leopard. In the statuary men appear; youthful, riding on bulls or leopards, or accompanied by a bird of prey and an old woman. It is difficult not to conclude that we are witnessing a moment of transition, when the old fertility beliefs, centered on the woman, are under direct threat from the newfound power and confidence of the male.

Among the wall paintings (the earliest yet discovered) are crowded scenes that appear to represent the celebration of animal games [58]. Small capering figures crowd around giant bulls, stags, and boar, pulling

58. Neolithic, Anatolia, bull, stag, and boar baiting, ca. 6000 B.C.

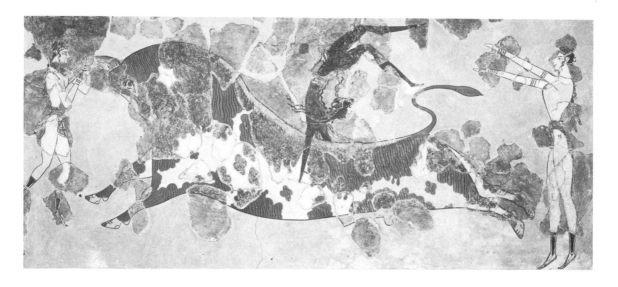

59. *Minoan Crete, bull leaping, ca. 1500 B.C.*

them by the tail, alarmingly touching them on nose or tongue, bending over and presenting a derisive backside to their gaping jaws. The plaster bulls' heads in the shrines often have red hand impressions on the nose. Perhaps they were touched by male initiates who then completed the rite of passage by blooding themselves in mock contest with the bulls; those same bulls that in adult life they would gain prestige by herding.

Whatever their purpose, the connection with the Minoan bull games seems clear. In these famous contests the young Cretans somersaulted over the horns of a charging bull [59]. If the fact that they occur some four thousand years later seems to make any link tenuous, we can visit the bull running at Pamplona, where scenes very similar to those on the walls of Çatal Hüyük are still enacted every year.

Festivals celebrating the power of the bull usually suggest a male-oriented society; yet the cult of the goddess has proved extraordinarily resilient and pervasive. Her image is found all over the Near East and Eastern Mediterranean. Deeply rooted in the agricultural life of small communities, she has been dispossessed, suppressed, harnessed into other religions, but never completely lost. Some of her liveliest representations come from Hacilar, another center in Anatolia [60]. Hacilar was a small village that was burned down about 5400 B.C., so the pottery figures are only a few hundred years later than those at Çatal Hüyük. There is a similarity in the treatment of the broad almond eyes and heavy thighs, but the Hacilar figures are altogether more sinuous and energetic. The leopards reappear, but here the goddess, while sitting on one, embraces the other. Its paws are around her neck, its hind legs against her abdomen. Another embrace is with a human figure half her size. It might be a child, but the tense counterthrust of the entwined limbs suggests a sexual encounter.

Over two thousand years later, Narmer, while opting to raise himself to godhood when he conquered the Nile delta, cautiously put the endorsement of a residing god on his palette. And he chose a female, bovine deity. The Pharaohs continued to succeed, at least nominally, through the female line, their sisters. And a number of goddesses retained their importance in Egypt, a country where at one time there were said to be 740 deities.

One, whose elongated body arches over many royal tombs, is the sky-goddess, Nut. She was originally a mother-goddess, but in the Egyptian cosmology is the lover of her twin brother, Geb, the Earth-

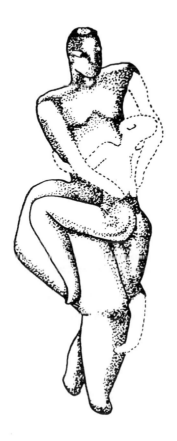

60. Modern drawing of Neolithic entwined figures, ca. 5400 B.C.

god. She mounted his prone body, a position which has been said to be ancient and matriarchal. Their father, Shu, the god of air, separated them [61], thus allowing space and light to be created, and the world as we know it to begin. (This story in itself may be symptomatic of the reduced role of the woman, as it is a patriarchal deity that keeps the goddess apart from earth.) The passion of Nut and Geb continued and each evening she descended upon him, bringing night to the earth. The interdict against the female dominant position still applies, apparently, in Islam: "cursed be he who makes the woman the sky and the man the earth."[3]

Nut was also connected to the idea of resurrection. Each night she swallowed the sun, which passed through her to be reborn in the morning. The blood she shed in giving birth was said to color the dawn. The friendly sky of her body, showing the sun in transit through it, was often painted on the inner lid of coffins to ease the soul of the deceased through the night of the afterlife [62]. By Geb she had five children, including Osiris, Isis, and Set. Osiris was originally a corn-god from the Delta. His fertility cult spread through Egypt. His image, made into a bag of seeds, was ritually buried to propagate the crops. It was from these simple elements that his myth grew.

In it Osiris was murdered by his jealous younger brother, Set, and his dismembered body scattered. His wife, who was also his sister, Isis, eventually found and reconstituted all the parts except the phallus. Set

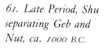

61. Late Period, Shu separating Geb and Nut, ca. 1000 B.C.

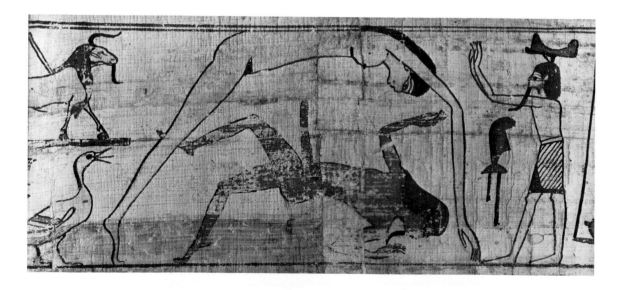

62. Late Period, the goddess Nut, ca. 600 B.C.

had thrown it into the Nile where it was eaten by a fish. (We remember the fish was a symbol of sex in the cave paintings. Also in ancient times the sexual parts of fallen foes were often cut off and scattered to aid fertility.) Isis was not defeated. She modeled another phallus for her husband. For the first time the rites of embalmment were performed and Osiris was restored to eternal life.

This myth probably gained its hold on Egypt initially due to the growth of elaborate funerary practices meant to preserve the body. First carried out for the nobility and priesthood, they gradually spread downward through the community. Osiris, because of his resurrection, became the center of Egypt's preoccupation with immortality. His temple at Abydos, built by Seti I in about 1300 B.C., still has a remarkably charged atmosphere. In a side chapel two reliefs capture the tragic pathos and triumphal regeneration of Osiris. In one the dead god lies prostrate [63]. Isis stands behind him, supporting his head with one hand and stroking his brow with the other. Osiris is stirring. In a gesture of touching weakness that signifies his returning consciousness, he raises his left hand toward his head. His right hand instinctively clutches the upright phallus which Isis has given him. Bending over his feet and reaching toward the right hand of Osiris with his own is a powerful man with a hawk's head. This is Sokar, the god of the

63. Drawing of New Kingdom relief, Isis tending the dead Osiris, ca. 1300 B.C.

necropolis at Sakkara. So this shrine unites elements of creation and resurrection from widely separated centers. There is a Mozartian vitality in the classical restraint with which all the rhythms of the relief are connected and revealed through the movements of the hands: soothing and tender for the wife, pliant and weak for the husband, beneficent and strong for Sokar.

On the opposite wall there are no such contrapuntal energies. Everything is poised on a single moment: that of creation [64]. Osiris is now in his mummy wrappings, wearing the white crown of Upper Egypt. Once more Isis stands protectively beside his head. The loss of her husband was more poignant for her because they had no child. This is about to be rectified. In the guise of a hawk she also flutters above the upright phallus, her wing tips brushing the body of the dead god. At the foot of the tomb, Horus, the god who is being conceived, looks on majestically, his right hand raised in benediction.

Time has damaged the reliefs, though not enough to conceal their grandeur. But in both cases the phallus has vanished completely, leaving the reverse image of its absence, a gap in the stone. What Set could not achieve, the gullibility of many generations has managed, chipping away to carry off a fragment of fertility as sympathetic magic. Nor in the 1980s is the age of Osiris over. As I left the chapel I came across a

64. Drawing of New Kingdom relief, conception of Horus, ca. 1300 B.C.

group of fashionably dressed Egyptians watching in amused embarrassment as one of their party walked round and round a small standing stone, raising her skirts provocatively. She wanted a child and was invoking the aid of Osiris: a perfectly natural, time-honored practice.

Isis hoped that Horus would grow up to avenge his father's death. So he did, but only after many vicissitudes. Fleeing from Set, Isis had to beg to support her child; time and again she had to use all her ingenuity to save him. From being the faithful wife she now becomes the prototype of the protective mother [65]. Horus grew strong and fought terrible battles with Set. Before he regained his rightful kingdom, his father had to return from the underworld and intervene crucially on his behalf.

65. Late Period, Isis with the infant Horus, ca. 300 B.C.

It is easy to see why the family-loving Egyptians embraced the story of Osiris. The Greeks recognized the connection with their myth of Dionysus. The Romans set up temples to Isis, and her cult in Rome probably influenced the early Christian veneration of the Virgin Mary. As for Osiris, the spread of warfare made the image of the fallen hero appropriate for all later nations. From Greek and Roman monuments to victory, up to countless war memorials in this century, the urge to commemorate those struck down in the flower of manhood has retained its power. We wish to believe, as Isis did, that the sacrifice of loved ones has not been in vain. Like her, we want to keep alive the compassion generated by past suffering.

Through the myth of Osiris, an entirely new sentiment permeated mankind. This was of profound importance in art, but crucial to religion. The unifying urge of the Egyptians had cast local gods, originally animal fetishes, into a human, universally recognizable image. Now they created a spirit, suffering as we suffer, who would be the intermediary for our redemption and resurrection. For Osiris presided over the judgment of the dead, which preceded the deceased's entry into the afterlife. Eventually the weighing of the soul involved the need to lead a virtuous life on earth —quite a different concept to simply paying dues to Caesar for material well-being on earth. Morality had a pragmatic purpose, to ensure a happy immortality.

The growth of the Osiris myth can be seen as the success of reconciling opposing sexual attitudes. By his suffering, Osiris abrogated the conventional female role, even to the point of losing his manhood. It was a woman who remade it. Moreover, with a typically Egyptian grasp of practicality, it was the woman who needed it most, his wife, Isis. The part Osiris plays in the myth is almost entirely passive, whereas Isis is energetic, resourceful, and brave. It is a complete role reversal, down to her assuming in the sexual act the matriarchal position. But at the same time all her actions are to support her husband, and later her son. She has plenty of initiative, but she uses it selflessly in the masculine cause.

When Osiris graduated to become the principal intermediary between humanity and the afterlife—all prayers for the dead were addressed through him—he lifted the authority of the masculine principle a further notch. Woman's initial authority rested on her ability to give life. But it was only for an earthly span. Now a male deity was granting eternal life. Because Osiris was thought in some sense to have once been an earthly king, his power in the afterlife added to the prestige of the Pharaoh, his present proxy on earth.

Just as the corn sprouting through his linen effigy was ritually sheared to encourage the harvest, so men saw the restoration of Osiris to his full powers after death as a hopeful omen for their own future. Osiris was often portrayed supine in funeral wrappings, but sexually vital. The *Book of the Dead* requests of the afterlife: "May I be able to make love there." In the New Kingdom the penis of the dead man was often preserved in a small obelisk in the tomb. The obelisk was decorated with the image of Osiris and Isis, a symbol that the dead man also hoped to be reunited with his earthly partner in the afterlife.

The spread of the Osiris cult through the lower levels of the community may have accelerated the practice of one of the most bizarre of male customs, circumcision. Inspection of mummies suggests that the operation was carried out even before the formation of the Old Kingdom, but not universally. Probably it was a distinction awarded to caste; a blood brotherhood that drew together priests and princes. They may have had a precedent in the behavior of the sun-god, Ra. As the father of the Egyptian gods he had the responsibility for the creation of the world—always a problem with a masculine-orientated religion. Alone in the inchoate waste of waters Ra produced children either through union with his shadow; masturbation; or a self-inflicted wound. "These are the drops of blood that flow from Ra's phallus when he has mutilated himself. They have turned into gods who find themselves in Ra's presence."[4] His priests may have emulated his injury as a visible demonstration of their dedication to his service.

This is speculation. But by the Fifth Dynasty, around 2500 B.C., circumcision is so frequently illustrated in reliefs and papyruses [66] that it must have been widely practiced. Herodotus thought that the Egyptians had originated the custom.[5] The adolescent age of the candidates, their isolation in some scenes behind a fenced enclosure, with whitened faces, forced to submit to severe physical ordeals such as flogging, all suggests affinities with the ceremonies that continue in much of East and Central Africa to this day. These rites of passage into manhood are deeply ingrained into tribal life. They have proved hard to eradicate. A significant reason comes from the Dogon tribe of West Africa: "A boy is female by his foreskin, while a girl is masculine by her clitoris."[6] It seems likely the foreskin was another price man had to pay in his assertion of godly dominance over the female. He removed the flaccid folds that in the naked male could look disturbingly similar to the labia. Later he began to shave off the tip of the clitoris as well,[7] to ensure the total femininity of his partner. A survey conducted as recently as 1979 by the Cairo Family Planning Association showed that 90 percent of the girls interviewed had had some part of the labia and clitoris removed.[8]

66. Old Kingdom, circumcision, ca. 2350 B.C.

Osiris took on many of Ra's functions, including his symbol of the sun. A splendid pectoral that once adorned the chest of Tutankhamen shows Isis and her sister Neftis protecting the djed-column of Osiris [67]. The djed-column represents the tamarisk tree in which Osiris' body was hidden when Isis was searching for him. Topped by the solar disk and stroked by the wings of the goddesses, it seems the apotheosis of masculine power. The sloping, transverse pattern of the wings sweeping up to a peak—the column itself with its four horizontal lines, said to represent the lopped branches of the tree, but suggesting rather four successive horizons over which the orange disk rises—conveys a sense of effortless uplifting vitality. This is contained, first within the feathery solicitous wings of the female deities and finally by the reassuringly solid palace which outlines the jewel. The effect is erotic, beautiful, and soothing all at once. If there is an emotion for the experience of resurrection, this is its anagram.

Only a society with a wealthy leisured class would produce such assured elegance. The treasures of Tutankhamen's tomb continue to excite amazement. Yet he was a very minor Pharaoh, who died too young to have amassed much. These were the boom years of the New

67. New Kingdom, Isis and Neftis protect the djed column of Osiris, ca. 1360 B.C.

Kingdom. Under Tutankhamen's successors in the fourteenth and thirteenth centuries B.C. Egypt reached the zenith of her material power.

The well-to-do had never had it so good. Many of the young nobility look straight out of the pages of a 1920s *Vogue*. Feasts would be enlivened with the music of harp and flutes and the sinuous shimmy of youthful dancing girls [68]. The Pharaoh interrupts his game of draughts for a little dalliance with one of his concubines [69], of whom he has several hundred. All rich men had a harem, and few of any class were monogamous. But the family was sacrosanct, and the status

68. New Kingdom, dancing girls, ca. 1500 B.C.

of the chief wife assured. Children were as well loved as dancing girls.

No society until nineteenth-century Europe and America has paid so much attention to the delights of being young. One of the few physical embraces in Egyptian art is the innocent kiss of nurse and child. She was the daughter of an exceptional Pharaoh, Akhenaton. But the daughters of an ordinary man, Nakht, a middle-range civil servant of the New Kingdom, would have the fun of going with him on a hunting trip in the marshes [70]. The eldest steadies her father for the throw, the middle one, a bit apprehensive, hangs on to his knees, and the youngest, anxious to be noticed and helpful, points to where the fish are jumping. Of course those poses became as conventionalized as photographs of family seaside holidays have in our time. But their similarity to each other does not mean that they are any less genuine records of individual pleasures.

A loving zest for life. It colors the New Kingdom recording of experience as much as it did the reliefs in the Old Kingdom tombs fifteen hundred years earlier. A sure sign of contentment must be that the Egyptians wished the afterlife to be exactly like life on the Nile.

69. New Kingdom, Rameses III and a concubine, ca. 1190 B.C.

70. New Kingdom, Nakht and his family on hunting trip, ca. 1410 B.C.

They wanted their bodies preserved for their future enjoyment, down to every last wart and blemish. The final words of the embalming ritual were: "You live again, you live again forever, here you are once more for ever."[9]

It is strange that such a materialistic people should have produced a profound leap of the imagination like the wounded hero. But of course a practical acceptance of life involves recognizing the thousand natural shocks the flesh is heir to. The Egyptians had to take what steps they could to alleviate the effects of these shocks. Creating a myth that allowed them to turn death into victory was the *coup de foudre*.

Isis and Osiris maintained their hold on the popular imagination for nearly three thousand years. They survived the social collapse of the Old Kingdom, and the empire building of the New. The temples and palaces grew larger and grander than ever, and so did the statues of the Pharaohs. Though divine, they had remained human in scale in the cheerful days when civilization was beginning. By the thirteenth century B.C. Rameses II at Abu Simbel towers over eighty feet high even when seated. Standing, his queen barely reaches to his knee [71]. Perhaps she is admonishing him for his ardor; in his long reign of over sixty years, he sired more than a hundred sons.

No other human being can have been carved so often on such a scale. It is possible to sit comfortably on his little toe at his mortuary temple on the edge of the desert at Thebes. The rest of the body lies in a vast broken hulk nearby [72]. It was this memorable illustration to collapsed vanity that the English poet Shelley commemorated:

> *'My name is Ozymandias, King of Kings:*
> *Look on my works, ye Mighty, and despair!'*
> *Nothing beside remains. Round the decay*
> *Of that colossal wreck, boundless and bare*
> *The lone and level sands stretch far away.*[10]

Though Rameses' image is shattered, his physical body survives. I have held it in my arms: it was light and brittle as a dry stick, and brown as the inside of an old teapot. The mummy was discovered in 1881, survived being unwrapped, and is now on exhibit in the Cairo Museum. By their skill in evisceration, painting, and embalming, the Egyptians turned the body itself into a work of art.

Rameses also cultivated a reputation as a warrior. In the early days of the Old Kingdom there were few images of battle. Egypt had no foreign rivals to speak of, and was absorbed with internal construction. Moreover the benign charm of the fertile river, protected on both sides by the desert, made, and still makes, for an easygoing acceptance of life. Even today the most vicious elements at the mortuary temple seem the small African bees that shrill like bullets in and out of the tamarisk trees above the broken feet of Rameses' statue. But they fly in front of a huge stone relief of fearful carnage [73]. Here Rameses, jaunty in his war chariot, is showering death and confusion on the tumbled masses of his foes. This is a spruced-up version of a real struggle between the invading Egyptian army and the Hittites that took place at Kadesh in Syria in 1286 B.C. It is the first battle in history of which we have a detailed account. Characteristically, both sides claimed Kadesh as a victory. As in all later battles, it was the ordinary man who suffered

71. New Kingdom, statue of Rameses II with a queen, ca. 1250 B.C.

72. Colossus of Rameses II, photograph of 1867

the losses. From this time on the history of art is full of monuments to those who have died in wars they little understood, for causes following generations have barely comprehended and remembered with indifference.

73. New Kingdom, Battle of Kadesh, ca. 1280 B.C.

"But what good came of it at last?"
quoth little Peterkin.
"Why that I cannot tell," said he:
"But 'twas a famous victory."[11]

Despite the bombast of Rameses II, Egypt herself soon suffered invasion. In the following thousand years of decline and disorder, the precepts of Osiris came to express the concerns of the time: "Give food to the hungry, drink to the thirsty, clothes to the naked, and assist the traveler."[12]

The evocation of Osiris as the voice of the poor and needy shows that the glorious dawn of civilization was over. Humanity was beginning to learn the price. Organized society increased the opportunities for social advancement but also for social aggression and exploitation. Yet there were compensations—for the affluent. City life brought the opportunity to cultivate sensibilities which earlier generations had not had the time to dream about, and introduced a new element of erotic pleasure to the image of the body.

4

THE PERFECTION OF PLEASURE

Sailing around the headland we saw a naked man on the brown rocks. His tanned body gleamed like a seal in the sunlight. A group of women leaped from point to point laughing breathlessly, and young men ran, wrestling and shouting, into the dark magenta sea. It might have been a scene from the dawn of the classical world, and was in fact a nudist beach on the Cyclades.

The quality of light, unique to islands in the sun, has often been commented on. Henry Miller, a twentieth-century recorder of sensual pleasures, savored it some forty years ago: "The vault of blue spreads out like a fan, the blue decomposing into the ultimate violet light which makes everything Greek seem holy, natural and familiar. In Greece one has the desire to bathe in the sky. You want to rid yourself of your clothes, take a running leap and vault into the blue. You want to float in the air like an angel or lie in the grass rigid and enjoy the cataleptic trance. Stone and sky, they marry here. It is the perpetual dawn of man's awakening."[1]

Greek civilization played a large part in the recognition of the hedonistic enjoyment that the body could yield. No longer the mere receptacle of generation, or simply a cog in the hierarchy of gods and human society as in Egypt, the body was seen by the Greeks as a unique gift to be exercised, cherished, and admired. It was an instrument which could be taught a variety of sensual tunes—not out of duty or necessity but simply for pleasure. So with many fits and starts and back-slidings it has remained.

The Cyclades are a link in a complex chain that connects the sensual experience of the body with trade, wine, religion, and the development of theater. The island of Delos is stone proof that the pleasures still

74. Indian, prince and dancing girl, tenth century.

pursued on neighboring shores have gone on for a long time. A relief of the third century B.C. shows a naked Dionysus, god of enjoyment and festivity, accompanied by one of his bare-breasted female followers and his old tutor, Silenus [75]. The carving is on the plinth of a giant marble phallus. Once there was an avenue of these monuments to male fertility, rearing proudly upward like the seated lions we find nearby. Now there are only two, broken in mid-shaft. Like everything in this once teeming city, they are reduced to fragments.

In its prime Delos was a meeting place for many cultures. Despite the continuous winds that whip the sea horses into foam around the

75. Delos, Avenue of Priapus, third century B.C.

coast, the island was a trading center from archaic times—the stepping-stone between Europe, Asia, and Africa. It was trade, not sex, that first brought Dionysus to these shores.

A mosaic in one of the ruins, itself damaged but still brilliant in color, shows the god riding on a snarling tiger wreathed in vine leaves. Ripe grapes hang in clusters from his furry neck. To make the point even clearer, a wine chalice lies overturned beneath his upraised paw. Like the tiger, wine is seductively glamorous, destructive, and exotic. And just as the tiger came from Asia, it was from there, somewhere on the mountain slopes between the Black Sea and the Caspian, that the vine was first cultivated.

On the southern foothills of the Caucasus in the Soviet state of Georgia lies the rose-gold city known to history as Tiflis, now called Tbilisi. Its dark-complexioned, convivial inhabitants believe theirs are the earliest wine cellars. They point out that the Georgian name, *ghvino,* has been adapted by all other nations. Another legend suggests that the Greek adventurer Jason brought his Argonauts here, after navigating through the Bosphorus and across the Black Sea. The practical basis of that mythical journey would have been trade, not pillage. The truth of the Golden Fleece was that the natives used the long-haired sheep pelts to sift particles of gold from the fast-running mountain streams, a practice continued to our own day. With the returning Greeks would have gone not only precious metal and fine Caucasian wool but amphora of the golden elixir. Wine has always been prized if it has traveled from afar.

The oldest vineyards still under cultivation are south of Tbilisi on the Armenian slopes of Mount Ararat. Noah is said to have planted them on his descent from the Ark. And in the very next verse of Genesis he provides us with the earliest recorded case of the effects of imbibing: "And he drank of the wine, and was drunken; and he was uncovered within his tent. And Ham, the father of Canaan, saw the nakedness of his father and told his two brethren . . ." Turning their faces away, Shem and Japhet covered their father with a cloak [76]. When he woke up, Noah cursed Ham's offspring. And indeed they turned out to be a bad lot, creating Babel, Sodom and Gomorrah, and many of the warring tribes that threatened Israel. They continued to use wine to excess in the orgiastic pagan rituals that accompanied the

76. Michelangelo,
Noah's Drunkenness,
ca. 1510.

worship of the Golden Calf (according to Exodus, this involved feasting, drinking, singing, dancing, and nakedness). These offerings to Baal were considered so seductive that the Orthodox are still abjured from drinking with non-Jews for fear of being led astray, even though partaking of wine in strictly prescribed amounts is an integral part of most Jewish ceremonies.

Christianity also acknowledged the gravity of Noah's lapse. As the example of merely sensual enjoyment, it signified the second fall of man. In the great theological drama that Michelangelo painted on the ceiling of the Sistine Chapel the panel of Noah's drunkenness is chronologically the final episode. But it is the first to be seen by the congregation, as it is immediately above their heads as they enter the chapel. Appropriately so, as humanity is still sinful.

The Greeks soon recognized the ambiguity of the Dionysiac gift. Wine could promote conviviality but also rage. It loosened reticent limbs in dance and raised amorous desires [77]. Here Dionysus is still seen in his earliest manifestation as a grave, full-bearded Asiatic. He carries not only the drinking bowl but the *thyrsus,* an ivy-twined staff tipped by a pine cone. This is said to represent wine's triumph over an earlier beverage: spruce beer which was spiced with ivy and sweetened with fermented honey.

In myth Dionysus was a son of Zeus, the father of the Greek gods, and a mortal woman. Like Osiris he was torn apart, but when only an infant, by Zeus's jealous wife, Hera. Reconstituted by his grandmother, an earth-goddess, he was brought up in the women's quarters, disguised as a girl. In a later attempt to escape Hera he transformed into a goat or ram. Both disguises, as female and animal, affected the way he was perceived, and the character of his followers. Euripides in his play *The Bacchae* immortalizes the equivocal nature of the wine-god. He is handsome, almost feminine in appearance; subtle and soft-spoken compared with the rough Thebans, but he carries a goatish power to drive men (and especially women) to frenzy.

Like the Egyptians the Greeks evolved a complicated pantheon of gods and goddesses. Like the Egyptian deities the Greek divinities could assume animal shapes and characteristics when they desired, but such metamorphoses only personified the emotional drives, which normally needed to be kept in check. Dionysus was a late arrival among the gods, an Eastern reaction against the excessive Greek veneration of

77. Greek, the Kleophrades Painter, Dionysus and Revelers, *ca. 490 B.C.*

78. Greek, Makron,
Maenad and Satyr, *ca.*
480 B.C.

reason, order, balance. He represents a return to the older forces, which man ignored at his peril. Like the felines—leopards and tigers—who often accompany Dionysus, man's animal nature can be beautiful in its strength and freedom from conventional shackles; it can also be as pitiless and unbridled in cruelty as a beast of prey.

Euripides emphasizes the new cult's appeal to women. Dionysus was also a corn-god, in touch with the springs of fertility which the old earth-goddess had commanded. The seasonal ceremonies of rebirth and renewal, their celebration with dance and ritual, increased his hold on the feminine sensibility, which was undervalued in the male-orientated city-states of Greece. Euripides describes how the female followers of Dionysus would take to the hills in groups, at first behaving modestly, sleeping quietly on beds of pine needles. Then, loosening their hair, they would dance and sing, waving their *thyrsus* wands until they had danced themselves into a frenzy. Possessed, they would tear apart cows and even bulls with their bare hands, devour their flesh raw, and terrify the mountain villagers.

In other words, under the influence of the god and his potent force, wine, these women, known as maenads, behaved like male marauders.

Hence it was natural that the portrayal of the god's followers in art should make the maenad more effective than her male counterpart, the satyr [78]. With her curled locks flowing over her shoulder, her ivy-leafed garland, and diaphanous robe covered by a leopard skin, she is shown continuously getting the better of the bumbling beast-man. A deft poke of her prickly *thyrsus* will quickly deflate his ardor. In the lively pictorial style of Greek vase painting the behavior of the mythical satyr and maenad follow as closely defined conventions as do the characters of Punch and Judy in our own day. Satyrs, despite their brawn and the agility which must come with their horsetails, practically never make it. Their sex perpetually engorged with drink, they are forever on the prowl—unsuccessfully. No whit abashed, they are reduced to playing adolescent games together [79], or even, occasionally, taking

79. Greek, Douris, Reveling Satyrs, *ca.* *485 B.C.*

their monster members in hand. Yet they never really lose their fuddled good humor, are never seen, as the maenads are, dancing in frenzy, brandishing the haunches of young animals they have massacred with their bare hands and are about to eat raw. The evidence of art suggests that the Greeks thought booze made men bestial, amorous but ineffective, and released unexpected aggressive energies in women.

Perhaps the Greeks also retained a lingering subconscious fear that women would reassert their old power. The conflict of ancient instinctive forces and new hard-won rationality is one of the themes of the great trilogy of plays, *The Oresteia*. Orestes has avenged his father by murdering his mother. He is pursued by the avenging Furies, demanding blood for blood: the old pitiless code of tribal justice. The Furies are the embodiment of the all-consuming female principle, giving life and taking it away. But in the final act they are opposed by the goddess of the new order, Athena. She is not born of womankind, but sprang fully formed from the brain of her father, Zeus, the Lord of Heaven. Procreation had given magic power to the woman, but now rational, civilizing man wanted to wrestle that unique gift away from her. As Apollo, the god of reason, tells the Furies:

> *The woman you call the mother of the child*
> *is not the parent, just a nurse to the seed,*
> *the new-sown seed that grows and swells inside her.*
> *The* man *is the source of life—the one who mounts.*[2]

Athena, the patron goddess of Athens, is the fulfillment of this one-sided diagnosis. Unmarried, cool, balanced, usually portrayed in masculine armor, she is every inch her father's daughter.

At the time Aeschylus wrote the plays, women in Athens had no more legal rights than slaves; they were subject to the absolute authority of their male next-of-kin. Married off by parents, they were largely confined to domestic quarters, allowed no formal education, rarely dined with their husbands, and were lucky to have sex three times a month.[3] Of course different laws applied to the different Greek states. Relations between the sexes seemed much more free and easy in the territories of Ionia, toward the Asian mainland. "In the island of Chios it is delightful just to walk to the gymnasia and running tracks to see the young men wrestling naked with the young girls, who are also naked."[4] If the evidence of a sixth-century pottery fragment is to be believed, they may also have allowed girls to ride naked and seated astride, like a boy jockey.

Even in Athens the Dionysiac rites came to be celebrated openly in annual festivals. They were broadly related to events in the wine calendar, such as the vine harvest and the first drinking of the new vintage. The followers of the wine-god now danced in procession and in great gatherings. The swirl of body-clinging drapery, the hypnotic tossing of long haired heads, the stamping of feet, the repeated wild movement of limbs, the leaping and bending to the mesmeric beat of tambours and drums and the shrilling of pipes, produced a spectacle of unparalleled visual excitement. Sculpted by great artists like Scopas [80], it defined a new aspect of the human body: the ecstasy of dance. The maenad is wearing her single garment, the Doric *peplos* in the Spartan style, leaving one thigh bare. The thrown-back gesture of the head entered European art as *the* pose of violent sexual abandon.

Inevitably, with wider participation ecstasy became less induced and more produced. The priapic element that had been present in the fabled orgies described by Euripides was maintained by carrying enormous phalluses in procession. The knob was often decorated with an eye, as ships' prows were, to help find the way to a sheltered inlet. Set up to be danced around by female acolytes [81], and later lengthened, formalized, and beribboned, the phallus is still with us as the maypole. It performs the same function, as a focal point for festive dancing welcoming spring fertility. The human males who took the part of satyrs in the Athenian ceremonies could not be expected to be so long-standing. They were provided with a loincloth which incorporated a horsetail behind and a dummy erection in front [82]. Similarly, the girl who was to dance the role of the frenzied maenad was kitted out in a sexy panther skin, without having to go to the trouble of tearing the animal apart first [83], thus leaving her hands free to click the sticks in time to the fluting of her young partner.

So costume and performance become part of the spectacle. They are still evident in such spring festivals as the Carnival at Nice. The floats, rearing high and decked with thousands of flowers, are the direct

80. *Greek, after Scopas,* Maenad, *fourth century* B.C.

crowd's boos and scorn after giving up three runs in ninth

By Larry Stone
OF THE EXAMINER STAFF

The boos for Mike LaCoss we loud and unrelenting. In light the circumstances, and consideri the incendiary nature of Cand stick Park fans, they also were be expected.

LaCoss had just undone a b liant effort by Trevor Wilson giving up three ninth-inning runs that turned a tense scoreless tie into a past-tense 3-0 Expos victory. That

enough to set off most of the 1 fans, who endured what ma Roger Craig called one of the est nights in recent memory.

The crowd booed when L unleashed a two-out wild pitc let in the game's first run, an turned up the volume when Walker followed shortly two-run homer that put it reach.

"I'm used to it," LaCo

FOR COLLECTORS

---

nt ly her his ons last

5, af- hich start- d had in the 09-105 Lewis

away. he shot jumper the Pis- -111. ave De- Brown Moments per over r a five-

d a sea- Boston's nds re- uled by w with 14 the final

wn said. in a big- ive me his aught out and I paid r it, and it

or the sev- he selection raft will of a d

to Bakersfield

FROM EXAMINER STAFF AND WIRE REPORTS

THE SAN JOSE franchise in the Continental Basketball Association plans to move to Bakersfield, team owner **Dom Cortese** said Friday.

Cortese, a Democratic state assemblyman from San Jose, signed a three-year contract with the Bakersfield Convention Center last week. He formally announced the planned move, subject to league approval, at a news conference in San Jose.

The team played two seasons in San Jose as the Jammers, but a new nickname will be chosen before its first season in Kern County.

The Big West Conference has delivered a double blow to UNLV, barring the Runnin' Rebels from the league's basketball tournament and billing the school for $100,000 in legal fees over a television flap.

The action at the conference meeting in San Jose means the Rebels will end up netting only $57,000 for eight national TV appearances and a trip to the Final Four this season.

RACING

Roberto Guerrero led the way among non-qualified drivers in the final day of practice for the Indianapolis 500. Guerrero, who lost his ride in **Danny Sullivan's** backup car earlier this week, ran an Alfa Romeo-powered Lola at 5.941 mph on Friday before rain cut short the session by an hour.

After the first weekend of qualifications produced 22 qualifiers, leaving 11 positions to fill in the 33-car lineup Saturday and Sunday.

TRACK AND FIELD

Zach Ci

81. *Greek,* Dancing Around a Model Phallus at a Festival, *fifth century* B.C.

82. *Greek, Makron,* A Satyr-Player, *ca. 480* B.C.

83. Greek, Epiktetos,
Musician and Dancer,
ca. 505 B.C.

descendants of the phallus carried in procession. Just as the costumed girls dancing down the Promenade des Anglais and tossing blooms to the crowd have a link with the followers of Dionysus dancing around the symbol of fertility. Primal violence has been gentled into jollity.

Soon pseudo-satyr and pseudo-maenad were enacting vigorous short scenes together. Out of wine, manic dancing, and sexual arousal theater was born. So far this speculation derives from the archaeological evidence and the interpretation of myth in art and in the plays of Aeschylus and Euripides that were written about an already legendary past. But now we enter the realm of history. Peisistratus was the tyrant of Athens between 542–527 B.C. He gained power on a wave of economic hardship and land hunger. Greece was a country of barren hills and mountains. Peisistratus encouraged the cultivation of vines and olives, both of which flourished on much steeper slopes than could support grain. Increase in exports of wine and oil brought prosperity and added prestige to the god of the vine, Dionysus. Recognizing the influence local worthies gained from patronizing the Dionysiac rites, Peisistratus gave the principal festival official recognition, thus greatly elevating its importance. He gave a decisive impetus to the dramatic representations which were part of the cult. A patron of the tragic poets and said to be one of the first collectors of the Homeric epics, he had them sung during the festivals. "The genius of that protodemocratic tyrant saw that if ritual, epic and tragedy could fuse—if tragedy could harness the collective force of Dionysus to the wilfulness of Homer's heroes, all might be enlarged."[5] And so it was.

Traditionally it was at the Dionysiac rites in 534 B.C. that the leader of a chorus, Thespis, produced a performance in which he not only had exchanges with the chorus but also with a further single voice. This voice was called the Answerer (in Greek $\nu\eta o\kappa\rho\iota\nu\eta\zeta$). Afterward this became the word for actor. Now to the static element of the declamation of blank verse—Homer's poems had been read aloud from archaic times—was married the swirl of movement that was the chorus, and the psychological give-and-take of dialogue which grew ultimately out of the dramatic opposition of satyr and maenad. Their initiating parenthood is recognized in the early versions of the twin masks which have always represented theater [84]. Significantly, the maenad has

84. Roman, theatrical masks, first century B.C.

taken on the mask of tragedy while the jovial satyr, wreathed in grapes, grins away as comedy. Incidentally, on the stage all parts would have been played by men, suitably masked and garbed.

The development of acting and its observation by a wide spectrum of the local populace must have had a further effect. We have only to watch our children to know that humans are naturally imitative. The simulation of feelings portrayed on the Greek stage must have had a similar influence on behavior to that exercised by the performances of favored actors on screen and television on the manners and attitudes of modern youth. The mere fact that, for the first time, emotions were demonstrably shown to be imitable must have affected the way people behaved on social occasions. In particular, such awareness must have diversified the game of love. Not love itself—there instinct always was our guide. But all those games played under the banners of flirtation, courtship, or, as here [85], "having a little bit on the side." These amiable youths are indulging themselves with hetaerae, professional courtesans. Their antics would not have been so comfortable before

85. Greek, the Dikaios Painter, Lovers at a Symposium, *late sixth century B.C.*

cushions and soft furnishings had entered society (like wine, from the East); not so prolonged without the idea of role-playing, which came with the mysteries; not so stimulating without wine; and not possible at all until there was a leisured middle class (helped by the growth in trade, including wine).

From this distance, the hetaerae cast a refreshingly joyful light on the austere Apollonian world of Greek achievement. They seem to have had a role not dissimilar to that of the free-thinking blue-stockings who attached themselves to the Pre-Raphaelite movement. They were expected to participate in the stimulating topics that interested the men who were their companions. It can be no coincidence that Plato puts the crucial arguments for the forms of love in *The Symposium* into the mouth of a wise woman. Diotima is probably a fictional character, but the Greeks were familiar with such women as priestesses of the mysteries. These cults, like that of Dionysus, were intimately connected with sexuality. Some temples, such as that of Aphrodite in Corinth, maintained professional courtesans. They led a life dedicated to devotion, poverty, and sex, which Pinder praised in a poem in the fifth century B.C.

> *Young hospitable girls, beguiling creatures in wealthy*
> *Corinth,*
> *You who burn the amber tears of fresh frankincense*
> *Full often soaring upward in your souls to Aphrodite,*
> *Heavenly Mother of loves;*
> *To you girls she has granted*
> *Blamelessly upon lovely beds*
> *To cull the blossom of delicate bloom;*
> *For under love's necessity all things are fine.*[6]

Hetaerae, like the geisha in Japan, were woman's answer to a masculine society. Trained in the art of pleasing men, they were essential adjuncts to the symposia, those long all-male parties which Plato extolled, but which must have been dull affairs without their provocative presence. Of course, some symposia were just gay parties. The Greeks accepted pederasty with youths. Sixteen was said to be the divine age for a boy [86]. The admirer was usually a mature man, presumably a confirmed homosexual. His tastes would have been understood because

86. Greek, the Brygos Painter, Man with Young Boy, *ca. 490 B.C.*

87. Greek, the Briseis Painter, Man with Hetaera, *ca. 485 B.C.*

of the veneration of the naked male form, at the peak of athletic beauty in the late teens. For the boy there was a substitute for the warm feeling he would not get at home in a society where family affections were little valued. The older man, if influential, would give him an entry into the adult male world of the city.

Youthful gay affairs do not seem to have had a lasting effect on the majority of young Athenians. Painted vases show a preponderance of heterosexual scenes. This is not conclusive evidence, but it does suggest where customer demand lay. Women writers have argued that the vase scenes were meant for the edification of men; as they were often painted on drinking vessels, they might have been intended to stimulate. Postures which are thought more enjoyable for men than women are cited as confirmatory evidence of masculine chauvinism [87]. But professional ladies usually choose for themselves positions they know their clients like, especially if it means they don't have to look them in the face.

However there are a number of paintings which imply affection between hetaera and customer [88]. This couple seems rapt in mutual enjoyment, even if his stick leaning against the wall suggests he is not

88. Greek, the Triptolemos Painter, Lovemaking on a Bed, ca. 470 B.C.

going to stay long. Lusty vitality and an unabashed grasping for erotic experience are sustained through every posture and every shape of vase. The men are of all ages, from portly elders, bald-headed and bearded seniors, to youthful striplings. The girls are of course nubile; that is the way the world has always been. When Aphrodite, the Goddess of Love, was angry that there was a young woman called Psyche on earth whose beauty was drawing attention from herself, she sent her son, Cupid (or Eros as the Greeks called him), to punish the girl. Aphrodite's plans went awry because Eros fell for Psyche's fresh and innocent charms. The child of Love and Psyche was a daughter, whose name was Pleasure. Such a very young pair of lovers are portrayed in one of the most charmingly tentative scenes [89].

89. Greek, the Shuvalov Painter, Young Lovers, *late fifth century B.C.*

Masculine society prescribed the extent of hetaerae freedom. Groups of women, mostly precluded from lasting relationships with the opposite

sex, tend to form them among themselves. The red figure vases show hetaerae having a relaxed gossip together over a bowl of wine [90], sometimes pleasuring each other by the light of an uplifted oil lamp. Such scenes were certainly recorded for male delectation, but it would be extraordinary if they had not taken place.

90. Greek, Phintias, Two Hetaerae, ca. 510 B.C.

Nuns and whores are usually debarred from the common pleasures of womankind, the family hearth, the cares and rewards of parenthood. Even the most famous inhabitant of Lesbos, Sappho, who wrote so many fiery lines to her own sex, reserved her most tender feelings for motherhood:

> *I have a child; so fair*
> *As golden flowers is she,*
> *My Kleis, all my care.*
> *I'd not give her away*
> *For Lydia's wide sway*
> *Nor lands men long to see.*[7]

Despite changes in morality and social custom, the courtesan has maintained her place in society down to the present day. In widely different times and cultures she has continued her connection with performance, dance, and theater. Over a thousand years after Athenian society reached its zenith, at Puri and Khajuraho in the valley of the Ganges in India were built the temples that are the masterpieces of Chandella art. They appear to Western eyes amazingly sophisticated for the eighth to eleventh centuries. Most of them are not large. Nor are they awe-inspiring like Charlemagne's chapel at Aachen or Durham Cathedral, their European contemporaries. Rather they suggest that they have grown by accretions—like a beehive full of individual cells each with its own sweetness [91].

Decked in provocative strings of beads and jangling bracelets, the women cavort in their stone niches. Long-limbed and firm-breasted, they look down on the dancing floor where once their human counterparts performed. These temple girls, the *devadasis,* fulfilled the same dual functions as the sacred courtesans had done in Greece. They danced the elaborate rituals that were carried out on the open stone stage outside the holy of holies, the inner sanctum where the lingam, the emblem of the phallus, was displayed. They served this symbol of creative power, but they also satisfied the needs of the priests and the righteous. Symptomatic of the demand on them was the provision of 400 *devadasis* and 212 male ancillaries (dance masters, musicians, garland makers, and servants) at one temple alone.

The Indian carvers were adept in combining sensuous appeal with realism. The girls bang tambours, play the flute, practice the pirouettes and complex arm movements of their profession. They smile, yawn, paint the soles of their feet red and their eyelashes black; they trim their nails and braid their long hair [92] and then deck it with jewels while looking in a convex hand mirror. Lips pursed in a half-smile, they are engrossed in writing a love letter. Bending one foot up to the other thigh, they put on the ankle bracelets whose bells will jingle to the slap and stamp of their bare soles on the dancing floor. Teasingly, they unhitch the girdle which is their only garment. If the movements of the hetaerae are infused with energy, all these are languorous as befits a more tropic clime. Such girls were considered the ornament of civic life, "that lovely coloured, scented flower that the city puts in its hair for all to see, when a festival or some other joyous event is being celebrated."[8]

Indians often say that romantic love does not exist in India. Arranged marriages are still the norm, even among the intelligentsia. Practical matters, the assessment of bank balances and horoscopes, take precedent over transient emotion. Similarly, the largest of the temples, Konarak, seems more a palace than a religious shrine. Near the Indian Ocean, surrounded by green fields and great banyan trees, approached by a

long avenue leading to an imposing gateway guarded by crouching stone lions, it is a manifestation of earthly splendor rather than divine glory. Covered in horizontal tiers of carving, the erotic sculpture is only one aspect of the pleasures of a king. It takes its place along with splendidly caparisoned horses, prostrate foes, sages and courtiers, and thousands of elephants (a continuous frieze of them circles the whole

91. Indian, Markandesvara Temple, tenth century.

building, symbolically holding it up). This is reminiscent of the riot of invention to be found in the cloisters or around the cornices of Gothic cathedrals. But closer inspection reveals that the apparent diversity is in very constrained and formalized limits. There is nothing like the individual creations—amounting to whimsy—of the northern European carver-craftsmen. Even the sexual poses, startling in their graphic detail and sensual abandon, are repeated over and over. Nor is there the recognition of the diversity of society that was one of the achievements of the Western mind at that time. At Konarak and the other temples the beings portrayed go up in registers from the human nobles, through the semidivine, to the celestial. The lower orders are only there as soldiers, hunters, carriers of stone: accessories of power.

Despite their reputation for mystic contemplation, the majority of Indians do not appear to think profoundly about their faith. Rather, its acceptance permeates their every action. So there is no opposition between the grandeur of Konarak, said to represent a vast chariot to the sun god with its twelve rearing horses and twenty four wheels of stone, and the rats scurrying unhindered in the inner sanctum of the Brahma Temple at Khajuraho. The continual cycle of being means that the rodent might house the soul of a former emperor. Spiritual materialism makes all things sacred. Hence the embodiment of sexual acts, an essential part of life, on temple walls.

These scenes reach their apogee at Khajuraho. The complex of temples, placed between hills on the fertile central plain south of the Ganges, were the manifestation of an increasingly wealthy feudal society. Great landlords built them as houses for the gods and to legitimatize their own credentials. The earliest have a warm optimistic humanity reminiscent of the Old Kingdom tombs in Egypt, but there is a much greater emphasis on the sensuous aspects of experience. There are few studies of old age or childhood or the trials of life. Predominant are the athletic forms of youthful nobles and complaisant dancing girls [74], potent gods and avid *apsaras,* celestial girls said to be filled with inexhaustible sexual desire. Grace and elegance hold sway even in potentially torrid scenes [93]. Two courtesans are lowering a third onto the prostrate body of a noble. He has already coiled his legs around her with the assistance of one of the attendants. His heel in the small of her back is pressing his partner into position, leaving both hands

92. Indian, Dancer Braiding Her Hair, *tenth century.*

93. Indian, Figures in
Complex Embrace,
tenth century.

free to play with the girls-in-waiting. The mastery of the carver has
transformed the sweat and strain into a satisfying rhythm of contrapuntal
limbs.

These stone embraces seem at first sight similar in feeling to the
sexual encounters on Greek vase paintings, but they are subtly different.
Imbued with a sense of the value of existence in all its forms, the
Hindu was bound to rate women—half the human race—more highly
than the Greek had done. In the dark womblike sanctum of the Indian
temple the lingam, the symbol of male generative power, grows *out* of
the yoni, the stylized form of the female genitals. Constrained though
a woman's lot might be in feudal India, she was thought to have the
more passionate nature. No matter how bad she had been, or what
adventures she had experienced, the menstrual flow was believed to
wash her pure again. Woman, water, and pearls, it was said, were
never spoiled. Her kiss was always clean [94], as she was herself, during
the pleasures of love. Participating with her, the man experienced a
godlike draft of immortality, because at climax its intensity produced a
temporary loss of self.

The carvings in fact reproduce positions described in detail in the
Hindu sacred books. Every requisite movement, pinch, and bite is

categorized like the spices required to perfect a series of flavorsome curries. Hindu literature dwells graphically on the copulations of the gods. Here from the *Gita-Govinda,* a classic song cycle of the twelfth century, is a verse in which Radha, the wife of Krishna, describes their coming together after a separation.

94. Indian, Lovers, *tenth century.*

95. Indian, Krishna
Surprises the Gopis,
eighteenth century.

The bejeweled anklets on my feet will tinkle:
He will complete the demonstration of coitus.
My girdle will jingle and become torn:
He will pull me by the hair and give me kisses.[9]

Ankle bells not only gave a melodious punctuation to the stamping feet of temple dancers; they were a valued ingredient in the music of love. The poet is not resorting to hyperbole with his description of tinkling and jingling. Learned commentators have agreed that the first line implies a position in the *Kama Sutra* in which the woman sits on the man and, with her knees bent, rotates her hips in a semicircle from side to side. Because this was very tiring for her, "He," Krishna, in the second line, resumed the dominant role. The third line shows a further reversal, and the broken girdle indicates a vigorous movement listed in the *Kama Sutra,* involving the woman in waving her hips forward and backward and from side to side. (I am indebted to Nirad C. Chaudhuri for the analysis of these verses.)

Like Dionysus, Krishna was a late arrival among the pantheon of gods. Like Dionysus, his message of love brought him many followers, especially among women. Like Dionysus, he was not an inaccessible distant deity but dwelled in the forest grove of Vrindavana, dancing with his devotees, and raising them to ecstasy. In his earthly guise, he was not above playing games with them. The legends of the *Bhagavata Purana* describe how he heard the *gopis,* the milkmaids of Vraja, singing his praises. Approaching, he finds them bathing in the river Jamuna. He steals their clothes, and hides with them in a tree [95]. Emerging from the water, clad only in their bracelets and necklaces, the *gopis* are embarrassed when they spy the god. Some shyly plunge back into the river. Others plead with him to throw down their clothes. One is about to obey his request that they come forward with clasped hands. There can be no shame for true believers in baring themselves to the Lord.

Krishna will possess them each and all individually. Later texts make clear the universal nature of his message. "Wherever you are [says Krishna] there also am I, and verily there is no difference. As whiteness is in milk, power to burn in fire, scent in earth, so am I invariably in you . . . You are the basis of creation by me. I am the imperishable seed . . ."[10] This general love had a corporeal outlet. Desiring to satisfy the *gopis*—there were nine hundred thousand of

them gathered together in a park—Krishna cloned himself into nine hundred thousand different forms of man. The park resounded with the copulation of nearly two million people.

The power of Krishna is still manifest. Traveling across India in the mid-eighties one saw springtime commemorated with red smears on his statues, twists of bright cloth, or garlands of fresh flowers. Modern re-creation of the temple dances shows they were a way of embodying the divine legends. Highly stylized mime and ritual gestures retold the stories of the loves of the gods. Inflamed by the seductive movements of the performers, the faithful were able to possess them in their turn. Because the *devadasis* were dedicated to the rituals of the god, copulation with them could be seen as a holy act. Human sexual love prefigured divine union. As with the Dionysiac festivals, music, dance, mime, and story developed together in the service of sex and religion.

There are many similarities between classical Greek and Asiatic depictions of erotic encounters; but the tranquil joy of the latter and the frenzy of the former seem profoundly different. Probably the Hindu carvers were influenced by the conventions of Jain sculpture. The Jains were—and are—an Indian sect of dissenters from Hinduism. They eschewed ownership of everything, including clothing. Their naked ascetics were dedicated to a life of contemplation. Like the Buddhists, they believed enlightenment would release them from the endless bondage of rebirth. Their sage, Bahubali, towers more than fifty feet high in a characteristically stiff frontal pose [96]. Carved in the tenth century in southern India, he represents the first soul to reach enlightenment in this cosmic cycle. Spirit could be disentangled from matter only by avoiding injury to all living things. Bahubali must remain forever still because creepers twined themselves around his arms and legs while he was rapt in meditation. Such quietism would have been unthinkable to the restless Greek mind.

The erotic carvings also suggest a knowledge of Tantra, another cult which sought to short-cut the eternal repetitions of being. Unlike the Jain, the follower of Tantra sought release by harnessing sexual energy through an elaborate set of rules and rituals. At a profound level this meant breaking many of the prohibitions and prescriptions of Hindu thought and practice. Superficially, it involved some of the most esoteric sexual activities ever devised. Not surprisingly, this brought Tantra into vogue in the permissive sixties. It is doubtful if many Californian acolytes knotted themselves into the sorts of postures [97] necessary to increase appreciably the sum of cosmic energy.

The belief in the possibility of attaining spiritual ecstasy through detailed instructions involving the physical manipulation of the body seems peculiarly Eastern. So does the idea that a cup of tea will provide a stimulating intermission capable of upholding the tension between the acts [98]. The ideal of maintaining intercourse over long periods of time without orgasm implies a life of uninterrupted leisure, tranquil

96. Indian, the Jain saint Bahubali, 981.

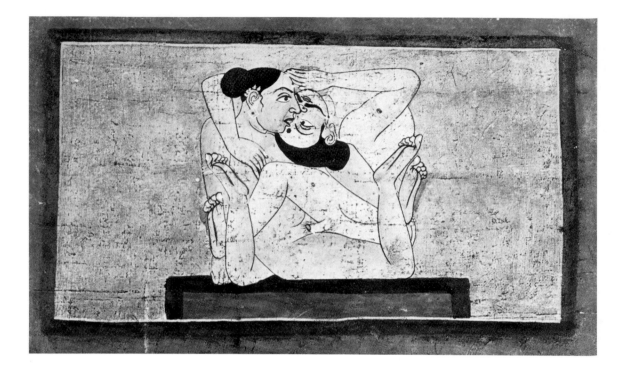

97. Indian, The Sexual Posture Cakra Asana, *eighteenth century.*

surroundings, and a continuously avid partner. Something we may have to wait for until we meet one of the heavenly *apsaras* in Paradise.

The refinement of sex demanded a well-endowed middle class, educated, idle, and sophisticated. The social intercourse of city life created such a class in many societies: dedicated followers of fashion in erotic pleasures as in other sensuous activity. It was manifest in classical Greece and medieval India. Five hundred years later and some two thousand miles further east the graphic art of Japan reveals a culture with both similarities and differences.

Penetrating this society (almost entirely closed to foreign eyes until the nineteenth century) poses a severe test on Western understanding. No culture is so opaque to our sensibilities. Yet superficially there seem many common elements. As in Greece and India, theater, religion, and art are intimately linked to private enjoyment. Like the Greek drama, the Kabuki theater of Japan owed its origin to dances of a religious nature. Similarly, as the performances gained in popularity they became more secular, elaborate, and dramatic. There was a similar cross-fertilization with the visual arts. Interest in the theater and its actors led to a flourishing business in wood block prints of them. The exaggerated conventions of Kabuki affected the style of the artists, even when they were not illustrating scenes from the stage, just as the frenzied gestures of Dionysiac dancing gave new postures to Greek sculpture.

But there were also striking differences. Theater flourished in Athens because it became a means to express the profoundest feelings

98. Indian, Prince and Lady Prolonging Intercourse with a Cup of Tea, *eighteenth century.*

of the newly burgeoning democracy. In the enclosed world that was Japan, with its rigid hierarchies and patriarchal conventions, the theater ran into frequent opposition. The ruling oligarchy of warlords was scandalized, not only by the subject matter, but by the dubious morality of the performers. The Kabuki plays were often banned, but were continually revived by public demand.

Rigidly formalized societies usually require some permitted anarchic outlet to syphon off suppressed energies. So it was with Japan. The city of Edo (Tokyo) was founded in 1600 A.D. at much the same time as Kabuki was first being staged in Kyoto. Within two hundred years Edo grew to a million people. Much of its wealth flowed into the center of the Floating World, that district devoted to the transient pleasures of life. This was Yoshiwara, a separate quarter with its own gates within the city of Edo. Here in the teahouses and brothels gathered the musicians, the geishas, the prostitutes, and actors, the pariahs of society; and, incognito, many of the ruling class, the samurai. It was an area where the normal conventions of Japanese society could be ignored. The green houses provided a lucrative trade in the unwanted, but attractive, daughters of the poor. They were given expert training in lovemaking, deportment, music, and poetry. With these skills they might, with good fortune, raise themselves above the lowly status they shared with actors. "Paradoxically it was precisely this pariah status, and the consequent freedom from the rigid moral code of the respectable classes, which was responsible for their appeal. The merchants' wives, although not so strictly cloistered as the women of the aristocracy, were nevertheless inexperienced creatures in comparison with the gorgeously attired and worldly courtesans."[11] Not for the first time, a masculine-dominated society allowed outcast women privileges of culture and education which were prohibited to the mothers of its children.

From much earlier times, manuals of sexual knowledge had been common in Japan. Sometimes these pillow books (so-called because they were often scrolls of prints which would fit into a wooden pillow box) were instructional. One, printed for a brothel-keeper, categorized forty-eight different positions. Increasingly, under the influence of the free-ranging theater, such books showed dramatic or violent scenes. Sexual encounters rarely have the relaxed sensuality or the emphasis on physical beauty of the Indian sculptures. They express the urgent necessities of desire [99]. Perhaps this couple had been studying together when master suddenly leaped on pupil. Their books lie abandoned on one of the powerful diagonals that complement the fierce upward thrust of the male. The axis of his pushing feet continues through his forceful thigh and genitals, the hand throwing her legs apart, his chest pressing down on her ineffective little hands, his greedy bald head biting at her ear and other arm pulling her to him, and comes to a halt in the upright painted screen where two tiny figures seem to be watching with interest from a balcony. The slotlike gap in the house is a psychic echo of the feminine space he is about to invade. We are reminded how seldom we are alone in Japan, how narrow are the spaces between elbowing, inquisitive others. Sexual partners rarely seem to have time to disrobe. The swirl of ruffled silk gives added movement to the scene, which appears the very opposite of the Tantric ideal of leisured, planned immersion.

99. Japanese, Harunobu, Lovers by a Landscape Screen, *ca. 1768.*

100. Japanese, Koryusai, Lovers Behind a Folding Screen, ca. 1770.

The few totally naked lovers inevitably seem more relaxed [100]. The apparent trancelike state of this couple is aided by the calm oval shapes which recede from their piled-up heads and shoulders, back through the curve of his bottom to the piles of bedclothes like a range of distant hills. On the other hand, if we reverse the movement of the eye these successive rumpled folds of coverlet become the equivalent of a line of railway trucks adding shunting power to the jutting buttocks. Noting their closed eyes and her curling toes we realize that we, and the peeking servant, are witnessing the moment when they are mutually pierced by orgasm.

The relative sparsity of sex without wraps in the pillow pictures is often explained by the casual propinquity of the communal bathhouse [101]. The sexes were so used to seeing each other naked on the scrubbing board that there was no new thrill in mutually disrobing. The eighteenth-century artist has chosen to show what could not have been an uncommon event, a young man's evident excitement at rubbing a young woman's back. Despite the feigned indifference with which he turns his head, he cannot conceal his body's involuntary reaction from the gaze of an older couple. The woman continues to towel herself disapprovingly while the man leans forward in prurient interest. Another young woman looks away demurely, but her posture suggests that she too has been sexually aroused by what she has seen.

There are other likely reasons for the Japanese preference for clothed encounters. Partial nudity can be more titillating than the whole thing. And the flow of draperies enhances the energy of pattern and movement which are such a powerful ingredient in Japanese prints.

Arguably the greatest master of *shunga,* "spring pictures," that is, views of sexual dalliance, was Utamaro. His life covered much of the eighteenth century and roughly coincides with that of George Washington. But while revolutions changed the political face of distant continents, Utamaro remained a willing captive within the confines of the Floating World. Like the nineteenth-century poet Baudelaire in the

101. Japanese, Koryusai, The Baths, ca. 1770.

102. Japanese, Utamaro, frontispiece from The Poem of the Pillow, *1788.*

streets of Paris, Utamaro was content to wander the narrow alleyways and teahouses of Yoshiwara, finding in this single quarter limitless subjects for his art.

Like Baudelaire, too, he was able to draw significance from the mundane. His delicate brush could invest a transient moment with gravity [102]. It has been suggested that the man absorbed in amorous *tête-à-tête* is a self-portrait. Despite the fluid lines of varied pattern that fill most of the picture, it is the relatively small areas of flesh that anchor the eye and give the dominant mood of still expectancy. Was human feeling ever so clear with so little facial expression available? Mutual happiness emanates from the silent regard of the two heads, in the touch of her hand on his jaw, and the tender line of her neck. That this mood will shortly be succeeded by others we know from the glimpse of her naked thigh. Her leg, marvelously concealed yet revealed under the transparent folds of the spotted silk scarf, has been thrown negligently across his. Shortly he will put down the fan with which he is bringing a cool flutter to the damp heat of her inner thigh, and turn to other matters. But for the moment time was away and somewhere else.

My love
Knows no destination
And has no goals;
I think only
Of meeting as its limit.[12]

With pictures such as these we seem to have matured a long way from the boisterous antics of the Greeks.

Utamaro was equally adept at turning the depiction of sexual desire from realism to fantasy. The hardy women of the tiny province of Shima, who used to dive more or less naked for awabi shells, were often the subject of prints. Their fortitude in withstanding extreme cold was legendary, but Utamaro has provided them with an additional hazard. At the bottom of the sea, where she has to grope for the large platelike shells, one of the divers is surprised by a couple of water-spirits [103]. As lecherous as monkeys, but equipped with webbed feet and ribs on their backs (presumably to aid the gills on the top of their

103. Japanese, Utamaro, Fishergirl Ravished by Water Spirits, 1788.

heads in the process of breathing), their faces reveal a gloating wickedness. One holds the poor girl down and licks her cheek with his long tongue, while the other is about to force an entry, to the flickering interest of a shoal of small fish, who swim forward eager to explore the new grotto which is opening up. Above the surface, the diver's companion crouches on a little island, guarding the basket of shells. She can see down through the drifting kelp and the cloudy mass of her friend's floating hair, brilliantly suggested in Utamaro's sensitively varied line, to what is going on below. Pulling at a strand of her own hair she watches with a mixture of alarm and excitement. Once again, the curious observer holds a dominant seat in the picture. Is it simply because, in small areas heavily encroached by water like Japan and Holland, voyeurism is perforce inflicted on everyone? Or that, arising as the prints do, from the traditions of Kabuki, the spectator in them implies that all the world is a stage? Plato, we remember, maintained that the enlightened observer was on a higher level than the performer in the games. In this case the viewer in the picture is a surrogate for us, the later viewers, who look into it. The diver may be about to lose her chastity but we shall gain the modicum of understanding and enjoyment art brings us by observing it.

The arrival of Western influence in the mid-nineteenth century was ultimately fatal to the culture of the Floating World. The prints had already become more sensational and fantastic. Sadistic rape, ghostly visitations, blood-curdling combat, elbowed out the scenes of actors and courtesans that Utamaro had immortalized. Art mirrors life in seldom maintaining a balance.

Yet there is a true advance that is related neither to the instability of politics nor to personal emotions, but to technology. Women's hopes of liberty have been much increased by more secure methods of contraception. In the mid-twentieth century the idea that all of us, male and female, have the right to choose the sort of private games we play began to be seriously considered, at least in the Western democracies. Hence pictures such as we have been looking at, long banned except for the wealthy connoisseur, have in recent years appeared openly in the West. They are undoubtedly works of art, but they also represent the most zestful and guiltless depictions of sexual enjoyment that we shall find in the long story of the image of the body.

The perfection of pleasure remains a fragile mutual enterprise: hard to achieve, harder still to maintain. It has constantly been threatened by puritanical societies and, even more intractably, by disease. The fount of love can bring forth pain, a harsh truth that has been central to the Christian portrayal of the body, to which we now turn.

5

PILGRIMAGE THROUGH PAIN

The dome of St. Peter's seen from afar, floating above the Eternal City of Rome, has hastened the footsteps of generations of pilgrims. On entering the great square, embraced by encircling colonnades and saluted by tiers of stone saints, the faithful must feel themselves at the triumphant heart of Christendom. And yet at the center of the square stands an Egyptian obelisk, which once stood at the center of the circus built on this same spot at the time of Caligula and Nero. Here countless Christians were butchered. The Church was forged in opposition to tyranny and terror. This birth in suffering had a profound effect on Christian attitudes to pleasure and pain and influenced the manner in which the body was depicted in Christian art for many centuries.

Another reminder of the founding days lies below St. Peter's. An unobtrusive side entrance leads to a flight of steps down onto a street running beneath the main nave. It is a narrow street. Once the Via Cornelia, it flanked the north side of Nero's circus. In that time and in the following century this area became a necropolis. The modest buildings of characteristic Roman brick that border the street are mausoleums. They harbor the sarcophagi and funerary urns of moderately well-to-do families. There are sculptures and frescoes to Dionysus, to Jupiter and Minerva; even a few to Egyptian gods and one or two Christian. In the center of a mosaic of vine leaves, Christ is seen as the sun, driving Apollo's chariot of rearing horses [105].

The road slopes up a hill, masked from above ground by the forty thousand cubic meters of soil that the Emperor Constantine deposited on it in order to make a level platform for the first Christian basilica in the fourth century. Climbing the slope brings the ceiling of the

104. Grünewald, Crucifixion *(detail), 1513–15.*

105. Roman, Christ the Sun Rising, *third century.*

excavations lower and a distant but continuous whisper becomes audible. Grilles overhead tell what it is—the feet of the faithful, passing and repassing on the marble floor of the modern St. Peter's above.

This underground area was rediscovered only by chance less than fifty years ago. Excavations went on from 1939 to 1950. We are the first generation to pass this way for sixteen hundred years. But in the humblest part of the necropolis ancient and modern worlds meet. Here, in about 160 A.D., two small pillars were put by a niche in a wall. More than a hundred and fifty years later Constantine covered this undistinguished fragment of architecture in marble. He went to the enormous trouble of leveling the hillside so that he could build his basilica around it. It is still at the heart of the gigantic Renaissance cathedral that towers above us. It is directly under the high altar. Above the altar rears the giant spiraled columns of the baldichino, the largest bronze structure in the world. And above that billows the immensity of the dome. The contrast between humble memorial below and opulent grandeur above is overwhelming. It is here, by tradition, that Peter, the fisherman from Galilee, was buried after his martyrdom in the neighboring amphitheater.

There is no direct evidence that Peter was ever in Rome, but it has been believed by generations of Christians since the earliest days. That many of the first Christians of Rome met agonizing deaths here is without doubt. The account written by Tacitus is well known but worth quoting as the first circumstantial report of the new religion by an outsider. In July 64 A.D. fire devastated Rome. It was widely believed to have been caused by the emperor, Nero. He wanted the glory of rebuilding a new city. But the outcry was so great he had to find a scapegoat.

"For that reason," Tacitus writes, "Nero made public those responsible and condemned them to the most refined execution, men, hated for their crimes whom the masses called 'Christians.' The one from whom they took their name, a certain Christ, was executed under Tiberius by the procurator, Pontius Pilate. Repressed at first, this execrable superstition broke out again not only in Judea, the cradle of this scourge, but also in Rome where everything which is most atrocious, shameful, and evicted elsewhere, finally settles. First those who confessed to being Christians were arrested; then, based on their depositions, a great multitude was accused not so much for the fire as for their hatred of the human race.

"Mockery of every sort was added to their deaths. Covered with the skins of beasts, they were torn by dogs and perished, or were nailed to crosses, or covered with pitch and used as torches to light the arena after dark. For this reason the condemned were pitied, even though they were guilty and merited the torture, because they were sacrificed not for the common good, but because of the sadism of a jealous tyrant."[1]

Despite his low opinion of the Christians, Tacitus was disgusted by the manner of their execution. And this was in an exceptionally brutal period; eleven thousand people and ten thousand animals were killed in one set of games shortly afterward. The games had begun as straightforward contests between groups of armed men, the gladiators, but as time went on the audience demanded more and more ingenious and excruciating debaucheries. It was a common practice to throw condemned criminals to wild beasts. In a Roman mosaic from Zliten in Tripolitania, which shows incidents from the games, a black panther is leaping on a man who has been tied to a chariot [106]. The persecution of the Christians had the great advantage of making available considerable numbers of victims at one time. Bets could be laid on which person would be eaten first, and which last. The big cats share with their domestic cousins the habit of chewing on their prey without

106. Roman, Leopard Attacking Condemned Man, *first century.*

bothering to kill it. As whole families and groups of friends were sacrificed together, the audience had the added piquancy of being able to observe the reactions of those still untouched.

Prurient interest in the misfortune of others is a persistent attribute; witness the crowds who gather at a road accident. But in the Roman Empire this latent taste was raised to a pitch of refinement and intensity unequaled in any other epoch. Animals were caught all over the known world and the means found to transport them live, in the relatively small ships of the time, to Rome and the other cities in Europe where there were amphitheaters. Many of the more exotic specimens, such as rhinoceros, polar bears, and hippopotamus, were not seen again in Europe for over fifteen hundred years. The animals were then starved or otherwise enraged to the point where they would fight each other or, more frequently, molest human victims. Vast amounts were spent to make these horrors more intriguing. The arena of the Colosseum could be flooded for sea fights, or have mock fortresses or islands rapidly erected in it by armies of slaves. During the Christian era the games occupied over a hundred days a year. Only the Nazi extermination camps surpass in evil this methodical demonstration of man's capacity for beastly ingenuity and skill.

Finding new methods of death racked the invention of impresarios. One popular device was to reenact in reality incidents in popular mythology. Thus one of the condemned would be flayed alive like Marsyas; another, in the guise of Adonis, would be torn apart by wild boars. A punishment that became popular for the younger, female Christians was based on the story of Dirce. It is shown on the largest sculptural group to come down to us from antiquity [107]. Dirce, the Queen of Thebes, her robe torn apart, reels back under the flailing hooves of a wild bull, which has been captured by the muscular twins Amphion and Zethus. In revenge for Dirce's cruelty to their mother, they are about to tie her to the bull's horns.

In the arena lightly clad girls were hung in nets to be tossed and gored by the bulls. Sharp horns could tear through garments as well as flesh, thus giving the spectators a double excitement. We have a detailed account of two Carthaginians, Perpetua and Felicitas, who were martyred in this way on March 7, 203. Perpetua was twenty-two, of good family, well educated, married, with a small baby which was brought to the prison every day for her to feed. Felicitas was eight

months' pregnant, and according to the chronicler, anxious that this could delay her from sharing the fate of the other prisoners. Another explanation might be that she did not want the child to suffer with her. Her wish was granted, she was brought to birth shortly before the execution date. When Perpetua was tossed her tunic was ripped away by the bull's horns. Her first thought was to try and conceal her nakedness from the multitude. A Christian should appear composed and joyful in martyrdom.

Perpetua survived the bull's horns, but was so shocked that she continually asked, "When are we to be tossed?" unaware of the wounds that covered her body. She recovered sufficiently to call out to her

107. Roman, The Farnese Bull, *third century.*

108. Roman, Crucified Man, *second century(?).*

comrades "to stand fast in the faith and love one another," before being stabbed to death by gladiators. The chronicler does not record what happened to her infant. On the day of her trial her pagan father appeared at the bar and held out the child, beseeching her to have pity on it and recant, as it would die without her. Perpetua was able to deny what we would consider her natural instincts by her radiant conviction in a future life. Jesus had been crucified, was dead and rose again. So redemption through a death of suffering was an appropriate Christian end.

Executions, such as crucifixion, were a routine item in the games. The evidence from skeletons of those crucified is confirmed by a drawing discovered at Pozzuoli near Naples in 1959 [108]. It was scratched on the wall of an inn near the amphitheater, along with other rough images from the arena. A man is shown nailed through each wrist. His legs are bent apart and the heels brought together with one great nail which is driven through both. So he is spread, like a frog under dissection. The crude drawing catches the distorted position and the

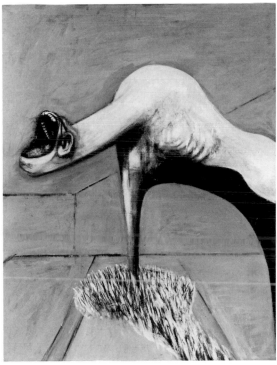

109. Bacon, Three Studies for Figures at the Base of a Crucifixion, *1944*.

frantic struggle for breath it causes. Quite apart from the agony, it was a punishment that invited the abuse of the mob. The authorities were much too practical to waste large amount of wood on the crosses; hence the victim would be at the eye level of the onlooker, naked and splayed apart, entirely defenseless against every sort of abuse and physical assault.

So fearful was the reality of a crucifixion that it was a thousand years before it was adapted as the central image of Christianity. By then long out of favor as a punishment, it could be viewed with equanimity by the faithful as a consoling symbol of general suffering. Only occasionally did artists allow themselves to portray its more revolting aspects. The modern artist Francis Bacon has painted many pictures of the Crucifixion, some of the most horrifying of which are of the spectators [109]. Mob reaction is a lowest common denominator of human emotion. "The baiting crowd is very old. It goes back to the most primitive dynamic unit known among men: the hunting pack."[2] Just as the onlooker is morally degraded, the victim ceases to seem a

110. Bacon, Three Studies for a Crucifixion, *right-hand panel, 1962.*

human being. "His permitted murder stands for all the murders people have to deny themselves for fear of the penalties for their perpetration."[3] In the various purges of Christians they were scourged till their bones and inner organs were revealed, had their feet burned off, their flesh torn away by red-hot pincers. Sanctus, a deacon of Vienne, had red-hot plates applied to his testicles. At the end of a day of torture, "his poor body was one whole wound and bruise, having lost the outward form of a man."[4] A number of Francis Bacon's paintings show sides of bleeding meat being crucified; "undulating," as he has said, "down the cross like a worm" [110]. Bacon's paintings are shocking, partly because of the violence of the technique, but partly because the crucified not only resembles a piece of meat but also seems sentient and suffering.

The Romans were able to get heartless enjoyment out of such suffering because from the beginning they did not perceive the victims as fully human. They belonged to certain categories that were exempt from normal consideration: slaves, barbarian captives, condemned criminals. Christians were added to the list. They were officially regarded as enemies of the state because they refused to recognize the divinity of the emperor. Had they done so, the authorities, tolerant of the many local religions that existed under the *lex Romana,* would, in general, have left them alone. As Gibbon put it cynically: "The various modes of worship which prevailed in the Roman world were all considered by the people as equally true; by the philosopher as equally false; and by the magistrates as equally useful."[5] It was the Christians' arrogant denial of all other gods but their own that roused popular fury. Regarded as atheists and anarchists, they could be summarily sentenced to death by a local magistrate. Equally, a routine prayer to the pagan gods and an act of libation would bring their freedom. The appalling torments were in part intended to enforce submission, in the same manner as the Christians later used the Inquisition against heretics. Many recanted, but others, like Perpetua and Felicitas, did not. Later, descriptions of their suffering were used to *inspire* the faithful.

But at first the main strength of the new religion came from its emphasis on resurrection. The belief in an unverifiable future reward has a potent attraction for the hopeless. So it was among the poorest of the poor that Christianity gained its earliest converts. By the end of the first century it also had many followers from the well-to-do. A

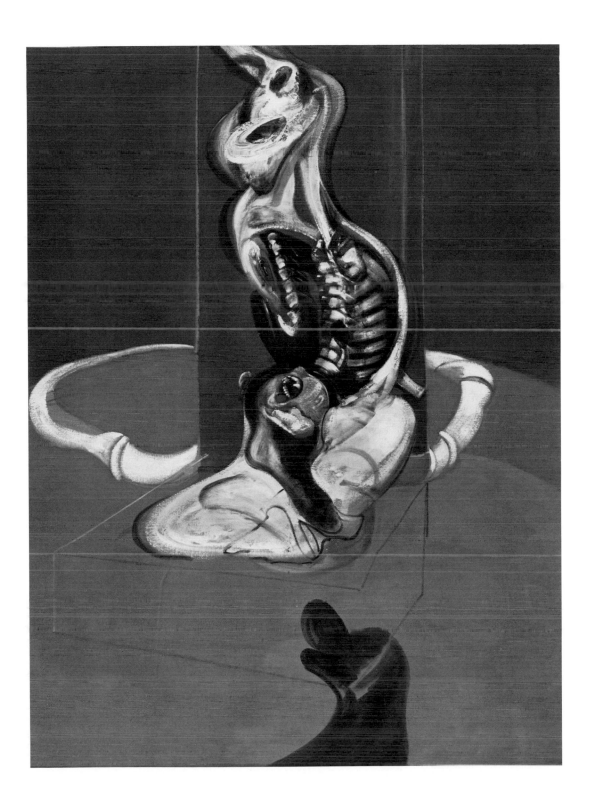

creed of love, sacrifice, and faith appealed especially to women in this grossly masculine society where Hercules with his brute strength, lion's skin, and club personified the popular hero [111].

The time was ripe for a new faith. Rome under the early Antonines was exceptionally licentious; a tone set by the emperors. Nero slept with all three of his sisters and his mother. Eventually he had his mother poisoned and then examined her body at length, pointing out its better features to his attendants. Dressed as a woman, he went through a marriage ceremony with a notorious pervert and was then publicly sodomized. "He was convinced that nobody could remain chaste or pure in any part of his body, but that most people concealed their secret vices; hence if anyone confessed to obscene practices, Nero forgave him all his other crimes."[6] Perhaps no other society has ever been so obsessed by the phallus. Its image was turned into doorknobs, oil lamps, table legs, amulets, jewelry of all kinds, wall brackets, floor mosaics, and road signs, and was also used to designate property boundaries. Phalluses grow other phalluses, penile tails, and legs; they sprout wings and are hung with bells [112]. A gladiator strikes out at a canine animal that rears to attack him. It is his own penis, grown monstrous and aggressive. This is the heavy-handed humor of a society which gloated over the sexual violence of the arena.

No wonder the early Christians stood out against the excesses of the flesh. Austerity came naturally to a religion whose founder had said his kingdom was not of this world. The old gods with their family feuds and sexual conquests and petty vengeances seemed selfish and venal compared with the pale Galilean. Even pagans envied the beauty of the Christian service with it mellifluous singing and chanting. Despite centuries of intermittent persecution, converts continued to grow in numbers and influence. As the Empire itself began to tatter under the inroads of barbarians and the strains of an overstretched economy, the Christian passport to a future life of bliss grew more attractive. In 313 the Emperor Constantine passed the Edict of Milan, establishing toleration for Christianity. His convening of the Council of Nicaea in 325 confirmed the dominant influence and growing authority of the new religion.

Oddly enough, the Church then rapidly became very worldly indeed. It accepted many aspects of the Empire, including the games, the

111. Greek Lysippos, Herakles (copy by the Athenian Glykon), fourth century, B.C.

112. Roman, tintinnabulum, first century.

ostentatious display of wealth in the churches, the exercise of power by the clergy, the persecution, torture, and execution of heretics, including members of rival Christian sects. Almost the only early tenet the burgeoning Church still clung to was the idea of sex as a display of natural evil in man (or more particularly woman).

There had been more than a hint of misogyny in St. Paul: man was not created for woman, but woman for man. Women were ordered to keep quiet at gatherings of the church. "It is not permitted unto them to speak; but they are commanded to be under obedience, as the law enjoins."[7] Origen, the first great philosopher of Christianity, castrated himself to escape the temptations of the flesh. Jerome saw all sex as physically dirty, though it did not stop him from bewailing the temptations of lust.

Perhaps Jerome, with his hair shirt and unwashed body, was afraid that the new, fashionable converts would dilute the original purity of the faith. The evidence of costly artifacts of the time suggests he might have been right. The splendid silver casket that commemorated the Christian marriage of a woman named Projecta to Turcius Secondus also shows naked pagan deities [113]. On the lid, bride and bridegroom stand soberly with clasped hands in a wreathed medallion. The inscription exhorts them to "live in Christ." But they are surrounded by voluptuous Nereids and cavorting Tritons. Venus, goddess of love, reclines sensuously on her shell, regarding herself in a mirror, just as Projecta does immediately below [114]. She is braiding her ornately coiffured hair, while handmaidens bring her the unguents and ornaments that will complete her toilet. Peacocks and doves flutter among the ornate arcades, bordered with vine leaves and pendulous with grapes. It is all a dream of earthly delights of the sort guaranteed to make such resolute puritans as Jerome squirm. "Marriage," he said, "is only one

113. Roman, Projecta's casket lid, ca. 380.

114. Roman, Projecta's casket side, ca. 380.

degree less sinful than fornication."[8] Augustine, his contemporary, was of the same opinion. He identified the male genitals as the place from which the first sin was passed on. "Adam had defied God—and for every man born, the shame at the uncontrollable stirring of the genitals was a reminder of, and a fitting punishment for, the original crime of disobedience."[9]

Self-hatred is not a good beginning for brotherly love. Augustine believed in coercion to obtain converts. Better torment on earth than to be damned for eternity. Of course, he was writing in a crumbling world. The author of *The City of God* died while his own city of Hippo in North Africa was under siege from the Vandals. The sophisticated society that admired Projecta's marriage casket was swept away. Illiterate barbarian kingdoms replaced the Empire. They soon converted to Christianity. They needed all the help they could get. As well as taking on priestly administrators and legislators, they also absorbed and expanded the grosser superstitions of the Church.

The only bodies to be coveted in the Dark Ages were bits of saints and martyrs. Enormous prices were paid for the jawbone of St. Bridget, the hand of St. James, a twist of the Virgin's hair. I myself have seen the brain of Thomas Aquinas; it resembled a moldy Camembert. For eight hundred years some of the most precious and costly artifacts made in the West were the repositories for these unsavory morsels [115]. They

115. German, golden reliquary designed to contain Charlemagne's arm, fifteenth century.

brought great kudos to the places that owned them and made them lucrative centers for pilgrimage. There was intense competition for the more enticing items. No less than fifteen establishments, including Chartres, claimed to possess the foreskin of Jesus, presumably the only part of him left on earth after the Resurrection. The reliquaries themselves were often created out of antique gems and golden fragments of classical sculpture. At the same time, the beautiful gods of Greece and Rome became pagan idols to be destroyed. They were thought to be occupied by demons who had diabolically assumed their form. By association all comely mortals were suspect.

"All that beauty consists but in phlegm and blood and humours and gall," wrote Odo, tenth-century Abbot of Cluny, in a famous diatribe against women. "If a man considers that which is hidden within the nose, throat, and the belly, he will find filth everywhere; and if we cannot bring ourselves, even with the tips of our fingers, to touch such phlegm or dung, wherever do we desire to embrace this bag of filth itself?"[10]

116. German, Adam and Eve Reproached by the Lord, *1015.*

117. German, Expulsion from Paradise (detail), 1015.

Not surprisingly, one of the first considerable works of Western art from this time deals graphically with the Fall. The great bronze doors at Hildesheim Cathedral in Germany were cast in 1015 for an Abbot Bernward. The crouching, cringing hulks that are Adam and Eve pay scant respect to human anatomy but are masterpieces of expressionist art [116]. God, with countenance severe but sorrowful, points the finger at Adam. Bowed with guilt, without looking around, Adam gestures toward Eve. She, in an attitude that recalls the silent but stubborn denial of an accused peasant, points down to the serpent (in this case a small dragon) between her feet. She, we feel, is less repentant than he. On the expulsion from Eden, Adam trudges doggedly forward, accepting his lot; Eve looks back with a gesture that mingles grief and regret [117].

118. English, Adam and Eve Getting the Forbidden Fruit, *twelfth century.*

Suffering humanity: the dark centuries knew all about pain. The expression of pleasure in a carnal form was quite beyond them. Eating the forbidden fruit should have caused Adam and Eve at least a momentary spasm of delight. The painter of the wall panel in a village church in Sussex [118] has given them the wide-eyed look Genesis describes, but can only manage a simpering prissy reaction. As for their bodies, they are like butchered carcasses of beef, inarticulate and formless. Nothing could demonstrate more clearly the chasm into which Western culture had fallen with the breakup of the classical world, and out of which it was just beginning to climb. The twelfth-century artist has lost the knowledge of proportion and its background in mathematics and geometry that his classical predecessor a thousand years earlier would have taken for granted. Instead he has acquired a Christian distaste for the manifestations of the flesh. Only her hanging dugs differentiates Eve from Adam.

Human sexuality must be revealed only as a source of anguish, not joy. Thus, in another village church, this time in France, at about the same date, a naked woman was sculpted in stone [119]. As a human portrait she is even cruder than the Eve in Sussex, but her sex is more

119. French, Woman Tormented by Lust, *twelfth century.*

explicit. St. Bridget had a vision in which a soul in torment described a similar condition: "A serpent creepeth forth by the lower parts of my stomach unto the higher parts, for my lust was inordinate; therefore now the serpent searcheth about my entrails without comfort, gnawing and biting without mercy. My breast is open and gnawed with worms, for I loved foul and rotten things more than God."[11]

The Church gave women an impossible exemplar when it hailed Mary as perfect. Growing girls were told they must be both mothers and supporters of mankind, and also pure and virginal. No wonder the early Fathers, like Jerome, recommended a life of chastity for women as the only answer. In that way, it was thought, they would escape the demands of the body that made them inferior to men. Unsullied and free of marital chores they would be able to participate in the same activities as the other half of the human race. In turning against marriage, Jerome was anticipating the position Engels reached fifteen hundred years later: that it was the source of women's enslavement. Neither of these bachelors suggested how women were to satisfy their own desires.

Jerome believed in the mortification of the flesh (he used to beat his chest with a stone), and that, by and large, has continued to be the Christian answer. Cold baths, simple food, and plenty of exercise would keep the old Adam at bay. The Church teaching was particularly hard on women. Male desire was undeniable and uncontrollable; Augustine preached on the recurring shame of wet dreams. But women produced fewer visible symptoms when sexually aroused, and were assumed not to have such feelings to the same degree. A sexy woman was being perversely provocative. Even good looks were an unfair temptation to poor weak man; Paul ordained that women should cover their heads in church.

So the only physically attractive females in medieval art are bound to be temptresses, like the Eve who peered over a lintel in Autun Cathedral [120]. It is not only the long strands of hair which frame her pert little face, or the coy gesture with which she catches the attention of the passerby, but the way her plump body emerges from the tree of knowledge that confirms her sensuality. We empathize with the broad palms of the leaves which have just brushed the firm curves of her breasts and are still caressing her stomach, hips, and thighs. *We* see her as sinuously peering through the branches to attract us. But medieval

man saw her body undulating like the wicked snake she was. The master-mason who carved her, Gislebertus, sought to make an image that would rouse both lust and righteous condemnation. In other words he wanted to have it both ways; a hypocrisy which has been necessary to many artists in Christian societies since.

The Gothic obsession with luxuriant detail gives multiple footnotes to the preoccupations of the times—comic, savage, sometimes irreverent, often mysterious. Small carvings of ill-favored crones can be found in inconspicuous corners of a number of churches across northern Europe. Each has its individual ugliness, but all have in common the fierce stare, the gaping mouth, and hands stretching wide the labia [121]. It has been suggested that they hark back to earlier fertility goddesses and were put up by superstitious masons to ward off evil luck, as the phallus was thought to do in classical times.

It seems more likely these unsettling little figures were meant to prohibit sin; pointing out the first tunnel that man could enter en route to Hell. Hell was something the religious imagination could really get its teeth into: the invention of torments even worse than those in common practice outside the monastery walls. Most well-endowed

120. French, Eve, *twelfth century*

121. Irish, female exhibitionist, twelfth century.

churches, especially in Italy, had their Last Judgment, and there, opposite the chaste troops of the saved wanly ascending, were the gross masses of the Damned getting their just desserts [122]. We respond to the plastic energy of the invention, and laugh at the sooty demons and all-too-literal misfortunes they are inflicting. But they were no joke to their creators. The medieval world lay under the shadow of this dreadful future life. *"PER ME SI VA NELL' ETERNO DOLORE"* (I am the way into eternal grief), Dante read above the gateway to Hell.[12] Only one person in a thousand was expected to qualify for the other place, the Heavenly City.

Death, the great leveler, came to obsess the Middle Ages more and more. The plague, which reached Europe in the fourteenth century, carried off a third of the population. Whole villages died. For four hundred years this unpredictable scourge dominated all other fears. Perhaps it was familiarity with disease in a horrifying form—the ulcers of the victims emanated a peculiarly disgusting smell—that led to the preoccupation with physical corruption that occupied the creative consciousness during these centuries. The maggot would eat up mortal beauty: "then worms shall try that long preserved virginity" [123].[13] This rotting corpse, still erotic in decay, lies beneath the charging hooves of St. George, off to avenge her on the dragon. It was painted for the

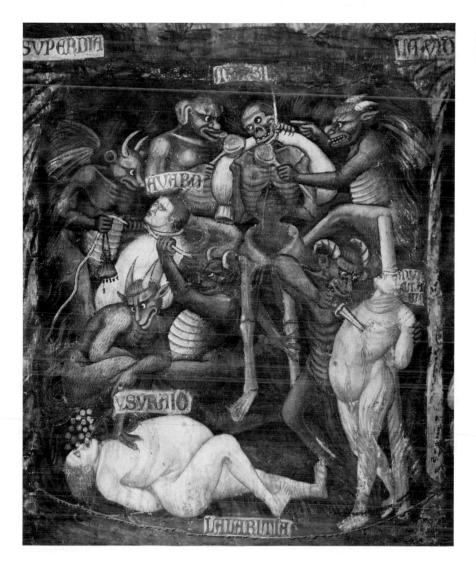

122. Di Bartolo, Hell: Punishment for Sinners, *1393*

123. *Carpaccio*, St. George Slaying the Dragon *(detail), ca. 1500.*

124. Baldung, Death and the Woman, *ca.* *1517.*

saint's chapel in Venice by the Italian artist Carpaccio, in the fifteenth century. Similar displays of putrefaction could be found in churches all over Europe during the period when King Death and his minions, disease and famine, held sway.

The fourteenth century invented the dance macabre, a celebration of horror and loathing. The figure of Death coming to claim new victims was also ourselves in our future state of corruption, still avid for life, struggling back to embrace the living [124]. It is not so much a kiss that the corpse bestows as a gluttonous bite. He grapples greedily with the warm flesh. As for the woman, she is not at all averse. She tears off her shroud; she must grasp what pleasure she can, before she too rots away.

God also must be shown to suffer. The agonies inflicted on Jesus in the stations of the Cross grow more cruel, especially in northern art. Often he is shown humiliated, defiled. The most terrible of all Crucifixions was painted in Germany between 1513 and 1515 [125]. The artist has come down to us as Grünewald, though his real name was probably Mathis Gothardt. Jesus is not a god but a dead man. Only recently dead, because a viscous flow of blood still issues from the wound in his right side—but dead, the blue pallor of the lips, the flaccid fall of the features, tells us without doubt. His body has been defaced by the manner of his death. He might be a plucked fowl hanging in a market, but when we look closely, nothing is carried beyond the bounds of the probable. This is how flesh that has been scourged by thorns must look, manifold small bloody slits, with here and there barbs that penetrated more deeply, broken off and sticking in the wound. The arms are wrenched out of their sockets. The hands and fingers, despite the tension of the nails through the palms, are twisted grotesquely by the final spasms of agony. The emaciation of the body reveals the skeleton it will shortly be, as do the blackening feet, already turning gangrenous.

Grünewald knew gangrene. The painting was commissioned by the Abbot of Isenheim, a monastic hospital. It was founded for sufferers from St. Anthony's fire, or the burning sickness. Spread by fungus that afflicted rye, the main source of bread for the poor, it was a common disease in the Middle Ages. "The victims' blood was affected by a poisonous inflammation which consumed the whole body, producing tumours which developed into incurable ulcers and caused thousands

125. *Grünewald,* Crucifixion, *1513–15.*

of deaths."[14] In the late stages gangrene rotted the arms and legs from the body. There was no cure. Surrounded by such patients, Grünewald was not likely to minimize the physical suffering that the Son of God was said to have borne for them. Probably Grünewald had seen too much suffering to believe in its expiatory force. In another wing of the *Isenheim Altarpiece* he shows a figure pullulating with ulcers, bloated and green with gangrene, still alive and looking hopelessly to a Heaven peopled with demons. Nearby on a paper is written: *"Ubi eras Jhesu bone, ubi eras, quare non affuisti ut sanares vulnera mea?"* (Where were you, good Jesus, where were you? And why did you not come and dress my wounds?)

A religion that began in pain and death continued for many centuries to praise sacrifice and portray the trials of the body with zest. Looking to the afterlife for principal rewards, Christians were bound to be suspicious and negative toward acts of spontaneous joy and creativity. Yet as they grew ever richer and more powerful through the Middle Ages, there seemed few of the seven sins that churchmen themselves had not embraced. Avaricious pardoners, slothful friars, greedy abbots, lustful templars, proud bishops, envious sacristans, and choleric deans; a monstrous regiment, they still live in the pages of Boccaccio and Chaucer. Even in their day a wind of change was stirring. It rattled the coffin lids of the kings, lords, ladies, and commonality emerging at the Last Trump on the tympanum of Bourges Cathedral [126]. They are about to suffer the usual probing, gnashing, and boiling by the demon host, but they are a remarkably handsome lot by thirteenth-century standards. In this they were obeying the behest of the Church

126. Bourges Cathedral, The Last Judgment, *thirteenth century.*

authority Vincent of Beauvais. When portraying the Resurrection, the figures rising from the grave should not only be naked, but each should be in a state of perfect beauty. Unfortunately, few artists had the skill to achieve such grace. The unknown master of Bourges must have studied classical models and from life, unusual disciplines for a medieval craftsman. But if the muscular back of the man pushing up the lid of the tomb on the left is two hundred years before its time, the girl stepping confidently forward can be found in Chaucer.

> *For hadde god comanded maydenhede,*
> *Thanne hadde he dampned wedding with the dede;*
> *And certes, if ther were no seed y sowe,*
> *Virginitee, wher-of than sholde it growe?*
> *In wyfhode I wol use myn instrument*
> *As frely as my maker hath it sent.*[15]*

She is the new woman of the late Middle Ages, earthy, cheerful, and practical, sure of her charms and skeptical of all authoritarian dogma. Her body, slender, with small high breasts and long waist, was to become the soul mate of the cautious, pragmatic reformers of the north whose belief in themselves would crack the autocracy of the papacy and usher in the divided world we have inherited. That new world would not banish pain. Far from it. The rival sects of Catholic and Protestant proved as vindictive as Nero, burning each other with the sanctimonious self-righteousness that had aroused the animosity of the pagan Roman mob. But artistically the new age dwelled less on torments and instead exalted the portrayal of the body to heights of unprecedented magnificence. Even so, the greatest protagonist of human beauty remained a devout Christian.

At first sight, Michelangelo Buonarotti might seem an unsympathetic intermediary for the Man of Sorrows. He was an egoist, proud, ambitious,

---

* *Nevill Coghill's paraphrase:*

> *Had God commanded maidenhood to all,*
> *Then marriage had been damned beyond recall;*
> *And certainly, if seed were never sown,*
> *How ever could virginity be grown?*
> *In wifehood I will use my instrument*
> *As freely as my Maker me it sent.*

127. Michelangelo, Pietà, *1498–99.*

contentious, scarred with guilt over his own nature, no lover of humankind in general, a complex individual living through a time when certainties were dissolving. Yet at several crucial points in his long life he turned to the consideration of Christ.

Like all the greatest artists he was able to remake a hallowed theme in his own likeness yet retain its universal command. As a young man of twenty three he was commissioned by a French cardinal in Rome to carve a pietà [127]. It was the work that established his reputation. Michelangelo has created a paean to lost youth. It is the most sweetly gentle of all his themes. Jesus lies back as though peacefully sleeping in the arms of his mother. She is freshly beautiful enough to be the Bride of Christ indeed. She looks down in tender resignation at the slender unscarred body. Only the fall of the limbs, the slant of the head, reveals that this is the sleep of death.

Six days before his own death, Michelangelo was working on another pietà—he had struggled with it intermittently for years [128]. The

128. Michelangelo, Rondanini Pietà, *1555–64.*

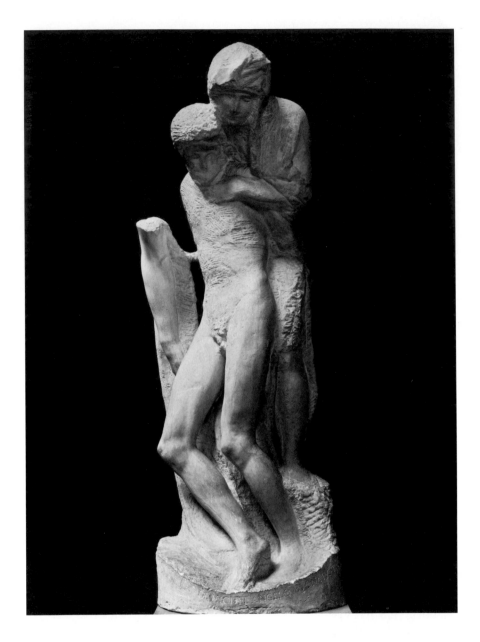

distance between the slim legs echoes in reverse the pose of the earlier Christ. Everything else has changed. This is an old man, his body rough-hewn and skinny. The Virgin clings to him with sorrow; she both supports him and cannot bear to let him go. The contrast with the smooth finish of the first pietà highlights another truth. The young can die carelessly; the old hang painfully to life.

The unfinished carving imparts a modern poignancy similar to that of *The Captives* [44]. There, the figures struggle to be released from the stone; here, they are subsiding back into it, growing together in their grief, which is also the sculptor's for lost time, for tasks undone. It seems appropriate that it should not be finished as so many of his works were not: Michelangelo attacked every task as a challenge to be carried beyond the limits of previous achievement. He was not interested in the creation of a circumscribed perfection.

In middle life, shortly before painting *The Last Judgment* in the Sistine Chapel, and in the years when Luther was preaching in Germany and reform was in the wind, Michelangelo made a number of drawings of the Resurrection. In them Christ is an elemental force bursting out of the earth and scattering slothful, stupid, and lustful humanity with irresistible energy [129]. Nature is rendered coherent by classical order. The adversaries fall away like the linked entrails of some bovine sacrifice while the divine executioner soars upward, an exultant Apollo.

129. Michelangelo, Resurrection, *ca. 1530s(?).*

130. Michelangelo,
Risen Christ, *ca. 1530
s(?).*

Another drawing strips all extraneous detail from the risen god, save the vacated tomb [130]. Christ the Tiger juggles with the thunderbolts of freshly assumed power. He is the idea of human perfectibility, hurling defiance at time and the elements, sloughing off the dross of the past. The spirit has become flesh, purified and triumphant. But that reminds us of Blake and the innocence of the newly created:

> *What shall I call thee?*
> *I happy am*
> *Joy is my name—*
> *Sweet joy befall thee!*[16]

For each reborn soul, a return to the body but made anew, without its poor tormented imperfections. Here is the ecstasy of resurrection that the faithful hoped to experience through their martyrdom. It recalls the early Christian mosaic encountered on the narrow street beneath the Vatican: Christ the sun-god, driving Apollo's chariot.

Each generation of believers views the Savior in the light of their needs and to the limits of their understanding. It was natural for Renaissance artists to see Christ naked and risen—as triumphantly reborn as was their own culture. In that new vision the old certainties of the medieval world vanished forever, leaving each individual soul to find his particular road to salvation. Then and now, the pilgrim must take his own way forward.

> *Forth, pilgrim, forth! Forth, beste out of thy stal!*
> *Know thy contree, look up, thank God of al;*
> *Hold the hye wey, and lat thy gost thee lede;*
> *And trouthe shal delivere, hit is no drede.*[17]†

---

† *Nevill Coghill's paraphrase:*

> *Forth, pilgrim, forth! Forth, beast, out of your stall!*
> *Look upward, know your home, thank God for all;*
> *Hold the high way and let your soul lead clear;*
> *Truth shall be your deliverer, never fear.*

6

THE WAGES OF FAME

Custom dictates that as soon as I have left my baggage in the *pensione* where I usually stay in Florence, I take the iron cage lift back to the entrance. Walking along the Arno away from the Ponte Vecchio, I quickly turn left under a stone arch. I am in a narrow passageway, dark and stinking of urine and rotting refuse. Just the place to meet one of those large rats that can be seen in the twilight, crawling over the lower piers of the old bridge. But two turns and a minute's brisk walk brings me out into brilliant sunlight. I have entered the Piazza della Signoria.

The Gothic arches of the Loggia dei Lanzi are beside me and beyond, the arrogant tower of the Palazzo Vecchio. In front of these tremendous medieval buildings stands the triumphant assertion of the Renaissance: sculpture by Donatello, Cellini, Giambologna, the enormous replica of Michelangelo's *David*. They seem to confirm the optimistic eulogy of the English poet Samuel Rogers:

> *Of all the fairest Cities of the Earth*
> *None is so fair as Florence. 'Tis a gem*
> *of purest ray; and what a light broke forth,*
> *When it emerged from darkness!*[1]

The reality was not quite so clear-cut. The *David*, fourteen feet high and triumphantly naked, seems with a disdainful glance to reject all those wincing, ill-formed, lost souls of the Middle Ages [150]. So modern is he that he has become the hero of Muscle Beach, the most famous masculine statue in the world. But if man has broken out of

131. Botticelli, Birth of Venus *(detail), ca. 1480s.*

his medieval shackles, what about woman? Near the *David* until recently stood the slightly earlier *Judith* of Donatello [132]. (*Judith* was moved after over four hundred years into the Palazzo Vecchio in 1980.) Not so large as the *David*, she is quite as stern and confident. Moreover, she is in the act of lopping off the head of Holofernes, with whom she has

132. Donatello, Judith and Holofernes, *ca. 1446–60.*

just spent a torrid evening. Opposite, under the arch of the Loggia dei Lanzi, the male gets his own back. Perseus lifts up the decapitated head of the Gorgon in triumph [133]. Her beautiful body, gushing bronze blood, lolls at his feet. The Gorgon, of course, could freeze an intruder with her look. Without such defenses, the Sabine woman nearby is

133. Cellini, Perseus, *ca. 1545–54.*

134. Giambologna,
Rape of the Sabine
Women, *1583.*

thrust aloft in the conquering arms of a burly rapist [134]. Women invite such behavior, so male thinking has often suggested, with their seductive ways. On *The Fountain of Neptune* one of the Nereids writhes her long limbs, to rouse the lascivious attention of the watching Tritons [135]. The evidence of stone and bronze suggests that the renewal of interest in the classical world did not greatly alter Christian society's attitude to woman. She remains goddess or temptress or both: delightful but dangerous.

In some ways, the Renaissance was the first of those false dawns with which the Age of Revolutions has made us all too familiar. It *did* produce a glory of art, architecture, and literature and some definite social change. Within a relatively short time the status of the artist altered beyond recognition. This in turn had a considerable effect on the view of the human body in art.

Even to those living through it, the fifteenth century in Florence seemed a unique moment. Returning from exile in 1434, the young Alberti, lawyer and humanist, was so struck by what he saw that he wrote the first treatise on art in modern times. He addressed it specifically to five men in whom he found "a genius for every praiseworthy thing. For this they should not be slighted in favour of anyone famous in antiquity."[2] Three were already in their fifties:

135. Ammannati, Fountain of Neptune, Nereid, and Triton, *1563–75.*

Brunelleschi, the brilliant architect, whose dome for Florence Cathedral, the first to be attempted since Roman times, was nearing completion; his "close friend" Donatello, the sculptor whose figures were adorning the campanile of the cathedral; and Ghiberti, the master craftsman who had already been working for over thirty years on the bronze doors of the Baptistry nearby. Of the others, Luca della Robbia was in his early thirties. His charming terra-cotta Madonnas became some of the most popular images of the early Renaissance. The fifth man, his contemporary, Masaccio, had died of the plague at twenty-seven, but not before he painted a series of frescoes in the Carmelite church in Florence that gave a new grandeur to art. It was the note of weighty achievement and high seriousness that Alberti responded to and extolled: "As you work from day to day, you persevere in discovering things through which your extraordinary genius acquires perpetual fame."[3]

Perpetual fame acquired by artistic genius: not a concept that would have been understood in the Middle Ages. Dante had recognized that his contemporary, the artist Giotto, outshone his fellows, but in general the medieval painter was as much a craftsman as the stonemason. Both were hired to carry out a specific task. They were paid for time and materials. Often they could turn their hand to neighboring skills. So indeed could Alberti's heroes. Brunelleschi, Donatello, and Ghiberti all served their apprenticeship to goldsmiths. There is a revealing story that Brunelleschi and Donatello went to Rome in early manhood to look at the antiquities. "Neither of them paid much attention to what they ate and drank or how they were dressed or where they lived."[4] They earned money when they needed it, getting work from the local shops, cutting and polishing precious stones. Such casual and unpretentious use of a craft skill would have been unthinkable to the successful artists of the next century who were enriched, acclaimed, and sometimes ennobled by their devotion to "High Art."

Recognition on this scale was in the future; and was part and parcel with the change of aspiration in the making of the work of art itself. In the fourteenth century, Andrea Pisano, sculpting a bronze door for the Baptistry at Florence, still worked within the accepted tradition of Gothic relief. Beautiful and expressive as are the figures in the *Baptism of Christ* [136], rocks, trees, hills, and river adhere to the formal iconography of the time. The water might be a tactful veil drawn across

136. Andrea Pisano,
Baptism of Christ,
1330–36.

the hips of the Savior. The result was very different when, in 1401, the city fathers decided to commission a companion door. "They resolved to invite to Florence the best craftsmen in Italy to make in competition, as a trial specimen of their work, a scene in bronze similar to one of those that Andrea Pisano had made earlier for the first door."[5] Seven artists, including Donatello, Brunelleschi, and Ghiberti, labored for a year. Ghiberti won the contract, and a lifetime's labor. His entry [137] is a masterpiece of design: the tumbling hillside, the beetling brows of Abraham above the pointing dagger, the descending angel, all carry us to the naked victim. Kneeling and bound, looking up at his father in mute supplication, he represents a grasp of anatomy that directly challenges the achievements of the classical world.

Beauty, elegance, and the display of superlative skill were Ghiberti's intentions. In this sense he was the quintessential craftsman. But when he was commissioned in 1425 to create a third door on the same pattern as the earlier two, he decided to outshine his own achievement. He radically changed the design. It has been suggested by E. H. Gombrich, one of the most influential of modern writers on the Renaissance,[6] that with this decision Ghiberti introduced the idea of artistic progress. "Henceforward there will be a growing gulf between the intellectual pursuits of Art and the applied art of the craftsman."[7] From now on it would not be enough for an artist to reach an accepted level, like a potter throwing another vase—individual, certainly, but similar to earlier vases. Increasingly, artists sought to show some new thing in

137. Ghiberti,
Abraham Sacrificing
Isaac, *1402.*

138. Ghiberti, The Creation of Eve, *ca. 1426.*

every work. A climate of hectic amazement grew around creative endeavor; necessarily so when artists were no longer assured commissions from conservative bodies like guilds and church orders, but were vying with each other for the patronage of wealthy but capricious individuals. Such connoisseurs acquired art as a means of displaying their taste and wealth in an era of conspicuous vanity. Naturally they wanted works that would astonish their peers and rouse their envy.

The general reaction to Ghiberti's new doors was unanimous. Successive generations have echoed Michelangelo's opinion: "They are so beautiful that they would grace the entrance to Paradise."[8] The first of the ten panels could symbolize the triumph of the artist [138]. Eve rises effortlessly at the behest of God from the earthbound side of the sleeping Adam, as her slender, beautiful form, precursor of the ideal of later ages, grows under the fingers of Ghiberti. Newly created, she faces her Maker without shame, "the first of the proud naked beauties of the Renaissance."[9]

Alberti recommended the fundamental importance of the naked figure in painting. "Before dressing a man we first draw him nude, then we enfold him in draperies. So in painting the nude we place first his bones and muscles which we then cover with flesh so that it is not difficult to understand where each muscle is beneath."[10] In this, as in much else, he forecast what was to be standard practice for artists in the future. Drawings show that Raphael made studies of his models naked [139] to analyze their postures before clothing them in the flowing robes of saints and prophets for the heavenly discourse on the walls of the Pope's apartments in the Vatican. Leonardo dissected corpses in order to gain a greater command of human anatomy. His drawings recording his discoveries uniquely combine art and science and were soon to be extended by the comprehensive mapping of Vesalius [140].

Alberti wanted this knowledge applied to the most elevated subjects, what he called histories. They were to be varied, dignified, and

139. Raphael, drawing for Disputa, *ca. 1510.*

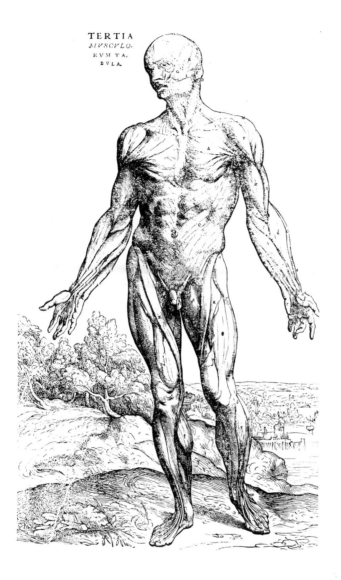

TERTIA
MVSCVLO.
RVM TA.
BVLA.

140. Vesalius, plate from De Humani Corporis Fabrica, *1543.*

harmonious, and would bring back to painting the renown it had possessed with the ancients. "The history will move the soul of the beholder when each man painted there clearly shows the movement of his own soul. For we are so formed by nature as to sympathise with what we see; we weep with the weeping, laugh with the laughing, and grieve with the grieving. These movements of the soul are made known by movements of the body."[11] Alberti's formula for a genre of painting that barely existed in his time accurately predicts the course academic art would follow for the next four hundred years. "A painting in which there are bodies in many dissimilar poses is always especially pleasing

141. Masaccio, Baptism of the Neophytes, *1425–27.*

. . . to each one is given his own action and flection of members; some are seated, others on one knee, others lying. If it is allowed here, there ought to be some nude and others part nude and part clothed in the painting."[12]

In 1435 when this was written only the frescoes that Masaccio had painted a few years before in the Church of the Carmelites in Florence came near to fulfilling Alberti's prescription. In one panel St. Peter is shown baptizing a group of young men [141]. The figure of the youth wincing and shivering on the edge of the water shows the precise observation that Alberti praised. Commanding the expulsion from the Garden of Eden [142], the golden-haired Archangel might have fluttered in from the previous century. But the figures below are as anguished as any by a modern Expressionist. "Who could ever without the greatest

142. Masaccio, The Fall, 1425–27.

study express faces in which mouth, chin, eyes, cheeks, forehead and eyebrows all were in harmony with laughter or weeping. For this reason it is best to learn them from nature and always to do these things very rapidly, letting the observer think he sees more than he actually sees."[13] In just such sure strokes, Masaccio catches the bitterness, fear, and undignified haste of the departure.

Vasari, the first chronicler of the lives of artists, draws a portrait of the young painter as a characteristic Bohemian; well intentioned, but erratic and absentminded. Devoting all his time and thought to art, he never cared about worldly possessions or even how he dressed. "So instead of calling him by his proper name, which was Tommaso, everyone called him Masaccio"[14] (as we might indulgently call someone "Silly Billy").

In his brief lifework he captured the realism, psychological truth, and high seriousness that Alberti believed were the essence of great art. So did the sculptor Donatello; but he added to it a restless unease of spirit that was his own. Donatello stood at the hinge between the anonymous craft-artists of the Middle Ages and the superstars of the next century. Like Masaccio (to whom he lent money) he was often hard up. A number of his sardonic wisecracks have been preserved. When he fell out with Brunelleschi over a crucifix Donatello had carved, his response to his friend's criticism was "Take some wood and make one yourself." It became a standard Florentine riposte. On the other hand there is much in his character which remains mysterious. We do not even know when two of his principal statues, the *Judith and Holofernes* and the bronze *David*, were cast. Both were probably commissioned by the Medici, the dominant merchant family of Florence. Most likely they stood in the courtyard of the new Medici palace in Florence. In similarity of subject—the beheading of a tyrant by a weaker but patriotic opponent—they seem linked. The date of building the palace (it was not finished until the 1450s) and stylistic evidence suggest that the sculptures were not completed until Donatello was nearing seventy. They were almost certainly the first free-standing figures to be cast in Europe for over a thousand years.

Nevertheless they seem a forbidding pair to decorate a private ambulatory; even though the *Judith* [132] was given an added inscription extolling the virtues of cities as opposed to the license of kingdoms.

This would have appealed to the Medici, the leading citizens of a powerful city-state. In the apocryphal Book of Judith she is a Jewish widow whose city is under siege. She visits the enemy commander, Holofernes, and captivates him with her beauty. After making him drunk, she cuts off his head with two strokes of his own sword. Donatello shows the moment between the strokes. Holofernes is already dead from a great gash in the neck. "One can see the effect of wine and sleep in the expression of Holofernes and the presence of death in his limbs, which, as his soul has departed, are cold and limp."[15] Judith is poised above him, her left hand hooked in his hair, pulling his lolling head back on her braced left thigh, while her foot presses down on his flaccid arm. Her expression is enigmatic. Perhaps she is steeling herself to strike the second blow, or she might be savoring her moment of triumph. There is certainly stern resolution in every muscle

After more than five hundred years the *Judith* remains an ominous and gloomy work of great power. When it was first moved to the Piazza della Signoria at the end of the fifteenth century, it was not readily accepted. It was thought "not fitting that the woman should slay the man."[16] There is something sexually disturbing in the clothed female executioner looming over the nearly naked male. The contrast between her fierce countenance and his, still carrying the relaxed anticipation of pleasure, increases our discomfiture. Noticing that her rigid right leg is jammed between his open thighs, we remember that decapitation is a symbol for castration.

The *David* is also sexually challenging [143]. There may be remote textual reasons why the defender of the Israelites goes into battle clad only in a saucy hat and kinky boots. The Bible does say he is a youth, but also ruddy from looking after the sheep. This lad's soft, hairless body appears incapable of kicking a ball across the Piazza della Signoria. Perhaps the pose, left hand on hip and other hip jutting, did not carry the provocative message that it does now. But the eroticism of each androgynous curve is unmistakable. Apparently Donatello loved to have beautiful apprentices (the only readily available models for artists in those days). When he was offered a boy who was said to be even prettier than his brother, already in the sculptor's service, Donatello remarked: "The less long will he stay with me!"[17]

In the Renaissance artists often included self-portraits in historical

143. Donatello, David,
ca. 1446–60.

and biblical scenes. Masaccio twice painted himself into the frescoes in the Church of the Carmelites. Even more often artists create a reoccurring egocentric type, based on their own features. Several clues suggest that both the *Judith* and the *David* contain an autobiographical element. No certain likeness of Donatello exists although a reliquary bust of San Rossore carried out some thirty years earlier may be a self-portrait [144].[18] Allowing for the difference in age there are similarities with the Holofernes and Goliath. Kenneth Clark has suggested that the features of Holofernes may be an ironic portrayal of the artist.[19] The likeness of the San Rossore bust to the severed head of Goliath seems even more striking. There is the same high-bridged nose, prominent

144. Donatello, Bust of San Rossore, *1422–27.*

cheekbones, beetling eyebrows, and full lips partially concealed by the luxuriant beard. A curious contrapuntalism has Judith burying her fingers in Holofernes' hair while David's naked toes probe playfully in Goliath's beard [143]. Both victims seem old to be conquering generals and all-powerful giants. They appear nearer in age to their creator, the sculptor.

Donatello has left us another clue. He has inscribed his name on the cushion immediately below the right hand of Holofernes [132]. Naturally he signed other works which were not so personal, but the position beneath the hand, once creative now prostrate, seems an extension of the theme of age defeated by youth and time. Many artists, including Michelangelo, have approached such a theme at the end of their careers. Kenneth Clark says the pathos in the head of Holofernes seems to indicate where the artist's sympathies lie. The woman has offered false hopes; man's dream of fulfillment is rudely cut off by the sword of righteousness. In the companion piece, David stands arrogantly on the wing of Goliath's helmet; the other wing curves up erotically to caress the inside of the boy's thigh [145]. Both victor and victim look down as though they were sharing some secret pleasure. Donatello has given us an indication what it might be in the relief inscribed on the front of Goliath's helmet. It shows the triumph of Priapus, the god of lust. Not an appropriate image for a bellicose Philistine, but close to the imagination of an old sculptor, dreaming of the next beautiful apprentice he might immortalize.

Donatello was able to invest even more youthful figures with a joyful energy that has sexual nuances. The most original is the so-called *Atys-Amorino* [146]. Nobody knows its exact meaning with its small wings on back and heels, little tail, flowers in the hair, and snake on the foot. More than anything it represents a small boy, full of wicked, unbuttoned glee. Such uncensored delight, childish but knowing, is rare in earlier art.

The appreciation of children for themselves, and not as tiny adults, was one of the advances of the Renaissance. It sprang from the desire to record things as they were (so that even angelic cherubs have the chubby limbs of real infants), and also perhaps from a society with more space and leisure. Children become a pleasure, not only a potential work force, as witness the hosts of little sweetlings turned out in terra-cotta by the Della Robbias [147]. Victorian sentiment has fatally tinged

145. *Donatello, David, ca. 1446–60.*

these with sugar for us, but we can still delight in the decorative energy which clothes door mantels, window cornices, and fireplaces [148] with dancing sprites.

The building this chimney adorns, the Ducal Palace at Urbino, perfectly combines the two major expressions of Early Renaissance genius, gravity and grace. The gravity, which Alberti so applauded, is another aspect of the mentality which made Florentines the leading bankers of Europe at this time. Hard-edged realism in painting, the desire to record every detail with precise accuracy, is the other side of the coin to the invention of double-entry accounting and the mastery of the abacus. In the fifteenth century, the Florentine slang for being educated was "*sta al abaco*"—he is at the abacus.[20] It was a tool to harness mathematics for the benefit of man, in the way that perspective, based on geometry, was giving a new authority to art. And business was creating a new wealthy class, serious, independent-minded and yet with the Italian love of display. Alberti, himself the scion of a great

146. Donatello, Atys-Amorino, *ca. 1440.*

147. Andrea Della Robbia, Boy with Bagpipes, *mid-fifteenth century.*

banking family, wrote that "painting ought to have pleasant and graceful movements, suitable to what is happening there. The movements and poses of virgins are airy, full of simplicity with sweetness of quiet rather than strength."[21] The greatest exponent of such linear grace was Botticelli. A generation younger than Masaccio and Donatello, his contribution to the portrayal of the body was neither so forceful nor so psychologically complex. Deeply religious, he yet produced the painting that for most

148. Chimney piece, mid-fifteenth century.

of us summarizes our idea, perhaps mistaken, of the Renaissance as a return to pagan beauty.

The Birth of Venus [149] is one of the few paintings that everyone knows, if only through its constant reproduction in advertisements. Consequently, the original at first sight appears much larger than expected. Venus flows impetuously toward the viewer carried effortlessly on the vast scallop shell. The perspective is so shallow that the very next moment the shell will touch land and she will be in your arms. Yet she is advancing with that demure grace that you still see in Florentine beauties. All the energy of movement emanates from her attendants, the amorous Zephyrs who fly beside her. They are clearly lovers, their bodies sensuously intertwined. Their hot breath blows Venus across the rhythmic foam and sprinkles it with falling roses. Just so the scattered seed of castrated Uranus, god of heaven, fell upon the waters and conceived Venus. That act is now past. The goddess, fully formed, is about to step ashore in the shadowless, clear light of early morning. There have been complaints that it gives a cold color to the flesh, but anyone knowing the fierce heat of the Mediterranean noon will recall the moment before sunrise as deliciously cool,

149. Botticelli, Birth of Venus, *ca. 1480s.*

refreshing as the touch of Venus would be at this first hour of her existence.

The handmaiden of Spring awaits her on land with a mantle of flowers, her earthly dress. Her robe is caught by the wayward wind as are the tresses of the goddess's long fair hair. They toss in graceful confusion belying the calm of her face [131] and obeying the behest of Alberti, who wrote, "I am delighted to see some movement in hair, locks of hair, branches, fronds and robes . . . especially pleasing is hair where part of it turns in spirals as if wishing to knot itself, waves in the air like flames, twines around itself like a serpent, while part rises here, part there. Thus you will see with what grace the bodies where they are struck by the wind show the nude under the draperies."[22]

Unlike the sculptured Venus of classical times, whose traditional pose of modesty she assumes, she is not a creature in repose. We see her in the moment of transformation from sea to land, from spirit to flesh. Through the turbulence of motion and the conflicting character of her attendants, Botticelli conveys the dual allegiance of the goddess. She is both sensuous and chaste. Human love, as opposed to mere lust, partakes of both feelings. Venus has this dual aspect because, born of the celestial sphere, she is clothed in the perfect body of earthly beauty. So lovers venerate the ideal, given form for them in the human flesh of their passion.

It is often said that *The Birth of Venus* harks back to an earlier period of art. The shallow depth, the lack of perspective, the decorative use of flowers and waves, all recall tapestry, which is what an enlightened grand seigneur would have demanded to adorn a stony wall a century before. But tempera can convey a great deal more than wool. Perhaps the arced wavelets do set up a formal rhythm; they also resemble the narrow crests of the shallow Aegean when the hot winds of the south blow across that tideless sea. Perhaps the long neck, sloping shoulders, and sinuous body of Venus do recall the tender virgins of the later Middle Ages. But Botticelli has set her lips in a knowing independence of thought, not without sorrow (Ruskin said she has "the sad, passionate and exquisite Lombard mouth").[23] And he has given her abdomen a sensuous, fruitful volume that is far from the smooth ovoids of the Gothic style. Yet, despite her evident weight, she hardly seems to touch the scallop shell that bears her earthward. All the figures dance on the vernal breezes, which lift them like the airy rhythms of a chaconne by Dufay or Josquin des Pres.

Probably the painting was commissioned (by Lorenzo di Pierfrancesco de' Medici, a cousin of Lorenzo the Magnificent) to illustrate a poem, which was written to commemorate a joust held by another of the Medici in Piazza Santa Croce in Florence. The poem tells of the Palace of Venus and describes a painting showing her birth from the sea. The Neoplatonic philosophy popular at the time had rescued Venus from her medieval reputation as an evil temptress. Now she could appear as the form of perfect beauty, and hence of truth, since, as Socrates taught, all ideals unite at the highest level. The dominant scallop shell reminds us that this is also the symbol of another voyager, the pilgrim. In his disinterested quest for holiness he exemplifies the purest and most enduring form of love, the spiritual, to which human lovers can also aspire.

Part of the painting's magic resides in this combination of spiritual and profane. The genius of Botticelli was able to fuse together the rehash of classical ideas, an awareness of antique sculpture, his own medieval inheritance, and the requirements of the story into something entirely his own, and quite new. He created a truly original work. Like Picasso's *Les Demoiselles d'Avignon* it was without precedent or successors,* save in the artist's other mythological pictures. Later in life he appears to have fallen under the spell of Savonarola's severe religious revivalism, and his poetic gift waned. His pictures went out of favor and were virtually ignored until the nineteenth century.

In his prime Botticelli was listed in the top rank of Florentine painters, and was one of those commissioned to decorate the walls of the Pope's private chapel, the Sistine. The *Primavera* and *The Birth of Venus* were the two largest mythological pictures painted up to that time. Yet the price the Medici would have paid was probably only fifty to a hundred florins for each. For an altarpiece painted two or three years later Botticelli received thirty-five florins, rather less than the amount allowed for gold or lapis lazuli in the picture. This was less than a hundredth of the value of one of Piero de' Medici's antique cameos. Then, as now, connoisseurs put a higher value on the works of artists when they were dead. Some fifteen years before *The Birth of Venus* was painted, Donatello, already acknowledged as the greatest

---

* The later classical cubism of Picasso and Braque followed much more astringent principles of destructuring the object.

sculptor of the age, had died in poverty in Florence. In his declining years he was sustained by handouts from the Medici. Botticelli belonged to a later generation, the second wave of the Renaissance. Moreover, he appears to have been a careful man, frugal in his habits. Nevertheless, his talents were only sufficient to buy a modest farmhouse outside Florence.

All this was about to change. In 1504, when he was nearly sixty he was on the committee set up by the city fathers to decide on a site for Michelangelo's *David* [150]. What Botticelli thought of it we do not know. Vast and uncompromising, it was the antithesis of his own delicate art. But it was very much in tune with the mood of the new century. While Michelangelo was carving it, another erstwhile associate of Lorenzo di Pierfrancesco de' Medici sent a letter to Florence about his voyages. This letter, quickly and widely copied, got its author, Amerigo Vespucci, commemorated forever in the name of the New World, whose scale and reality were just beginning to dawn on European consciousness. The imperious gaze of the *David* might belong to a conquistador. The early decades of the sixteenth century put the imprint of Western man around the world, a commanding influence that has been maintained to our own day. Michelangelo's *David* personifies the ambitions of the time, and still catches the spirit that has now carried us into space.

The citizens of Florence, who had recently expelled the ruling Medici, commissioned the statue as the personification of a defender of Republican virtues. The huge block of marble, the largest to be quarried since antiquity, had been lying abandoned for nearly fifty years. In carving it, Michelangelo had to take account of a botched assault on it by an earlier artist, including a hole hacked between where the legs would be. In fact his statue only makes its full impact from the front. From the side the figure seems disproportionately thin for the breadth of chest [151]. Botticelli's committee (it included Leonardo da Vinci, Piero di Cosimo, and Filippino Lippi) tacitly recognized this in suggesting that it be positioned in a niche or against a wall. It was eventually placed on a pedestal in front of the Palazzo Vecchio. Transporting the fourteen-foot giant required an ingenious mobile scaffolding, much labor, and a triumphal procession. Not everyone approved of it, then or later. A nineteenth-century critic called it "a gigantic hobbledehoy, neither man nor boy, a stripling at the age when the body stretches

150. and 151
Michelangelo, David
1504.

itself and the huge hands and feet seem to have no relation to the size of the limbs."[24]

Yet to most, the *David* embodies a two-fold ideal of perfection: the perfection of male beauty, and the perfection of its portrayal. As with Botticelli's *Venus*, familiarity cannot dim the initial impact of the original. The very size of the *David* forces our awareness that the artist himself participated in the heroic aspirations he portrays. There can be no achievement without risk and, by taking on that damaged monstrosity of rock, Michelangelo, twenty-six years old when he began it, has triumphed as surely as David over Goliath. And yet he has given his hero, even in the moment of victory, an awareness of divine discontent. "And shall I die, and this unconquered."[25] Beyond the peak in Darien lie new oceans, fresh empires, but they will not assuage this boundless ambition.

The *David* was recognized as a new summit of art. The Florentines (who paid four hundred crowns for it; approximately eight times the price Botticelli got for the *Venus)* quickly commissioned Michelangelo to paint a vast battle scene for the Palazzo Vecchio. Leonardo da Vinci, at fifty-two the greatest painter of the age, was already at work on a fresco in the Council Chamber. The principal citizen, Piero Soderini, "recognising Michelangelo's abilities, had part of the hall allocated to him; and this was why Michelangelo painted the other wall in competition with Leonardo."[26] In the sixteenth century artists achieved a popular regard something like film stars and athletes today. Unfortunately, in this case nothing came of Soderini's imaginative matching except some superlative drawings by the two masters. Michelangelo chose as his subject an incident in the war between Florence and Pisa when some soldiers were surprised bathing. It was a minor episode in a small war, but allowed Michelangelo to create a cartoon of naked male figures in every sort of posture. For ten years they served as a paradigm for visiting artists; then the cartoon was torn to pieces by acquisitive hands.

Surviving studies [152] suggest the quality which carried Michelangelo to his next Herculean task, the painting of the ceiling of the Sistine Chapel in Rome. His encounters with Pope Julius II have become a legend: the despotic, anxious patron; the proud and willful painter. It epitomizes the modern role of the creator, which Michelangelo by

his achievements did so much to foster. Recalling in a letter his early arguments with the Pope, he wrote: "After I had made some designs it became clear to me the whole decoration would turn out rather meanly. Then the Pope gave me a new commission: to paint down to the histories [the already existing paintings] and to do with the vault what I liked best."[27] No longer was the artist a craftsman employed to carry out a preconceived design; his judgment and personal preferences had to be taken into account. Perhaps no other artist till Picasso achieved such immediate fame and dominance. Appropriately so, for Michelangelo and Picasso stand at the beginning and the end of the epoch of individual creative genius fed by individual patrons of great wealth. Ultimately this wealth stemmed from the new worlds overseas that were opened in Michelangelo's time to European trade and conquest.

For over sixty years his influence on sculpture, painting, and architecture was so pervasive that, touring Europe in the late nineteenth century, Mark Twain was driven to berate the local guides: "Enough, enough, enough! Say no more! Lump the whole thing! Say that the Creator made Italy from designs by Michelangelo!"[28] Nevertheless, for

152. Michelangelo, study for cartoon of the Battle of Cascina, ca. 1504–5.

most of his life Michelangelo worked to a commission, however much he might transform it by the power of his imagination. Only in the highly finished drawings of his middle years and the religious sculptures of his old age was he creating for himself.

He spent four years, on and off, working on the Sistine ceiling. Perhaps the first thing that strikes the spectator, craning upward, is the immensity of the task. The chapel is far higher, the sheer footage to paint much greater than book-size reproductions lead you to expect. Apart from the creative energy required, the physical difficulties were awesome. He recorded some of them in a well-known poem.

> *My stomach's pushed by force beneath my chin,*
> *My beard towards Heaven, and my brain I feel*
> *Is shoved upon my nape, and my breast is like a Harpy,*
> *And the brush, ever over my face*
> *Makes a rich pavement with its droppings.*[29]

Add to that the inadequacy of his assistants, the importunities of the irascible Pope, technical blemishes like the appearance of an unpleasant mold in the plaster during the early stages, delays in payment, his own total ignorance in working with fresco, and the difficulty, as he himself said, in making judgments when upside down. Yet he persisted. The result struck the first spectators "speechless with astonishment."[30] Nor has it ceased to do so. The youthful *Pietà*, the *David*, the cartoon for the *Bathers*, and the Sistine Ceiling put Michelangelo, according to the verdict of history, on a pedestal alongside Shakespeare and Mozart: one of those very few artists who transcend their own epoch and art form and appeal to every succeeding age, irrespective of the dictates of current fashion. Even so, he could write to his family, a few months after descending from the Sistine scaffold for the last time, about these years of his supreme achievements: "I lead a miserable existence and reck not of life nor honour—that is of this world; I live wearied by stupendous labours and beset by a thousand anxieties. And thus have I lived for some fifteen years now, and never an hour's happiness have I had."[31]

Would he have been happier as a simple stonecutter? Genius requires an excessive energy and imagination that will always be, in part, frustrated. Michelangelo was withdrawn from the common enjoyments of society. "Rich though I have become, I have always lived as a poor man,"[32] he said. But close inspection makes it impossible not to believe that working on the ceiling brought Michelangelo a fulfillment far greater than the pains that came with it.

A few years ago I was lucky enough to be on another scaffold in the Sistine. (I had been up before for two nights in 1967 on a rickety mobile perch, while filming details for the television series *Civilisation*.) But in January 1981 I was being shown the first results of the most thorough cleaning ever attempted on the frescos. There, immediately in front of me, were some of the ancestors of Christ. Soap and water made their colors gleam with unexpected brilliance. An even greater revelation was the breadth and attack of the brushwork. In some places, such as the fold of a robe or the line of a naked arm, the paint had been applied in slashing strokes, each one of which must have encompassed the whole sweep of the painter's arm. It recalled the free gestures of a Jackson Pollock rather than the infinite pains and often invisible technique of the Renaissance.

The clearest expressions of Michelangelo's personal involvement are the seated nudes. Flanking each of the central panels that tell the story of the Creation [153], they provide the link, through the columns on which they are seated, with the vertical architecture of the side walls. Pagan and sensual, they contrast both with the profundities of Genesis above and the severe wisdom of prophets and sybils below. But they are less arbitrary than might appear. Earthly beauty was held by the Neoplatonists to be "the ray of God infusing all creation,"[33] the reflection of Divine Truth. Michelangelo grew up in Florence under the influence of this philosophy. Modern scholarship has shown the wealth of religious allusion supporting each gesture. Yet in the end such justification seems unnecessary. The figures belong to the artist's personal vocabulary in the way that plump cherubs seem a natural adjunct to Rubens.

They serve another, more material, function. Many hold huge cornucopia of acorns, the symbol of the Rovere family, of which the Pope, Julius II, was the most illustrious member. To allow yourself to be glorified in the midst of scenes depicting the Christian version of the beginning of the world, in the central chapel of the principal church in Christendom, may seem strange to us, but was entirely natural to

153. Michelangelo, God Dividing Light from Darkness, 1511.

the High Renaissance. The oak was the Tree of Life. The acorn, with its phallic similarity, was the potential carrier of fecundity. So we might see the nudes as the future generations of mankind, in all their variety of mood, bearing the heavy burden of the seed of Adam, first planted by God in the moment of Creation.

The art historian Frederick Hartt has pointed out a further connection to the main theme.[34] The arm of the nearest figure touches the thigh of the supine Adam, awaiting the life-giving force of the approaching God [154]. The first man is conspicuously impotent, but immediately below his loins the bulging Rovere acorns burst forth on the barren ground. The Church under Julius II will revitalize the Christian message and continue to transmit the intentions of God. But perhaps the warrior-Pope, who often used to boast of his own physical strength and potency, would have been content for us to draw a more direct conclusion.

154. Michelangelo, The Creation of Adam, 1511.

The nude figures allow Michelangelo himself to express a gamut of feelings. They form a human counterpoint to the universal drama unfolding in the central panels. Michelangelo increased their size and importance as the work progressed. The earliest are perceived as pairs, their forms balancing each other, their function largely decorative [155]. In the first scene, the last to be painted [153], the figure on the left watches in tranquil contemplation the overarching form of God dividing the elements. His absorbed, almost dreamy, gaze is in accord with this opening moment of the universe. The other figures surrounding the panel seem to be stirring from some primal repose, and about to take on their burdens. By contrast the nude on the next panel [156] is almost blown off his perch by the hurricane of God hurtling past to create the plants.

In such violent expressionism, Michelangelo went far from classical proportions. Preliminary drawings show that when it came to the painting, hard knots of muscle and protuberant bones were smoothed away to produce a mellifluous impression of perfect strength and harmony. Just as different perspectives and different scales of figures reside easily together on the ceiling so also we accept the lack of any consistent light source. In fact the figures seem lit from within. They glow with a radiance that is not of this earth. Such is Michelangelo's mastery that we accept its rightness instinctively, and hardly notice how every blemish and imperfection has gone, along with idiosyncratic manifestations such as facial and body hair.

Michelangelo represented to an extreme degree the general Renaissance enthusiasm for the naked form. But very soon there was to be a change of mood. On October 31, 1512, the first Mass was celebrated under the completed ceiling. Five years to the day later, on October 31, 1517, Luther hammered up the notice on the church door at Wittenberg that heralded the Reformation. Religious conflict divided Europe, brought a less confident epoch and a reaction against the adventurous liberalism of the High Renaissance. Rome itself was sacked by the barbarous mercenaries of the Emperor Charles V in 1527; for a time the Sistine Chapel was turned into a stable for their horses.

155. Michelangelo, nude figures, ca. 1508–9.

156. Michelangelo, nude figure, 1511.

The great work of Michelangelo's late middle age, *The Last Judgment*, on the back wall of the Sistine [157], became the center of controversy, even while it was being created. Painted between 1536 and 1541, it reflected the mood of self-questioning among the faithful. But already the Catholic counterattack to the rising tide of Protestantism was being formulated. Artists were to take their part. Epic moments in the

Christian struggle were to be portrayed in an uplifting manner. Michelangelo's personal and gloomy vision made him vulnerable to criticism from the now militantism.

There is no rejoicing in the picture, even among the saved souls. A powerful beardless Christ looks down on the mass of risen bodies upon whom he is passing judgment. The movement of densely packed figures seethes like a whirlpool around his upraised arm. Saints and sinners are humped nakedly together, without any of the hierarchies of the faithful billowing triumphantly upward that were to be characteristic of the Baroque style of the next age. Such crowded nudity seemed scandalous, displayed above the Pope's altar, especially at a time when the Church was seeking to purge itself of the licentiousness that had made it infamous in recent years.

With strange but not uncharacteristic self-distaste, Michelangelo put his own portrait on the flayed skin of St. Bartholomew near the center of the picture [158]. This hideous, flaccid, and helpless image, like a dead toad, is made more disturbing because Michelangelo was already the most famous artist who had ever lived. His friend and biographer Vasari listed among the hosts of the rich and powerful who begged for the opportunity to commission a work from Michelangelo's hand, seven Popes, the Sultan of Turkey, the King of France, and the Holy Roman Emperor. Yet he was as little concerned with their approbation as he was with his own well-being.[35] Careless of health and appearance, preferring a solitary existence, he was perhaps the first to experience the disadvantage of artistic fame.

The grimacing figure of St. Bartholomew, who suspends the skin portrait from his fingers, looks remarkably like the lecher, blackmailer, and satirist Pietro Aretino. Throughout the five years that Michelangelo was laboring on the fresco Aretino bombarded him with unwanted advice and more and more threatening demands for a free sample of his work, even "two chalk marks on a sheet of paper."[36] When he got nothing he published a violent attack on *The Last Judgment,* saying it would be more appropriate in a whorehouse—a staggering hypocrisy from a writer whose books were so shocking that they were banned in Italy for hundreds of years after his death. But many others joined Aretino in expressing their disapproval.

When the Pope, Paul III, got a first glimpse of the work in progress on February 4, 1537, his master of ceremonies complained that it was

157. Michelangelo, The Last Judgment, *1536–41.*

158. Michelangelo, Self-Portrait (detail from The Last Judgment), ca. 1536–38.

worthy only of a bathhouse. For that insult, Michelangelo portrayed him as the Prince of Hell [159] with ass's ears and a snake gnawing at that part he had found offensive in the fresco. The furious chamberlain demanded that his likeness be removed, but the Pope is said to have replied: "If the painter had located you in Purgatory, I would have

159. Michelangelo, Prince of Hell (detail from The Last Judgment), 1541.

made every effort on your behalf, but since he has placed you in Hell, it is useless for you to turn to me, for there, there is no redemption."[37]

Michelangelo still packed a formidable punch. When a later Pope demanded that he "amend the fresco," he replied tartly: "Let the Pope amend the world and pictures will soon amend themselves."[38] The whole vast, darkly turbulent scene is like an admonitory roar of warning against all human privilege and expectation—and it is placed in the very heart of privilege, the private chapel of God's vicar on earth. Throughout the sixteenth century there were moves to destroy it. Only the artist's immense reputation preserved it in a gelded form. After Michelangelo's death all the male genitals were painted over and two of the figures completely changed.

Total masculine nakedness seems to be permissible in Western art only in times of radical change, such as the Renaissance, the early nineteenth century, and this century. Michelangelo's unprecedented fame permitted him to express his own vision on a scale never before allowed to an individual; but it also aroused jealousy and violent opposition. The controversy over *The Last Judgment* has continued for more than four hundred years. In the 1980s discussion is heated in Italy as to whether the overpainting should be stripped away, to reveal the figures as naked as the painter intended.

For future generations Michelangelo represented a lonely peak of achievement against which to measure all later aspirations. But the actual subjects that were to occupy the great majority of professional artists were more accurately forecast in the work of his great contemporary, the Venetian painter Titian. What the customer wanted from the developing art of oil painting was a record of himself and his family, his possessions, and those things he would like to possess. High on the list were beautiful women. The earliest reclining nude is credited to Giorgione [42], but the undoubted master of the genre in sixteenth-century Italy was Titian. There is an almost surreal quality about a painting such as *Venus with the Organist* [160], it is so full of symbolic meaning. There are the obvious sexual implications of the man playing on the instrument, with its upright pipes, a vertical motif which is continued in the long row of poplars, past which a pair of distant lovers stroll in close embrace. The avenue of trees can also be seen as a verdant, feminine cleft in the landscape. A cleft into which juts the head of the organist, and, immediately above the thighs of Venus, the phallic shape of the satyr on the fountain, holding aloft the vessel from which spurts of water shoot forth. Venus herself lies embowered in luscious folds of velvet. Clad only in jeweled bracelets and earrings, with pearl necklace and coils of pearls holding her auburn hair, her rich expanse of flesh is in sharp contrast to the soberly confining dress of the musician. A feminist might say she is posed for the delectation of the male, and indeed he turns to look directly at her sex. But there are other interpretations. The only point of contact between them is her elegant foot, which rests on the small of his back. Perhaps she has just prodded him to draw his attention to how clever their child, Love, is being. But he, turning, looks instead at the source of pleasure and life, through which that child made his entry. In which case the picture is an affirmation of marital affection.

There is the strong sense that she is in repose and he is alert, restless, at his business. As he is a musician, the painting might be an allegory on art and life. Busy though he is in creating music, he is drawn to look at her, as we are, by the power of her beauty. But she is almost completely absorbed in her own creation, her child. Not totally, because her foot keeps contact with him. She knows, without looking, that she can draw the male to her. His response shows she is right. In this sense the picture is a tribute to the power of femininity.

160. Titian, Venus with the Organist, *ca. 1548.*

Yet there is an undertow of melancholy in the painting. Those splendid strands of cloud in the background might precede the dawn. More likely the lovers are walking into the fading gold of sunset. Maybe the autumnal glow emanates from the body of Venus herself, so well fed, well used; content with herself in a way man, immersed with making his mark in the world, can rarely be. Titian was sixty-one when he painted this erotic allegory for the Emperor Charles V. A friend of the dissolute Pietro Aretino, Titian had a reputation for roistering and womanizing. Perhaps he felt the frustration that is said to accompany promiscuity: the repeated realization of our inability to possess completely the loved object. At the same time, and especially for a modern eye, the whole confection hangs on the brink of the absurd. Nowadays we have lost the confidence to carry out such literal evocations of feeling except through parody or quotation.

In the end it is the sheer quality of the painting that conquers reservations. The practice of mixing powdered color with oil, instead of with egg yolk and water, had spread only gradually in the fifteenth century. Botticelli painted all his principal pictures in egg tempera. This gave a thin, clear surface, and, because of the speed with which it dried, a somewhat hard-edged look. Oil, on the other hand, was infinitely adaptable. Oil pigment could be painted over and the previous surface modified. It lent itself to scumbles and glazes, frottage and sfumato. It could give an illusion of depth and shadow; the subtle color changes of sunset; the iridescent glow of human flesh. Its first, and in many ways greatest, master was Titian. He continued to experiment with ever-increasing boldness and freedom into his late eighties. By his genius, and his length of life, he, like Michelangelo, became a key figure in the rising status of artists.

In the Middle Ages when the principal patron was the Church, pictures were mainly wanted for a particular place: as a fresco applied directly to a chapel wall or a heavy wooden panel above an altar. Oil paint made pictures much more portable, at a time when secular customers were on the increase. They wanted something that could be brought into their own palatial homes wherever they might be. Oil could be applied to treated canvas, which could be rolled up and easily transported. Hence Titian's work was known and available across Europe. He became the friend of poets, dukes, and emperors. Charles V made him Count Palatine and a Knight of the Golden Spur. Nor did such patrons expect to dictate, as the Church had in the past, precisely what an artist would give them. Princes begged for any work, however small, from the creative hand. Characteristic was the Venetian cardinal who wrote to Michelangelo reminding him of his promise of an *objet d'art* "of which the choice of material and subject is yours, whether painting, or bronze, or marble—do whatever is most convenient to you."[39]

We know of such requests because the activities of artists were so much more closely recorded. Vasari went to meet Titian when in Venice in 1566. "He found him, despite his great age, busy about his painting, with his brushes in his hand . . . His house at Venice has been visited by all the princes, men of letters and distinguished people staying or living in Venice in his time; for, apart from his eminence as a painter, Titian is a gentleman of distinguished family and most courteous ways and manners."[40]

Artists did not quite maintain this exalted position in society. Perhaps they enjoyed the success of novelty in the High Renaissance. Succeeding centuries would honor the outstanding and fashionable but exploit the majority. But the concept of individual creativity survived and flourished; it was seen as a gift which the artist had to cultivate and express within the limits allowed by the dominant fashion of the day.

The influence of the Renaissance, particularly in the use of the nude in history and allegorical painting, lasted a long time. Some of its effects are still with us. Michelangelo and Raphael made drawings from the naked model the basis of their work. This has remained a standard discipline of most art schools to this day.

While their patrons, the European nobility and gentry, flourished, artists continued to portray the body within the range of subjects and conventions that the Renaissance had opened out. Yet from the beginning there were artists who were too individual to conform fully to the fashionable style. They produced, from time to time, unique works that speak directly across the centuries about the human condition.

7

THE HUMAN CONDITION

Stepping out of the darkness, the bearded man catches our eye [161]. The hint of an accusation in his tense, searching gaze makes him one of the most arresting presences to greet us from the past. The longer we look, the more complex he seems. His nakedness is uncompromising, sharply lit from some hidden source over his right shoulder, yet there is a deep unease in his stance, arrogance as well as intelligence in the eyes, selfishness in the fold of his heavy lips. He looks defiant, sorrowful, and sensuous.

Such complexities suggest a man of our own times. The drawing itself, with its sophisticated command of anatomical volumes, seems as modern as this century. In fact, it was penned over four hundred and eighty years ago. Even more remarkably, it is a self portrait, made at a time when few had ever been attempted.

Though many Renaissance artists put themselves among the spectators in their religious paintings, Albrecht Dürer was one of the first to create a specific picture of himself. Few artists since have gone so far in the revelation of their own temperament. Dürer, who was thirty-two at this time, had already portrayed himself beautifully garbed and exquisitely coiffured, and even in the semblance of Christ. Now he postured naked as Adam. Every fold and wrinkle was recorded with beady-eyed intensity. We may feel the self-love to be obsessive, but Dürer brought the same compulsions to recording the fur of a hare or the stalks of a clump of grass. The determination to make an individual judgment, to be true to the facts as he saw them, coupled with an exaggerated concern for his own psyche, was something he shared with his friend Luther, and seems characteristic of the northern temperament that produced the Reformation.

161. Dürer, Self-Portrait (Naked), *ca. 1503.*

162. Raphael, nude studies for the Battle of Ostia, *1515.*

Of course without the growth of individualism that was part of the Renaissance, artists would not have presumed to record themselves at all. They grew proud of their own achievement. Yet individual skill did not necessarily mean a unique attitude to art and life. Most artists were content to accept the styles and subjects that were fashionable and sought only to excel in portraying them. It has always needed a very powerful ego to go against the tide. The men of genius who have done so, even if only on occasion, have given us fresh insights into the image of the body and increased our perception of the human condition.

Dürer had the advantage of overweening egoism, and immense skill. On the other hand he was born in Nuremberg in Germany, far from the center of the Renaissance in Italy. It was less easy to accept the perfectability of man in those cold northern climes. Some of Dürer's reservations are obvious in his uniquely searching revelation of himself. It was sketched at the very time Michelangelo was carving his splendidly self-confident *David* [132] in Florence. Dürer was avid to be part of that creative crescendo. He read more widely than any German artist had ever done; he studied mathematics and geometry and twice visited Venice. He became the friend of one of the leading painters there, Giovanni Bellini. He corresponded with Raphael. The young Italian master sent him a nude study of soldiers [162] to show Dürer what he could do. Dürer himself copied anatomical drawings by Leonardo da Vinci and extended the latter's studies of the proportions of the human figure.

The polymathic attainments of Leonardo, his experiments with new techniques, his almost magic ability to interweave scientific research with fantasy to produce a unique work of art, must have been a compelling prototype for an ambitious outsider like Dürer. Above all, Leonardo had an insatiable curiosity. He was fascinated by the unusual, "by a strange head of hair or beard; and anyone who attracted him he would follow about all day long and end up seeing so clearly in his mind's eye that when he got home he could draw him as if he were standing there in the flesh."[1] He wanted to know the body beneath the clothes [163], the muscles beneath the skin, the bone beneath the sinew [164]. In his lifetime he dissected more than thirty bodies, both men and women. When he discovered a man aged a hundred in the Hospital of Santa Maria Nuova in Florence, he waited until the man died, and

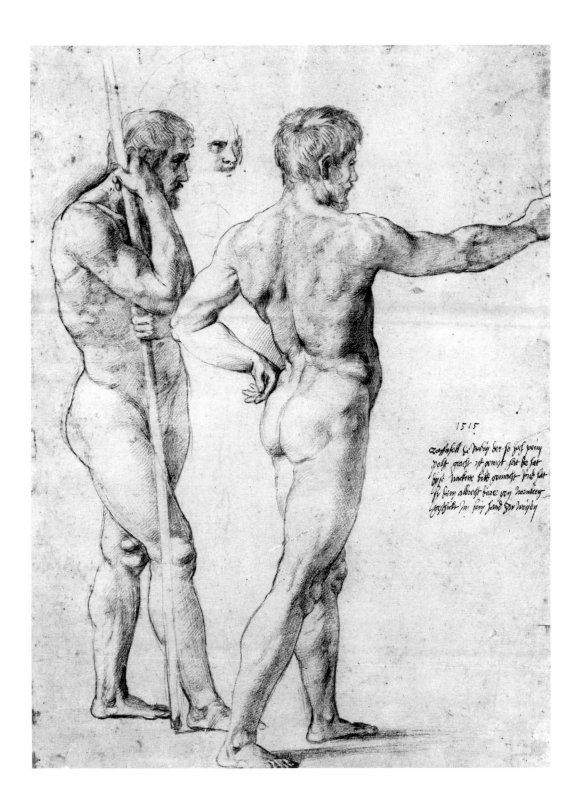

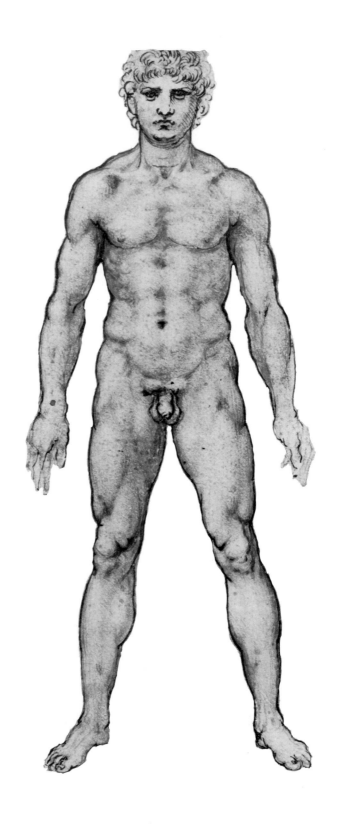

then carried out an autopsy on him. He decided that death was caused by failure of blood to the heart as the main arteries were "very shrunk and withered."[2] He was on the brink of discovering the circulation of the blood. He gained knowledge that in some cases was two hundred years ahead of his time. Everything he saw was recorded with extra-

163. Leonardo, standing nude man, ca. 1506–8.

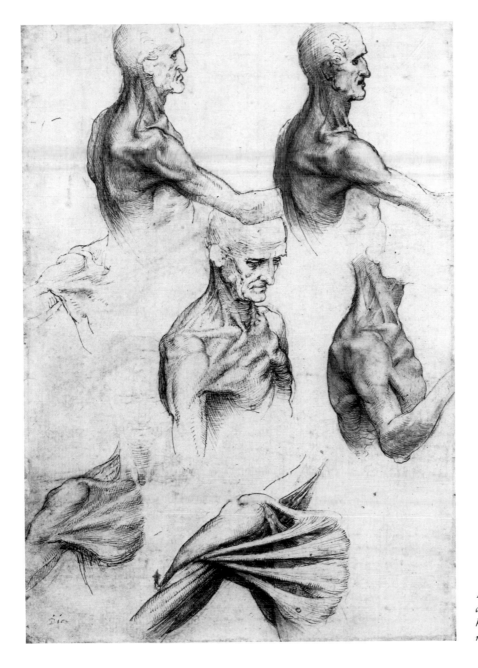

164. Leonardo, anatomical studies of head and shoulders of a man, 1510.

ordinary accuracy, but as none of his notebooks were published in his lifetime, it was of little use to his contemporaries. Often the studies were intended as the basis for major paintings. Many were never carried out.

Yet he left future generations a unique legacy in the drawings. No

165. Leonardo, studies of Madonna and Child with a cat, ca. 1478.

conventionally posed Virgin and Child in a formal painting would have the immediate charm of Leonardo's preliminary sketches [165]. He was fascinated by the rhythmic and symbolic potential of the double curve of the Madonna's arms holding the Christ Child, who in turn embraces a cat. But when it came to posing live animal and plump little naked boy, things did not work out the way he intended. Nearly twenty rapid studies reveal the enduring truth that animals and small children make unpredictable models. In some the cat stalks off haughtily or flashes a warning paw; not surprising, as the boy's response to being told to hold him still is to squeeze this delightful new toy as hard as possible. Leonardo unfailingly catches the child's gleeful zest and the ruffled affront of the suffering cat. Such casual informality was hardly recorded so directly again until the days of the box Brownie.

Leonardo was equally at home with the postures of young and old. At the time that he was observing the processes of aging and death on the centenarian, he was planning a painting on the mystery of generation itself. The subject must have occupied an area of deep tension in his emotional psychology. Illegitimate, the son of a well-to-do Florentine and a peasant woman, he spent his childhood in his father's country house in the Tuscan hills. "Marvelously endowed with beauty, grace and talent,"[3] as an adult he liked to surround himself with handsome young men. When he was twenty-four and living in an artist's house in Florence he was accused of sodomy. It was a serious charge; punishment for repeated offenses was death by burning. The case was dismissed but could have been revived on further evidence. Leonardo addressed an anguished petition to the head of the Florentine guilds. In it he wrote: "If there is no love, what then?"[4]

More than a quarter of a century later, on the ninth of July 1504, he noted "on Wednesday at seven o'clock at the Palace of the Podesta died Ser Piero da Vinci, notary, my father. He was eighty years old, and left ten sons and two daughters."[5] All the legitimate children were born after Leonardo reached adulthood. His father had married four times. Yet he remained on affectionate terms with his eldest, unmarrying, son. The death of a father is said to be especially traumatic in its effect on a firstborn son who is himself well into middle age.

Leonardo at fifty-two was about to undergo a peculiarly testing experience. He was painting a large fresco of a battle scene in the

Council Chamber of the Palazzo Vecchio in Florence. Later in the year he was joined by Michelangelo, who had been commissioned to paint a companion piece in direct competition with Leonardo. Michelangelo was only twenty-nine. The aging and youthful geniuses detested each other. Michelangelo is said to have taunted Leonardo with his inability to bring any work to successful fruition. It was to prove true of his battle scene; either his experiment with a wax medium or poor quality linseed oil rapidly deteriorated the fresco, which Leonardo left unfinished.

No wonder he became preoccupied with the mystery of creation and of his own entry into the world. Characteristically, he approached the problem from many directions and in oblique ways. He began to consider making a painting of Leda, the country nymph who was pursued by Zeus, the father of the gods. Zeus won Leda when he assumed the form of a beautiful swan. She bore him a clutch of several children. The story of a nymph of nature seduced by a potent, promiscuous, and distant being had an obvious relevance to Leonardo's

166. Leonardo, studies for kneeling Leda and horse for Battle of Anghiari, *ca. 1503–4.*

own parentage. He did his first sketches of Leda at the time of his father's death, while he was still working on the design of the battle scene [166]. The rearing horse was to be a central motif among the writhing, entwined soldiers who were in conflict on the fresco. Equally twisting in motion but bringing life into the world, not taking it away, Leda in the central drawing is as curvaceous as an Indian temple dancer.

In the myth she was a creature of the changing seasons and Leonardo, who loved nature as profoundly as Wordsworth, put the fecundity of leaves and burgeoning plants and water weeds into his studies. The pagan story of a woman's intercourse with a swan gave many Christian artists, including Michelangelo [167], the license to show an unusual erotic act. It allowed the portrayal of the pleasures of sex in a piquant form. No such directly sensuous message was available to Leonardo with his labyrinthine sensibilities. Perhaps his most passionate contemplation of female sexuality is his drawing of a Star of Bethlehem,

167 Copy after Michelangelo, Leda and the Swan, *sixteenth century.*

a preliminary study for the landscape of the *Leda* painting [168]. The thickly matted forms, the tender flowers growing from the dark, richly mysterious center, are expressed with an intensity that goes far beyond scientific observation. Leonardo used similar twisting coiled strands for the hair of Leda [169], which, a note tells us, he had designed as a wig.

In his notebooks Leonardo could write "lust is the cause of generation." He saw the desire for sexual intercourse as "the most important thing among the living."[6] Yet the evidence of his art suggests that it was something he contemplated with curiosity rather than

168. Leonardo, a star of Bethlehem and other plants, ca. 1506–8.

169. Leonardo, study for Leda's coiffure, ca. 1508.

170. Cesare da Sesto, copy of Leonardo's Leda and the Swan, *early sixteenth century.*

171. Leonardo, dissection of the principal organs of a woman, ca. 1508.

participated in with warmth. His very large painting of Leda soon began to break up and is now completely lost. Enough copies survive [170] for us to have an idea of its quality. It shows both the agent of creation—the uncoiling rising form of the swan—and its result, the eggs bursting open among the blossoming shapes of earth and water. In between, the act itself is suggested through the sinuous curving body of Leda, her eyes darkly downcast, her mouth conveying that contem-

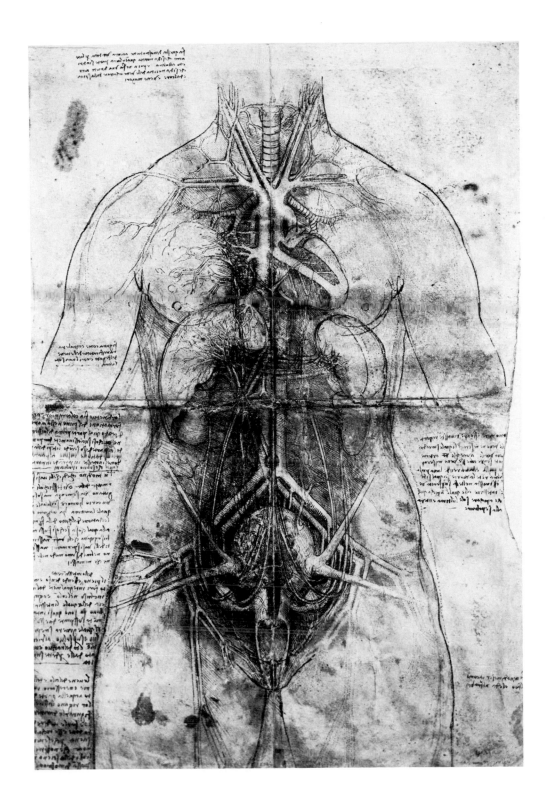

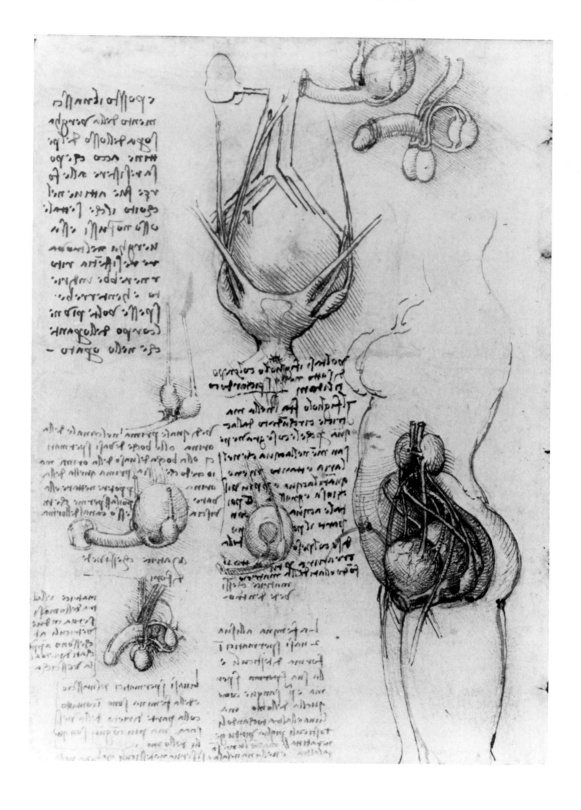

plative serenity which is more like a flicker of distant sunlight than a smile. She has already acquiesced and is drawing the powerful body to her, but her thoughts are on the glory of birth that will follow.

There is something about Leonardo's work that either captivates or sets your teeth on edge. One of his most famous anatomical drawings of a female torso [171] is related to Leda, as a note beside it refers to finding models for the painting. The intermesh of tubes, organs, and veins is shown beneath the outline of the fully fleshed body. The shape of the breasts and the general form suggest a woman of similar age and build to the Leda in the painting. So does another study [172] of the same time showing a woman in profile with the womb and lower organs revealed. The working of the male generative system is recorded on the same sheet.

Nothing shows more clearly the distance between Leonardo's interests and the average impulses of mankind. Leda was a theme that clearly meant much to him. It preoccupied him without any commission or patronage for over four years. The normal reactions of his contemporaries would have been to find an appropriate model; to have made drawings of her in order to decide on the suitable pose; and probably to have usurped the role of the swan with her. Leonardo must also have spent time looking for a model of the right age and physique— in the morgue; and when he found her he entered her with a dissecting knife.

Surely it must be the same preoccupations that led him to the most famous of all his anatomical drawings: that of the fetus in the womb [173]. He was the first artist to portray the opening stage of life. This drawing, marvelous in its wealth of scientific observation and delicacy of execution, is usually interpreted as a testament to the wonder of creation. We should remember that it is also a record of the triumph of death—the death of an unborn child and its mother. That the same Leonardo, who was gentle, fastidious, and so sensitive that he would buy caged birds in order to release them was prepared to undertake such a disturbing dissection of the freshly dead is another of his mysteries. His deep involvement is clear from the central drawing, but his pen never trembles in its recording accuracy.

While working on the Leda theme, he made a drawing of a small boy who would seem to be taking his early steps and hence about a

172. Leonardo, male and female organs of generation, ca. 1508.

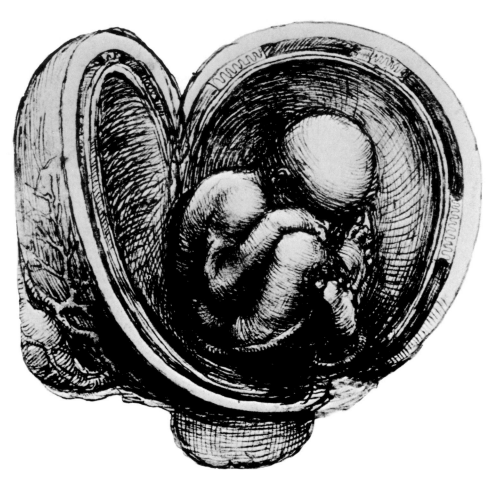

173. Leonardo, drawing of an embryo in the womb, ca. 1510.

year old [174]. His chubby nakedness allows the inclusion in this book of the cartoon, or large drawing, in charcoal for which he is a study. This family group of the Christ Child, his mother, his grandmother, and his infant playmate, St. John, is the most magical of all Leonardo's remaining works. That such a flimsy piece of paper (four feet by three feet) should have survived, when so many of his massive paintings, frescos, and sculptures have been lost, is itself a sort of miracle. The picture [175] is a reconciliation of many contradictions. The draped figures of the women are as solid as the marble reliefs on the Parthenon, yet they are also as airy and insubstantial as the spirits that must have first floated before Leonardo's imagination. Their complex posture, creating a contrapuntal liveliness of opposing angles, fits them with the ease of a familiar glove. They are held within the family circle that sweeps in a majestic ovoid from the compelling glance of the grand-mother, to the softer features of her daughter, down the warm curve of her shoulder and protective arm, along the stretched arm of the Christ Child that reaches out to clasp his playmate's chin. The sturdy little figure of St. John, grown a bit since the first drawing, leans inward to complete the movement. His devoted gaze carries us back to the central group.

174. Leonardo, studies of infants, ca. 1510.

Looming from the feminine circle but entirely contained within it, the infant Savior undulates like the fish that is to be his symbol. Soon he will no longer need the supporting hands of the Virgin. His face and upraised arm, shining in the crepuscular light, suggest a dawning awareness of his destiny. A fate that is confirmed in the ghostly pointing finger of St. Anne. Her face also has a noumenal quality, skull-like under its heavy shadows. She seems a wraith fading back into the rocks of the distant hillside. Yet she is the prop on which all the others lean. There is a spiritual strength in her regard that buttresses the tender joyful care of the Virgin.

Freud in his psychoanalytic study of Leonardo suggests a reason why the artist was able to invest these two women with such a powerful affection. He assumes that Leonardo spent his first years in the country with his real mother, the peasant woman. Then his father married and, being at that time without legitimate children, brought the little boy to live with him and his wife. So Leonardo had the benefit of two mothers. If this hypothesis has some truth, it also suggests that Leonardo would have a special feeling for St. John. Like him, the Baptist grew up in the country; like him he was a visionary and intermediary between man and creation; like him he was near to, but not the true (legitimate) son of the Father. So St. John is slightly outside the family circle, looking in at it from the countryside. Yet he has been accepted and blessed, as all humanity has, by the gift of life.

Memory is what gives the picture its preternatural glow. The memory not of a divine event, but the warmth of the charmed circle of domestic love. Leonardo never entered that circle as an adult, but he was able to recall it from his own childhood. To this strength of human feeling he brought his supreme gifts of draftsmanship, his knowledge of the body and the principles of balance, of the effects of light and shade, of mechanics and geometrical relationships; he has utilized his studies of drapery, of antique forms, and the formation of rocks. The drawing is a pendant to the painting of Leda, which he had probably recently completed.* If Leda examines the act of creation itself, the drawing is a demonstration of its effect, the generations of the human family in which we all share.

175. Leonardo, Madonna and Child with St. Anne and St. John, *ca. 1510–11.*

---

* In dating I have followed Professor Carlo Pedretti, rather than the earlier suggestions of Kenneth Clark and A. E. Popham.

176. Dürer, The Women's Bath, *1496.*

Leonardo was able, as all the greatest artists have done, to move from the visionary to the particular by his unique regard for the forces of nature. He not only penetrated the womb. He gazed at waterfalls so as to be able to analyze the vortices of cataracts. He climbed mountains to observe the massing and dispersion of the elements. Such a concentration on the most enclosed, the most transient, the most remote, implies a sort of intellectual pantheism, a perceptual identification with all things. He seems to have had little belief in the manifestations of religion. Man he thought universally vile. Curiosity drove him onward; the desire to master all knowledge, to experience all things. In this he intensified the preoccupations of his time and forecast interests that were to be harnessed by the Romantics three hundred years later.

Many of his preoccupations and even some of his attainments were mirrored by Dürer. He too could scrupulously record natural things and limn the changing mood of sky and landscape. Both believed in learning from experience, and in discovering things for themselves. But there were profound differences in the way their egotism emerged. Dürer reserved his greatest vitality for looking at himself. Leonardo's character evades capture. He revealed most in his drawings from nature. He could infuse life into the humblest sprig of blackberries. Dürer's botanical studies are as accurate and frigid as a specimen in a museum.

He turned the same cold, inquisitive eye on his fellow humans. Fascinated by each pore of his own skin, for the bodies of others he clearly felt both curiosity and disgust. This avid yet objective inspection is manifest in his drawing of women in a bathhouse [176] Such communal washing places must have been utilized by earlier artists looking for live models, but Dürer uniquely conveys the variety of female forms to be found squatting together in steamy proximity. An uneasy mixture of prurience and revulsion, his view balances precariously between memories of the classical veneration of the body and his eye for reality. The standing figure soaping her bottom on the left is an attempt at the smooth surfaces he knows to be fashionably appealing, but the three right-hand women are a surrender to the grotesque variety of shapes that actually bulged in front of him.

Lust and loathing often intermingle in the northern imagination. Yet the determination to show things as they really are has been one of the strengths of the reforming conscience. Northern art has looked at ugliness when it existed, and recognized emotions which the classical tradition might consider ignoble. Nor has its enjoyment been confined to the rich and titled. Printing developed in Germany, and it was there that the new techniques of woodcut and steel engraving were perfected, allowing the economic proliferation of many copies of an artist's work. Dürer was one of the earliest masters of both engraving and woodcut. His graphic work became known all over Europe. It was the exact opposite to Leonardo, whose drawings were entirely for his own use.

As had happened with the invention of fresco and oil paint, the development of the new medium led to an extension of the artist's range of subject matter. Dürer was the first artist to design, print, and publish his own book. He recognized that a picture held in the hand could be looked at much longer and more closely than one that was on a public wall. His images are dense with detail, sometimes open to different interpretations. Many embroidered religious or mythological themes. In any case, however remote and fantastical the subject, there was excuse for a wealth of human incident; something that the owner could browse over afresh each time he looked at it, or showed it off to his friends.

177. Dürer, Sea
Monster Abducting a
Woman, *ca. 1498.*

Perhaps the method of engraving encouraged the imagination, as
the hand followed the single line being scored in the metal. Any slip
would ruin the plate. So it certainly required intense concentration and
immense skill. These were qualities Dürer had in abundance. Observe
the pin-sharp pinnacles of the faery castle on the hilltop, or the gable
windows in the old town looking down on *The Sea Monster Abducting
a Woman* [177]. They have the clarity of images in a mirage.

There is something dream-like in the abduction itself. The old
monster, with his dark, scaly skin and fish-bone horns, swims on
determinedly toward the open sea. In contrast, the kidnapped woman
reclines almost negligently along his tail. She seems less perturbed than
the paddling companions she is leaving behind. Perhaps the two are

demonic accomplices. In which case he has returned to carry her back to her natural element. Her only mementos are her memories and her robe, which is drifting off into the water, and the ornate headdress, which had seemed so chic when she danced the galliard in the great hall, and had taken the fancy of the grand seigneur, now capering his grief on the shore. The ripple of foam and the angle of the monster's turtle-shell shield unexpectedly suggest a modern power boat, bouncing through the waves—an analogy heightened by the woman, lying back like some northern Bardot, sulkily enjoying the speed and the sensation caused by her nakedness. Her left hand trails languorously over the joy stick, ready to plunge her strange craft down into familiar depths.

This temptress and the woman looking at us from the center of the bathhouse scene have one thing in common: while discarding everything else, they have retained their headgear. A spectacular and towering confection crowning a naked body is a powerful sexual lure, as has been demonstrated from the banks of the ancient Nile to the Ziegfeld Follies. In consequence, the nudes of Dürer's contemporary Lucas Cranach have a piquantly modern appeal. Their willowy limbs and long waists are as much a convention as the more ample charms of Titian's beauties, but it is a convention closer to the slender looks favored today [178] The provocative twitch of the veil, which emphasizes rather than conceals; the hair piled up under the net of pearls, and the wickedly knowing, slanting eyes—all suggest a cabaret girl in Hamburg in the twenties: how strange that this apparition of decadence should originate in the sternly puritanical north, at the very moment when it is thundering against the moral corruption of Rome.

In fact Cranach was a personal friend of Luther's. He portrayed the great reformer and his wife, the matronly ex-nun, with perceptive clarity. He published many of Luther's books from his printing press. He also opened a tavern and a pharmacy from the proceeds of his painting. His work was greatly in demand among the increasingly affluent gentry of Saxony. They wanted portraits of their fiercely independent selves, displaying warts and all. They also had a taste for the lubricious female nude. The Renaissance made the naked body part of the general visual furniture of the age, as the phallus had been in Roman times. It was so common in decoration as to be hardly noticed. Even Erasmus' New Testament of 1519 had a frontispiece adorned with naked women.

Cranach gave a new twist to the genre. His slight figures derive more from northern Gothic cathedral sculptures than from classical Greece. Their imperfections give them an appealing vulnerability. They are more like real women undressed, with unathletic stomachs and bunions on their toes, than goddesses. At the same time they are definitely out to please. The three posturing charmers in *The Judgment of Paris* [179] might be shimmying hopefully on amateur talent night at the local strip club. They have achieved the appropriate provocative poses, throwing back their shoulders, pulling up one ankle, wearing

178. Cranach, Venus, *ca. 1530s.*

the flippant hat at a rakish angle, but they have not yet lost the last vestiges of their naïve innocence.

Provincial rusticity adds to the charm and takes us far from the sunburned hills of Anatolia, where, according to myth, Mercury descended on the unsuspecting Paris, bringing the fateful choice which sealed the doom of Troy. It is patently absurd to consider these armored and bearded old men as the youthful shepherd and the equally spritely messenger of the gods. However they were probably very similar in type to the newly Protestant nobility of southern Germany who would

179. Cranach, The Judgment of Paris, 1530.

180. Verrio, Heaven Room, Burghley House, England, 1686–97.

have admired the picture and commissioned more of the same from the artist, himself over sixty.

Cranach brought realism and fantasy together in an erotic mix rarely seen south of the Alps. In those sunnier climes imperfections were smoothed away; the object of desire would not often be seen only

in boots and pearls. Northern mannerism, the style that grew out of the late Renaissance, always had a higher-pitched note than its opposite number in the south.

Yet the well-to-do, both Protestant and Catholic, would for centuries move, work, and eat in rooms overlaid with underdressed images. The classical tradition, through many changes of taste and style, continued to license a host of naked woman and seminaked men cavorting across the ceilings of Europe [180]. Polite society viewed with equanimity activity going on above their heads which could only be hinted at behind the flutter of a fan below. It was as though the overdressed had a compulsion to dip their gaze in the purifying clarity of nakedness. As clothes became simpler the taste for this sort of decorative titillation waned.

The symphony of flesh was largely orchestrated from a male angle. Pagan mythology provided amorous nymphs and vengeful goddesses, and many of the Christian subjects that included naked women—Judith and Holofernes, Delilah and Samson, Salome and John the Baptist— showed them in an exciting but unfavorable light. Characteristic was the way artists treated the story of Susanna and the Elders.[7] In the Apocryphal Book of Daniel, Susanna is the epitome of a virtuous wife. She resists the blandishments of the lecherous Elders, who spy on her bathing. In spite, they falsely accuse her, but Daniel wisely recognizes the truth of her protestations. The Elders are condemned to death. The story is a clear-cut account of innocence steadfast against evil intentions. Yet the majority of painters chose to portray it much more equivocally. Tintoretto [181] makes the Elders comical voyeurs, groveling in the

181. Tintoretto, Susanna and the Elders, *ca. 1555.*

182. Gentileschi, Susanna and the Elders, ca. 1610.

shrubbery for a squint up Susanna's legs. She, fully aware of their presence, continues to dry her ankle with taunting disdain. The picture is not about virtue and vice, but the sweaty frustrations of voyeurism. Titillation is a male motive for enjoying paintings of naked women, and by recognizing this, the painting laughs at the viewer as well as nudging him in the ribs.

One version in the early seventeenth-century took a very different line [182]. Here the figure of Susanna is far from a cool temptress. Tormented by the whispered calumnies of the Elders, she twists away from them in a violent gesture of rejection. Her body is much less smoothly idealized than in Tintoretto's version. Perhaps this is not surprising, as the painter is a woman: Artemisia Gentileschi.

Virtually forgotten except by art historians, Artemisia has recently been resurrected by the feminist movement as one of the pillars of female art. Not only as a painter, where she was clearly outstanding, but because of the poignant facts of her life. Her father, Orazio Gentileschi, was eventually Court Painter to Charles I of England. Reputedly, his daughter showed talent early when they were living in Rome. Orazio asked a friend and fellow painter, Agostino Tassi, to teach the teenager perspective. Tassi first tried to seduce her, then raped her with the aid of a friend. Orazio brought an action against Tassi for damage to his property. Tassi countered by trying to prove that Artemisia was a whore. The trial, in 1612, lasted five months. Both sides denied the evidence of the other. Both agreed that Artemisia had frequently consented to intercourse after the assault. She said this was because Tassi had promised to marry her. Tortured by thumbscrews in front of him, she cried out: "This is the ring and these the promises you gave me."[8] She stuck to her story despite the torture; but so did he. He was acquitted. Her reputation was ruined.

It is difficult not to believe that the painting refers to this personal tragedy, though the date on it, 1610, is discrepant. Tassi was said to be handsome and black-haired. His accomplice, Cosimo Quorli, was older and was reputed to have also enjoyed her. The figures leaning over Susanna seem more related in age, energy, and appearance to the real rapists than to the doddering Elders of the story. Susanna, writhing in naked discomfort, appears to be seated on something more like a stone court bench than on the edge of a pool. Artemisia's greatest suffering came from the lies that were whispered about her during and after the trial. Lacking a Daniel, she had to marry immediately in a hopeless attempt to save her reputation.

A few years later she gained a proxy revenge. During the period of their intimacy, Tassi was said to have purloined a large painting of Judith and Holofernes by Orazio. Now Artemisia created her own version [183]. One of the few paintings portraying actual feminine violence, perhaps it is the only one by a woman showing a woman murdering her potential lover. It has none of the calm judgment of the Donatello sculpture [132]. Nor is Holofernes departing this life in besotted sleep. Held down by two stern avengers (as perhaps Artemisia had been held down), he struggles for every last breath, looking beseechingly at the onlooker. In vain; the hand has a strong grip in his curly black hair, the sword hacks through his throat, his blood sprays up over the body he thought to enjoy.

Tassi was rumored to have arranged his wife's murder. He was

183. Gentileschi, Judith Decapitating Holofernes, ca. 1614–20.

said in court to be a sodomite, his three sisters prostitutes; one brother had been hanged and another banished, and Tassi himself had debauched his wife's sister. Orazio must have known some of this when he entrusted his daughter to Tassi. But then Orazio knew she was likely to be tortured when he brought on the trial. Orazio was a close friend of Caravaggio, a painter who died in a tavern at the age of thirty-seven, burned out, two years before. Caravaggio's rage for living his art was such that he would turn his back on no experience however terrible. The Gentileschi circle has some of the same quality.

The human condition consists of murder, bestial agony, and revenge as well as love and trust. But frequently art turns war and pestilence and the other manifestations of sin into celebrations of painterly skill. This is especially true when the painter is as effortlessly exuberant as Peter Paul Rubens. His picture *The Rape of the Daughters of Leucippus* [184] was painted four years after the trial of Tassi. It portrays an event that would seem at least as disturbing as the rape of Artemisia Gentileschi: the abduction of two sisters. Rubens does not adulterate the fearful turmoil—the screaming women, their clothes ripped away, their hair falling awry, flailing unavailingly at their determined captors, whose wildly rearing steeds complete the image of brutal power. Yet all this expressive emotion does not disturb us a jot. It is not meant to. Cupids hold the horses' reins. Like the decorous tempests and lightning shafts that descended on the stage in the masques that were the fashion of the day, it is merely a storm in a paint pot.

In the seventeenth century the viewer would have felt enhanced by the splendidly assured upsurge of energy that spirals from the sprawling feet and cloak of the blond woman to the tossing mane and noble profile of the gray charger. These boisterous rhythms went with an age where the patrons of art were increasing and growing ever richer from the expansion of overseas trade and investment. Rubens mirrored the general affluence. He lived in a palatial mansion he had built in the great port of Antwerp, and was employed by the richest patron of all, the Spanish crown. He was prolific, brilliant, and well loved. His skill as an international diplomat earned him a knighthood from King Charles I of England.

Success glows through his pictures in halcyon color. No one ever caught the rosy bloom of healthy skin, the shimmering quiver of well-fed flesh with such lip-smacking skill. His women are displayed like

the great compotes of cream and exotic fruits from the Indies—kumquats and soursops and apricots, the flesh of melons and oranges from Seville—that the Dutch merchantmen were bringing back to the ports of northern Europe. It was an overdressed age, of velvets and taffeta and ornate brocades, when rich men habitually wore three topcoats, when even the walls of rooms were clothed in gold-embossed Spanish leather and the massive oak tables covered in heavy tapestries.

184. Rubens, Rape of the Daughters of Leucippus, *ca. 1616–17.*

The acquisitive burghers who owned such things would gain an additional *frisson* to see openly displayed the wide expanse of tender vulnerable bodies, their clothes torn away like the protective skin ripped off a ripe plum.

Similar atrocities might well happen only a few miles distant when Protestant cities of the northern Netherlands were sacked by the ruthless armies of Spain. But the painting was comfortably set in the mythological past. The stern abductors were in fact Castor and Pollux, two of the babies hatched from the eggs of Leda. They did the decent thing—married the girls, who each bore them a son. So the virtuous viewer could enjoy the triumph of rampaging masculine lust without a twinge of conscience.

Enjoyment was clearly Rubens' prime intention, in life as well as art. He liked his women to appear "comfortable," as they say in the north of England when they mean fat. In times when hardship and want were not so far away, excess flesh was a signal of prosperity. It has never been absent among the Flemish with their northern belief that a little of what you fancy must do you good. But if Rubens looks tolerantly at indulgence, he handles his paint with the discipline of a master.

He was an artist who did not mind showing crude things crudely. One of the greatest of his many gifts was his ability to do justice to a multitude of facets of life; to be true to them and yet to embrace them so warmly that we feel better for thinking well of them, even if they are not particularly to our taste. What we are really accepting is the good humor of his judgments. "Rubens leaves everywhere," wrote one of his nineteenth-century admirers, "the impression of the distinctness of his character, the warmth of his blood, the solidity of his stature, the splendid balance of his nerves, and the magnificence of his everyday visions."[9]

The most public of painters, distributing his largesse across hundreds of huge canvases with the aid of a workshop of assistants, he also could produce a picture so private that his wife wanted it destroyed after his death. Fortunately her wishes were not obeyed [185]. Hélène Fourment married Rubens when she was sixteen and he was a fifty-three-year-old widower. She crowned his life with a decade of happiness and gave him five children. Perhaps he painted this portrait of her when she was pregnant with their firstborn.

185. *Rubens,* Hélène Fourment in a Fur Robe, *ca. 1631.*

Why did she dislike it? Rubens, the master of scenes crowded with movement, has chosen to show his wife against an empty background. He painted her as she might be coming from the bath, wrapped in a fur coat, luxuriously braided at cuffs and hem. Underneath she is naked and as she turns to look at the painter the coat slips off her right shoulder. The effect is like a snapshot, where the exposure of the frame freezes the action. The positioning of the hands recalls the classic pose of modesty for Venus. It might be a static picture, but the implied fall of the cloak makes sure that it is not.

Hélène Fourment is not posed as a model, nor is she some timeless abstraction, a goddess or nymph. She is a real flesh-and-blood woman on her way from somewhere to somewhere else. Probably her feet are getting cold. Despite her youth she already has some wrinkles of spare flesh around her torso. She has ugly knees.

Nevertheless she is powerfully beautiful. She is beautiful because Rubens wraps her, like the cloak, in the warmth of his regard. The furry softness slipping over her skin is his imagined self. Knowing this gives the painting its erotic charge. A charge that is defused by her expression. It is neither teasing nor seductive. She looks at her husband the way happy lovers do, with a question. His answer is the manner in which he has painted her.

Probably it was the unguarded openness of her look, which was not within the range of conventional expressions thought appropriate for the portrayal of the nude, that made the young widow believe it too personal for public view. She had often served happily as a model for Rubens in mythological undress.

There could be no greater contrast between the radiant munificence of the Rubens family circle and the squalid disasters of the Gentileschi ménage. The human condition encompasses a gamut of responses and contrary twists of fortune almost side by side. Rubens admired the work of Caravaggio, the friend and inspirer of Orazio Gentileschi. Michelangelo da Caravaggio had no home life to speak of. A repeatedly erupting boil of brawls and scandals meant that he was constantly on the move around Italy and the Mediterranean islands in an attempt to escape arrest.

Violence did not prevent him from being a disturbingly innovative painter. Raking side light, dramatic foreshortening, and expressive gestures accentuated the melodrama he transferred from life into his canvases. A homosexual infatuated with delving in the dregs, he put the people he knew into his religious pictures with outrageous effect. He was just as iconoclastic with the characters of mythology. The god of love is turned into a provocative guttersnipe [186]. As with Hélène Fourment his look poses a question, but in his case it is brazen and provocative.

Caravaggio is an early example of the rebel in art, thumbing his

186. Caravaggio, Love Triumphant, *1598–99.*

nose at the accepted conventions of good taste and the hallowed achievements of the established style of the day. By giving his catamite a pair of unlikely wings he is making a mocking reference to his revered namesake, Michelangelo. That austere genius had made a drawing of

187. Barbizet (after Michelangelo), Ganymede.

The Rape of Ganymede for his friend Cavalieri. It would have been known to Caravaggio through an engraving [187]. Ganymede was a beautiful Trojan prince who was carried off by Zeus, the King of the Gods, to serve as cupbearer on Olympus. As with his drawing of Zeus as a swan [167], Michelangelo makes quite clear the nature of Zeus the eagle's passion for the mortal youth. His own letters show equal infatuation with his aristocratic young friend Cavalieri, expressed in elevated Platonic terms. Caravaggio characteristically brings this high-flown imagery down to earth, and teasingly mirrors the pose of Michelangelo's noble hero in the plump little legs of his streetwise young rascal.

Yet Caravaggio cannot deny the inheritance of the Mediterranean past. His urchin may be convincingly knowing and wicked, but his body retains the smooth finish of classic art. In the north artists were prepared to go further in their quest for realism. A generation later than Caravaggio, the young Rembrandt van Rijn produced his own version of *The Rape of Ganymede* [188] in Holland. He had obviously seen the engraving after Michelangelo; his eagle, though less imperial, spreads its wings and turns its head in much the same manner. But Rembrandt had considered the feasibility of the episode. Could any known eagle carry such a well-developed athlete as the young man in the engraving? Answer: no. Did eagles have a reputation for carrying off *any* humans? Answer: yes; traditionally the babies of peasants left outside their mountain cottages. So Ganymede must be an infant. Would he enjoy the flight? Definitely not. What would he do? Kick, scream, and urinate in fright.

The result is an almost comical piece of radicalism: a portrait of infant displeasure rather than immortal longings. In fact it makes Zeus's desire for Ganymede seem even more morally questionable.

No doubt that was part of Rembrandt's intention. He had already made two engravings of a man and a woman relieving themselves that must be among the first serious studies of this essential human function. All his life he drew the behavior of the poor people he saw around him in the streets of Amsterdam and the surrounding countryside. He caught the gestures of Jewish patriarchs, tinkers and small traders, peasants and their families, with a truth that instantly convinces.

Dutch painters often embellished a crowded fairground scene with saucy details—a boy stealing fruit, a couple stealing an embrace, a

randy tradesman putting his hand up a housewife's skirt. They frequently included a discreet view of an incontinent countryman turned to a distant wall. They wanted all aspects of human activity to be part of their pictures. The earthy, practical burghers who were their patrons approved of such realism when it was depicted within the limits of conventional propriety. Rembrandt goes further. His direct observation expresses his freedom to look at any subject in a uniquely personal way.

He put his own, deliberately unconventional interpretation on the goddess Diana [189]. She was traditionally the goddess of the hunt and was often portrayed bathing naked. Rembrandt dutifully shows her quiver of arrows and puts her legs in water; otherwise it would be hard to recognize the fleet-limbed virgin in his ungainly *huis-vrouw*.

188. Rembrandt, The Rape of Ganymede, *1635.*

189. Rembrandt, Diana at the Bath, *1630.*

He seems to be attacking the whole concept of the classical nude and the interpretation of the pagan gods as supremely beautiful human beings. His Diana is all *too* human with her pudding face and flabby body. Protestant Holland was still engaged in its eighty-year struggle for independence against Catholic Spain and perhaps this adds bite to Rembrandt's rejection of canons of art that had been conceived in Popish Italy. Certainly such etchings as the Diana were popular in Amsterdam when he produced them in the 1630s. Now they seem as overstated as most counterpropaganda. Those flaccid folds and wrinkles, the marks of garters and hemlines on pallid flesh, may be an accurate recording of the mature body of his model, but seem as inappropriate to suggest a fiery huntress as does her vacuous expression.

But Rembrandt was surely not wrong to pour scorn on all the beefy nudes who prance rhetorically through the fashionable Baroque art of his century. For him each body was unique and could not be fitted to a classical formula. When the subject made it appropriate, he could portray the human image with unparalleled sympathy. His etching of *The Return of the Prodigal Son* [190] shows a figure wasted with neglect and privation, a face riven with dissipation and despair. He seems the essence of failure, but Rembrandt has surrounded him with love and tender solicitude in an economic but strongly structured picture. The fallen son, the bowed shape of the father reaching to embrace him in one long step forward, make a powerful central triangle below the window shutter opening on the prospect of rehabilitating care. From the serving woman's anxious face one diagonal runs down through the interlocking, opposed heads of the two generations to the kneeling legs and abandoned stick of the son. This resolute geometry lifts the scene out of sentimentality to the simplicity of epic. How psychologically right is the stance of the busily helpful servant clattering down the stairs with the best robe. All the minor protagonists are in movement. The two central characters alone are frozen into the clasp of reconciliation. "This my son was dead, and is alive again; he was lost, and is found."[10]

Rembrandt matches, as he almost always does, the simple human message of the parable. He was one of the first and greatest masters of etching. The process is a refinement on the engraving directly onto a sheet of copper practiced so brilliantly by Dürer. In etching the copper is covered with a coating of resin impervious to acid; the etcher draws

190. Rembrandt, The Return of the Prodigal Son, 1636.

on the soft resin with a needle, which opens the surface down to the copper. The plate is then put into a bath of acid which bites the exposed drawn line into the plate. As with other methods of engraving any number of prints can be taken off the etched plate. So Rembrandt's line work was available for relatively modest homes while his paintings were in mansions and palaces.

Despite early success, he had a life checkered with much sadness. His wife and three of their four children had died by the time he was thirty-six. His mania for collecting art and objects of all sorts led to constant money problems. But his middle years were lit by the devotion of his housekeeper, Hendrickje. He painted her as *Bathsheba* [191] with the same solid realism he had applied to the curves of the baby

191. Rembrandt,
Bathsheba, 1654.

Ganymede. No doubt her chunky body, large feet, and massive hands are as truthfully observed as the gentle sweetness of her expression.

Bathsheba, it will be remembered, caught the attention of the middle-aged David. From the roof of his palace "he saw a woman washing herself; and the woman was very beautiful to look upon."[11] Having found out who she was, David sent for her. Does the paper she is holding contain a confession of his sudden infatuation? There is no mention of a letter in the Bible story. Its invention allows Rembrandt to heighten the psychological drama. Bathsheba was the wife of a captain of the Hittites, who was away on campaign for David. To get a love message from the King must have aroused mixed feelings. Her posture suggests submission. Her face is thoughtful and enigmatic; it might be read as conveying sadness as well as a pleasurable anticipation. Yet she holds firmly to the letter as the servant dries her feet. The sensuous curl of hair falling onto her bosom, the jewels that bedeck the rich curves of her body even here at her bath, imply the passionate narcissism that will take her to the King's bed and lead to the conception of Solomon that very night.

Rembrandt might have said with his contemporary, the English poet John Donne, that the body is the visible sphere of the soul.

> *To our bodies turn we then, that so*
>   *Weak men on love revealed may look;*
> *Love's mysteries in souls do grow,*
>   *But yet the body is his book.*[12]

No artist has been as profound as Rembrandt at interpreting the inner story of that book through gesture and expression. He represented to an exceptional degree the common Dutch curiosity about every aspect of the human condition, demonstrated all around them in their crowded little country. His art has never lost its appeal across all classes and creeds. But as the era of religious debate turned into the Age of Reason fashionable taste moved from massively expressive forms to elegant sophistication. The eighteenth century, exalting rationality, saw the body as merely decorative. The image of human beauty was appropriate to adorn the door of a cabinet, a china tea service, or a fan.

A characteristic exponent of this chocolate-box style was François Boucher. A painter at the frivolous court of Louis XV of France, his figures are as insubstantial as the heavens and oceans through which they float [192]. Their object is to charm away a yawn and make the viewer momentarily forget the effects of the previous night's dissipation. But occasionally Boucher had the opportunity to display, as here [193], a real body reclining, not on clouds or billows, but on the rich brocades of a solid sofa.

Marie Louise Morphy was the daughter of an Irishman and the sister of a young actress in comic opera. In his memoirs the Venetian rake Casanova describes meeting her in her sister's apartment in Paris. She was thirteen years old, "a pretty, ragged, dirty little creature."[13] He says he was the admirer who christened her "O-Morphi," the Greek for beautiful. Cleaned up, she gained the attention of Louis XV. When the King first sat her on his knee she burst out laughing. He was as like as two peas, she told him, to a six-franc piece (where his image was engraved).

Such ingenuous charm, combined with the kittenish appeal of her plump young limbs, gained the roving monarch's favor for a few years. Sprawling on her abandoned clothes, her own body temporarily discarded like the rose on the floor, she seems to be wondering whether her royal master will be returning for another bout of the war of love, or will be lost for the rest of the afternoon to boring affairs of state. Boucher catches a moment as transitory and delicious as the whiff of perfume drifting up from the incenser below the sofa.

If you had not lived in the eighteenth century, said that surviving

192. Boucher, The Setting of the Sun, *1753.*

193. Boucher, Miss Morphy, *1751.*

statesman Talleyrand, you would never have known the true sweetness of life. But already in the last quarter of the 1700s there were discordant rumblings across Europe. The developing technology of steam power began to alter the face of Britain, and with it came the first harbingers of social change, the earliest self-made tycoons, the iron masters. The American Revolution was a further potential lift for the common man. As though in recognition of this fundamental shift in the way of the world, the new French court at Versailles chose to play at being peasants. In society as a whole, the seismic shock of the approaching earthquake manifested itself in the renewed attraction of primitive beliefs. There was a revival of interest in witchcraft. It became fashionable to attend séances. Nightmares began to ruffle the smooth brow of reason.

An artist who mirrored many of these preoccupations was Henry Fuseli. Swiss-born, living mostly in England, widely read and traveled, he drew on a vast vocabulary of classical forms to stock the Gothic visions of northern poets and Germanic myths which he illustrated. This disjunction of styles contributes to the perverse impact of his phantoms. He turned many of the wilder scenes in Shakespeare into the hallucinations of his own fevered imagination. In the play, Hamlet's father's ghost tells his son how he was murdered while sleeping in his orchard. Poison was poured in his ear by his wicked brother, ambitious to gain his crown. Fuseli has transformed the sunlit fruit trees into a dark cavern of the mind [194]. Presumably the murder scene is a vision in the tortured brain of Hamlet, whose grief-stricken figure is on the right. The fatal brothers are no longer mature Danish royalty but naked personifications of light and darkness. Part of their corrupt evil stems from the fact that Fuseli has taken them from an antique vase painting of a homosexual encounter that was being watched by spectators.

Fuseli's obsession with madness, violence, and the perverse sexual exploitation that can appear in dreams caught the mood of increasingly uneasy times. Undoubtedly he was driven to create such imagery by his own obsessions, but now they seem like forecasts of what was shortly to come. The French Revolution brought in its wake the excesses of the Terror. The intellectuals of Europe had hoped for change, but were profoundly shocked by the form it took. They responded to Fuseli's glorification of ambivalent heroes like Lucifer, exiled by God to Hell, but still hurling forth lonely defiance of fate.

In the last decade of the century a greater artist turned his powerful imagination on the crumbling illusions of the old order. Like Fuseli, Francisco Goya had his own reasons for pain and anger. His career as court painter to the King of Spain was in jeopardy and many of his friends disgraced because the horrifying slaughter of the Terror had led to a Spanish reaction against reform. His brief liaison with the beautiful Duchess of Alba was over and a fearsome illness had left him permanently deaf and well stocked with a gallery of terrors of his own.

He let loose his night fiends, witches, and demons in some of the most searing images ever created in a graphic form. The series of aquatints known as *Los Caprichos* (literally *The Caprices*) owe their power to Goya's ferocious attack on all sides [195]. These bony, asexual old hags stand for the reactionary forces in society, the church, the military, and the administration. They literally feed on the children of the populace. But the gullible public do not mind; they push forward, greedy to get scraps from the feast. One child is pumped like a bellows;

194. Fuseli, The Dane King Poisoned by His Brother, *1771.*

his own wind fans the cooking fire. Goya took as his theme "the sleep of reason produces monsters."[14] He got the idea from Rousseau that "imagination abandoned by reason produces impossible monsters: united with her, she is the mother of the arts and the source of their wonders."[15]

The eighteenth century had not been strong on creative visual imagination. The nations of Europe had sought to maintain the old orders (and hence the established styles of art) against increasing pressures from revolutionary ideas and technologies. But now a real Lucifer arose, Napoleon, whose meteoric ascent and dazzling gifts mesmerized all sensitive observers, until he drowned adulation in the

195. Goya, Blow, *1799.*

torrents of blood spilled to further his ambitions. Within a decade of publishing the imaginary horrors of *Los Caprichos* Goya was witnessing the true horrors of war [196]. Such scenes were also part of the human condition. They were often to be repeated in the next two hundred years, but have seldom been set down with such searching ferocity.

The urbane sensibility of the eighteenth century was not adequate to cope with such experiences. Buffeted by the maelstrom of change, lashed to the frail plank of his imagination, the artist found himself carried out into unchartered seas. Each had to make his voyage on his own. As in the Renaissance, the body was often the chosen instrument for expressing unprecedented feelings. In the red dawn of the Romantic Movement the human image gestured with a new rhetoric to the far horizons; plumbed the mysterious depths of the psyche; occasionally confronted us with the level stare of an uncompromising truth freshly observed.

196: Goya, Bury Them and Keep Quiet, *ca. 1820.*

8

PATHOS OR PORNOGRAPHY?

In the eighteenth century the position of the artist seemed more secure than ever before. The establishment of the Royal Academy in England in 1768 under the patronage of the King, George III, continued the social advance. The first president of the Academy, Sir Joshua Reynolds, reaffirmed in his influential *Discourses* the aims for contemporary art that had been formulated initially in the Renaissance by Alberti and demonstrated by Raphael, Michelangelo, and others. For over two hundred years the academic style, broadly created by them, had reigned supreme in Europe. Even in the French Revolution, the leading painter, David, showed his radical convictions by an uncompromising delineation of those classical values that the Greeks and Romans had created and the Renaissance had extolled [198].

Yet the downfall of the *ancien régime* in France stirred more than political aspirations. Intellectuals everywhere hoped, like the English poet Wordsworth, that it heralded a new dawn in which the creative spirit would have a larger part to play. In a famous passage in his long poem *The Prelude*, written at the beginning of the nineteenth century, Wordsworth saw the artist as a privileged being. He was likened to the prophets of old as someone who could contribute to mankind's general understanding and knowledge: "he is enabled to perceive something unseen before." So the artistic work, "proceeding from the depth of untaught things, enduring and creative, might become a power like one of Nature's."[1] This assertion of the autonomy of the individual, based on his personal intuitions and his responses to his own sensibility, naturally ran into conflict with the cultural establishment. It helped to create the idea of the artist as a rebel, at loggerheads with the previous generation of practitioners. Many works by leading artists of the

197. Géricault, The Raft of the Medusa *(detail), 1819.*

198. David, Leonidas at Thermopylae, 1814.

nineteenth century were greeted with outrage when they first appeared. Was popular opinion right? Did the artists of the Romantic Movement and its successors debase the human body and deprave the minds of future generations with false sentiments? Or did they bring fresh pathos and newly charted areas of emotion to the portrayal of the nude?

Our first evidence comes from *The Raft of the Medusa* [199]. This very large composition, sixteen feet tall by twenty-four feet wide, occupied the young French artist Théodore Géricault for eighteen months. The *Medusa* was a frigate shipwrecked off the coast of Africa in 1816. It was part of a convoy carrying French soldiers and settlers to Senegal. A hundred and fifty people, including one woman, got away on a roughly constructed raft. It was so crowded that they were more than waist-deep in water. The seas rose and the weaker were washed away. There was no food or drink except a few barrels of wine. Many got drunk. Some went mad. Fighting broke out for the best positions near the center mast. Sixty-five died in this senseless struggle. Hunger drove the survivors to cannibalism. After six days the woman, who had been protected at first, was thrown overboard with all the other ailing or crazed survivors. The fifteen who remained lasted on a diet of human flesh, wine, and urine for seven more days. Five died after the rescue.

The disaster caused a political scandal in France. It was only a year since Napoleon had finally been defeated at Waterloo. Many disliked the restored Bourbon monarchy. One of the returned nobility was responsible for losing the *Medusa* through his incompetent captaincy. Nowadays there would be a fact-finding television documentary. In 1817 two of the survivors wrote a best-selling book and Géricault decided to paint a picture.

No one had ever attempted to paint such a recent and awful tragedy before. Moreover it was an event without an uplifting moral: there were no heroes on the raft. But Géricault had been attracted to violence

199. Géricault, The Raft of the Medusa, 1819.

from his youth. He had grown up under the last days of the Revolution and its Imperial aftermath. His early paintings were of fighting men and horses: charging chasseurs, wounded cuirassiers, trumpeters and galloping artillery teams, and carabineers standing defiant among the ruins of Napoleon's dreams of conquest.

Géricault showed some of the feverish energy and ruthless ambition of which the Emperor had been a supreme exemplar. When he decided to paint *The Raft*, he hired a large studio for eight months, had his food brought to him, and slept in the next room. He made a number of sketches of different episodes in the thirteen-day ordeal. He even tackled cannibalism, not a common subject in Western art. The early compositions all show the raft from some distance, to emphasize the dark wastes of the surrounding ocean. When Géricault decided to concentrate on the moment when the survivors first sighted another sail he shifted the viewpoint. The raft tilts up away from the onlooker. He looks beyond the frantically waving men to the infinitesimal patch on the horizon that is shortly going to disappear again below the intervening billows. The painting catches a moment of false hope and cruel fate, such as the French nation had recently experienced under Napoleon. Such conflict of emotion is characteristic of much Romantic art, as is the portrayal of an extreme situation.

Géricault went to great lengths to achieve authenticity. He consulted the survivors and sketched them. In order to understand what they had undergone he went to a hospital and studied dying patients. "He followed all the stages of suffering with ardent curiosity."[2] He acquired dissected limbs [200] and severed heads and carried them back to the studio. He painted them and watched their gradual decay. In the Renaissance Leonardo had gone to hospitals to dissect corpses, but no artist had pressed so close to the body's corruption before. For several months Géricault lived in the presence and stench of death.

There were stresses in Géricault's private life. He was in love with the wife of a kindly but unsuspecting uncle. In August 1818, while he was completing plans for *The Raft*, she bore him a son. The effects were permanent but hidden away: the mother sent to the country and the baby adopted.

In 1819 Géricault's huge painting was exhibited at the Paris Salon, to mixed notices. Most dwelt on the topical subject matter rather than its qualities as a painting. Exasperated, exhausted, and depressed,

200. *Géricault, study of dissected limbs, 1818–19.*

Géricault had a mental breakdown. He recovered to paint some penetrating studies of the insane and renew his obsession with horses. A series of riding accidents recklessly aggravated a spinal injury. The subsequent tumor brought him a slow and painful death at thirty-two. From now on the lives of artists are more and more part and parcel of their creation. Under the Romantic impulse artists pushed themselves to the extremes of experience they favored in their work. Keats, Lermontov, Shelley, Schubert, Byron, Pushkin, and Chopin all died dramatic and early deaths.

Time has been equally hard on Géricault's most famous picture. Wishing to accentuate the blackness of the shadow in an already somber color range, the artist resorted to bitumen. A pigment prepared from the resinous pitch asphalt, bitumen was often used in the early nineteenth century to ultimately disastrous effect. It never dries completely.

Chemically unstable, it has caused a decay as inevitable as that of the flesh of Géricault's cadavers. Patches of deterioration draw attention to the forced rhetoric of the postures.

Striving for naturalness Géricault painted most of the figures from life directly onto the canvas. The result is to make each seem a separate study. The reclining youth and his mourning father in the foreground, the headless figure trailing in the water, the back of the waving Negro, are individually superb, but their classical resonance works against the intended realism. These figures are not wasted with exposure, famine, and fear, but are riven with a theatrical Romantic agony. They are a monument to their creator's feeling for the fearsome situation in which they found themselves. His response includes savoring the ultimate demands the experience made on *him*, the artist; his relish for pitting himself, at least in imagination, against the Byronic challenge of the elements.

Despite his studies of death and decay, Géricault has not succeeded in conveying what such an experience would be like. The care with which he has arranged his composition and worked up each individual element gives the whole the feeling of that popular nineteenth-century entertainment the waxwork tableau. One of his models, for the figure in the foreground with his head fallen forward across a beam, was the painter Eugene Delacroix. He was twenty years old. Géricault was a powerful influence on his early development. Late in life when he came to examine some of Géricault's studies of horses he was struck by "the invariable lack of unity . . . the horses are never modelled in the mass; each detail is added to the rest, and altogether they make an incoherent whole."[3] His considered verdict was that Géricault's boldness of imagination was not equaled by his power of execution; a judgment with which we must concur.

Delacroix himself painted many similar themes: several shipwrecks and enough horses for a cavalry charge. The horse was *the* sacred animal of the Romantics. Not only was it a symbol of speed, energy, and beauty, but, more surprisingly, artistic sensibility as well. The rolling eye, twitching flanks, and foaming jaws suggest sensitivity, while prancing hooves, flaring nostrils, and switching tail convey poetic élan. The horse could add hauteur to his rider by his arched neck or pathos by his drooping mane. He could be a worthy foe [201]. His spirit had to bend to the will of the artist, just as the latter had to capture his rearing form in appropriately high-spirited strokes. These rising figures, already leaping upward before the close of the Century of Reason, presage the artistic revolution that is to come. The Romantics sought to push every emotion a notch higher and looked for appropriate subjects with which to do it.

Throughout the nineteenth century literature and the fine arts were closely interwoven; many of the themes of Romantic painting came from novels and poetry. One of the most popular concerned a fearsome ride. Voltaire had retold an anecdote about a Polish page boy, Mazeppa, who was caught in an affair with his countess. The vengeful count had Mazeppa tied naked on an untamed steed and let loose on the steppes. It was a quintessential Romantic image [202]. Bound together and

201. Gros, sketch for Bucephalus Vanquished by Alexander, *1798.*

202. Vernet, Mazeppa and the Wolves, 1826.

equally suffering the dangers of harsh nature and ravening beasts, horse and rider are a metaphor for the dilemma of the artist subject to the conflicting claims of emotion and reason. Eighteenth-century thought had exercised a controlling curb on the emotions, but the Romantic artist let them carry him away.

Delacroix, who himself had nerves as finely tuned as a thoroughbred, also painted Mazeppa. Unmarried, plagued since his youth by the tubercular fevers that eventually killed him, he fluctuated between elation and despair. "As soon as inspiration isn't there, I am bored."[4] Physically frail, he fell back on the dreams of the imagination. He found a ready audience in a society disillusioned at the failure of Napoleon's material dreams. It was the first era to luxuriate in the neurasthenic pleasures of illness. The liveliest passages of Byron's poem on *Mazeppa* describe the fainting hallucinations of the tortured hero. Delacroix deliberately evoked the phantoms of a mind overheated by sickness. Friends described how he would work in an obsessive frenzy. He praised the idea of being *beyond himself* in order to achieve his potential capability.

Yet there was a danger in such freedom. "Let those who work coldly and calmly keep silence, for they have no conception of what it means to work under the spur of inspiration—the dread, the terror of rousing the sleeping lion whose roarings move us to the very depth of our being."[5] Delacroix wrote this in 1824 when he was twenty-six and about to release the wild beasts as never before or after in an enormous painting twelve feet high and over sixteen feet long.

The Death of Sardanapalus [203] was probably inspired by Byron's insipid verse drama, which was translated into French in 1825, though for exotic violence the painting far exceeds anything in the poem. Delacroix wrote his own description of the scene. "Reclining on a superb bed on top of a huge pyre, Sardanapalus orders the eunuchs and palace officers to cut the throats of his women and his pages, and

203. Delacroix, The Death of Sardanapalus, *1827.*

even of his favourite horses and dogs; none of the objects that have contributed to his pleasures must survive him . . ."[6] The oriental tyrant lies back on one elbow watching with brooding pleasure the destruction of his playthings. All the lavish flesh, the cascade of brocade and jewels, the richly caparisoned horses, the faithful slaves, the golden elephants, and Sardanapalus himself will be consumed in the funeral fires, which are already sending their perfumed smoke across the scene. By that time the tyrant will have taken the chalice of poison waiting by his hand. But for the moment he is content passively to watch the frenzied passing of everything he held dear.

Never again did Delacroix reveal such a sensuous regard for death. Perversely, the whole paroxysm of destruction glows hot with life, the opposite of *The Raft of the Medusa* with its cold frozen energy. There, opposing forces are held in rigid tension; in *Sardanapalus* hair, blood, breasts, tasseled scarves, trappings, muscled shoulders, and flailing hooves flow together in a profusion of gorgeous color. By raising the color values, as he did during painting, Delacroix has made the scene more a vivid debauch than a somber tragedy. The vitality of invention continually titivates the eye, carrying it from the trousers of the executioner in the foreground, all splattered with tiny flecks of blood, to the impressionistic smears of color that suggest that his ankles are reflecting the rich glow of the velvet on which he kneels. The jutting curves of his victim accentuate the orgiastic tension of her pose, bent backward to receive the knife, contrasting with the abandoned release of the harem girl fallen forward on the bed, her auburn hair flowing away from her like the blood that will be pouring from her cut throat and emphasizing the slender arch of her neck. Around these two central forms, which suggest an erotic satisfaction in death, the writhing arms and abandoned postures of the other victims flail like a chorus of maenads. Across their ineffectual beauty the powerful pull of the naked black torso hauling in the terrified horse sets up a sinister counter-movement. *Sardanapalus* created such a stir at the Salon of 1827 that it was not exhibited again for nearly a hundred years. Yet in many ways it was the work in which Delacroix was most nearly himself. *Sardanapalus* was a metaphor of the destiny of the artist, brooding over the creatures of his kingdom and destroying them with a stroke of luscious color.

Many contemporaries remarked on Delacroix's affinity to the great cats of the jungle. It was said of him, "his deepset eyes and huge jawbones made one think of the muscles of leopards, and gave him a kind of energetic beauty."[7] His sketches of tigers are like psychic self-portraits. The cave painters had evoked the images of animals, no doubt to partake of their power. Delacroix painted lions and tigers to release the violence in his nature, which in life he increasingly kept hidden behind the bored mask of a perfect gentleman.

Voracious energy hungry for all experience, unbridled feelings pursued to the apogee: this was the Romantic aim. With it went in Byron and Delacroix a classically tuned intelligence which helped them steer away from false sentiment. They had the dandy's skepticism for the very experience into which they were determined to plunge. "Delacroix was passionately in love with passion, and coldly determined to seek the means of expressing it in the most visible way,"[8] wrote his friend, the poet Baudelaire. No one worked more delicately on the colors of his palette, so that it was like an expertly matched bouquet of flowers. "You might have called him a volcanic crater artistically concealed behind such bouquets."[9]

Among lesser artists the overheated emotions of Romanticism can seem bathetic. Many of the exotic themes reveal a sexual sadism that is only a little less than the general mayhem of *Sardanapalus*. Suitable subjects were easy to find in Egypt and the Near East. A French painter who paid many visits there was Jean-Léon Gérôme [204]. A generation younger than Delacroix, the photographic realism of his style and his provocative choice of imagery ensured his popular success. The inspection of a potential slave girl entails her being stripped naked under the searching gaze of a number of fully clad men. A prospective purchaser pushes his hand into her mouth to feel her teeth.

That the new bourgeois public of nineteenth-century Europe and America, chock-full of prejudices, inhibitions, and prudery, were able to accept such works is one of the strangest of those disassociations of sensibility which we perceive in every age except our own. Who would have thought that a chained and naked slave [205] would be a successful entry at the Great Exhibition in London of 1851, dedicated as it was to progress and education. The American sculptor Hiram Powers called the figure the "embodiment of enslaved Greek womanhood,"[10] so allowing her to be viewed with the righteous indignation which the

thought of their protracted struggle for independence produced in every democratic breast. The fact that her own breasts were very shapely was not considered relevant. As a contemporary sermon put it, *"The Greek Slave* is clothed all over with sentiment, sheltered, protected by it from every profane eye."[11] She was so popular that small china reproductions were soon gracing many Victorian homes.

Christian communities which made great play of venerating "the fair sex," modesty, and innocence, saw nothing untoward in canvases

204. Gérôme, The Slave Market, *n.d.*

205. Powers, The Greek Slave, *1843.*

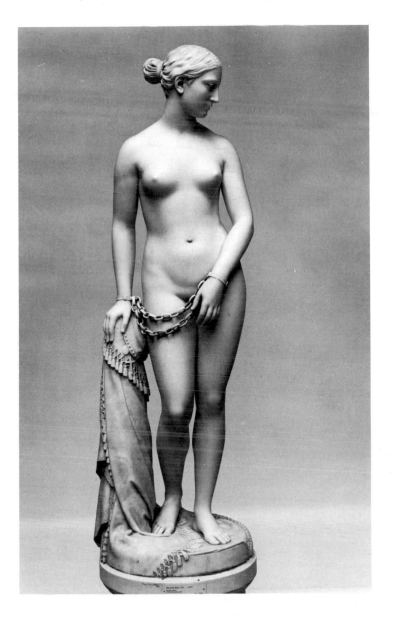

crowded with naked bodies: nymphs disporting themselves in sunlit glades, Roman maidens splashing in marble baths, sinuous Eastern beauties at the oasis. They were sanitized under the sacred banner of Art. Mock decorum increases our antipathy for their pallid abandon. So in Ingres' painting, Angelica chained naked to a rock [206], in danger of being torn apart by a nasty scaly monster with big tusks, is clearly fainting with shame as well as fear. The juxtaposition of her bare defenseless body and the well-armored frame of the hero with his thrusting lance adds to the piquancy. The emotions released are allowed free play only in rigidly circumscribed limits: within Classical mythology and fairy tale, or in a fabled Orient.

How thin was the veneer of acceptable conventions was demonstrated when in 1863 Édouard Manet's painting *Le Déjeuner sur l'herbe* [207] was declared indecent by no less a person than the Emperor Napoleon

206. Ingres, Roger Freeing Angelica, *1819.*

III. Its theme, of a picnic in a wood with one of the girls unclothed, had often been taken up in the Renaissance. Manet provided a similar pastoral calm, but he allowed the naked girl to look directly out at us, while dressing the men in modern clothes. These two breaches of taste were sufficient to reduce the majority of spectators to hoots of outraged laughter. To us it is hardly as disturbing as *The Slave Market*, where again a naked female is surrounded by fully dressed men. Nevertheless, if we try to look at *Le Déjeuner* without the covering of acceptability that long acquaintance has given it, it does appear a strange picture. Even today there is something provocative in these urbane bearded and trousered gentlemen lounging unmoved besides such cool nudity.

At the Salon of 1863, which rejected *Le Déjeuner sur l'herbe*, the most popular picture was *The Birth of Venus* by Alexandre Cabanel [208]. Another naked woman regards us, but this time dreamily through eyes almost closed. Venus lies back provocatively and without conviction

207. Manet, Le Déjeuner sur l'herbe, *1863.*

208. Cabanel, The
Birth of Venus, *1862.*

on a foaming billow. Her pose telegraphs sexual availability, but the waving cherubs reassuringly signal her descent from Raphael. One reviewer wrote: "Cleverly rhythmical in pose, offers curves that are agreeable and in good taste, the bosom is young and alive, the hips have a perfect roundness, the general line is revealed as harmonious and pure."[12] She might be a favored piece of blood stock. The Emperor bought her, Cabanel was awarded the Legion of Honor, elected to the Institute, and made a professor of the École des Beaux-Arts. Meanwhile Manet chopped up some of his pictures in disgust.

Two years later, when he submitted *Olympia* [209] to the Salon Manet appeared to be following an even more traditional form. The reclining nude with female attendant and small pet animal had been a standard subject for oil painting ever since Titian. Even the pose, with one hand protectively in the lap, was hallowed by convention. But once again the model looks at us; she is clearly the portrait of a real woman. Her expression is calm but challenging. Her body, we feel, is her own and she will choose to do what she likes with it. This is far from the coy submission that the age expected. The picture was described as a sham, a joke, a parody, a playing card, an attempt to attract attention at any price.

"The crowd, as at the morgue, throngs in front of the gamy *Olympia*" wrote one critic.[13] Manet was accused of lack of sincerity. The critic Gautier (who had once himself been a Romantic poet) said that the painting could not be understood from any point of view. "We would still forgive the ugliness, were it only truthful, carefully studied, heightened by some splendid effect of colour."[14] Looking at the self-contained elegance of that individualized body suggests that moral outrage is a poor microscope.

A painting like *Olympia* seems much less dubious in taste now than confections such as *The Birth of Venus* that were greeted with universal satisfaction. What seemed provocative now seems truthful; what appeared charming has become dishonest. Looking at the paintings of the body that were popular in the nineteenth century confirms the profound

209. Manet, Olympia, 1863.

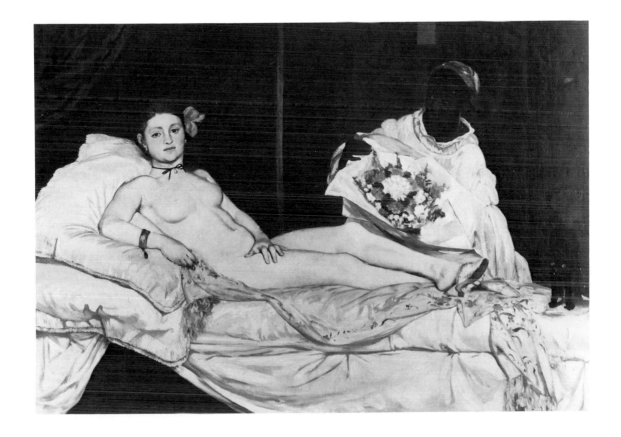

hypocrisy derided in the novels of Dickens and Flaubert. It was the great era for charades. Victorians loved dressing up just as they liked putting pretty fantasies around the weak—children, women, the poor. It was unacceptable to see them as they really were. That would have involved recognition of the exploitation on which society depended: of the underpaid, overworked masses, who provided the labor; of the rotten catacombs of prostitution which shored up the two-faced morality of the bourgeoisie. The chasm between conventional art and that of the avant-garde had become unbridgeable. (Though not necessarily recognized at the time; Manet continued to hope for the official commissions that fell to Gérôme and others like him.) Delacroix was the last great European painter to be employed on providing panels for public buildings. As for the academic art of the Salon, typified by artists such as Gérôme and Cabanel, it seemed to many young artists of the 1850s and 1860s to be sentimental and dishonest. An uncompromising realism, as in *Olympia*, is what the artists of the avant-garde sought to erect instead. That had been the goal of Géricault, and was not so easy to achieve. Once again the human body was the center of the battleground. A key witness is *The Bathers* [210], painted by Gustave Courbet in 1853.

Courbet was a true radical, involved in the politics of the 1848 revolution that toppled the last Bourbon king. He took part in pulling down the column in Paris commemorating Napoleon during the Commune of 1871. For this he was imprisoned, heavily fined, and as a result ended his life in exile. Born in a village near the Swiss border and largely self-taught, he had all the brash self-confidence of an exceptionally talented provincial. Bulky, bucolic, and pipe-smoking, he painted pictures that often seemed as vulgar as his manners. There is nothing elegant or winsome about the two women caught disporting themselves beside a weedy woodland pond. That great rump, gyrating up the slope like a cart horse, so outraged Napoleon III that he struck it with his riding whip—a reaction that must have greatly pleased Courbet.

Delacroix, who was fifty-five by this time, was amazed at the strength of the painting, but not sure what it meant.[15] He complained that the gestures of the two figures were unintelligible. The noncommittal stance of Courbet toward his subject was part of the realist approach. Courbet was avoiding the anecdotal. He was allowing the subject to

210. Courbet, The Bathers, *1853.*

speak for itself. Nevertheless, time has made the gestures of the two women seem as rhetorical as those of the castaways on Géricault's *Raft.* Most viewers must echo Delacroix's uncertainty as to the meaning. Perhaps its real intention was as an act of bare-bottomed provocation to all those genteel ladies splashing in the marble pools of Salon painting.

Delacroix's more serious charge was against the unevenness of the painting. Courbet sought to avoid the glossy finish that marked conventional professionalism, but his own technique was far from perfect. When his interest was not aroused the paint application could be clumsy and the color garish. What he did have, as Kenneth Clark noted, was a colossal appetite for the substantial. "Insofar as the popular test of reality is that which you can touch, Courbet is the arch-realist whose own impulse to grasp, to squeeze or to eat was so strong that it communicates itself in every stroke of his palette-knife."[16]

Bovine courage allowed Courbet to tackle subjects that were socially unacceptable. A picture of drunken priests—he was naturally virulently against the clergy—was submitted to the Salon in 1863, the same year as *Le Déjeuner sur l'herbe*. It was rejected by the jury and also by the Salon des Refusés, which was set up to take the works the Salon rejected. Eventually it was bought by a strict Catholic who destroyed it.

What could not be viewed publicly could be commissioned by a client with specialist tastes. In 1866, for Khalil Bey, the former Turkish ambassador to St. Petersburg, Courbet painted two naked women asleep on a bed [211], their limbs intertwined. Courbet said it should be called *Laziness and Sensuality*. The women are more comely than is usual in his work and the whole picture, opulent with flowers, pearls, and enameled flask, breathes an atmosphere of satisfied desire. It must be

211. Courbet, Sleep, *1866.*

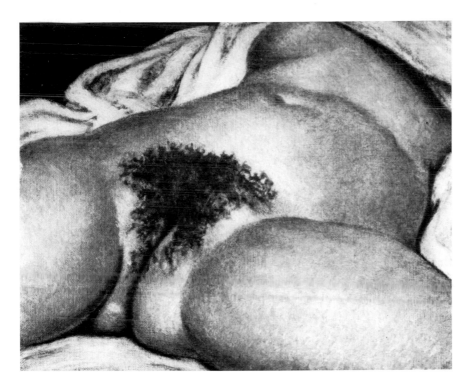

212. Courbet, The Origin of the World, 1866.

one of the few major works of Western art dealing with lesbianism. Even more provocative was Courbet's second picture for Khalil Bey. Entitled *The Origin of the World*, it was a straightforward view of the female sexual parts [212]. It vanished from Budapest at the end of the Second World War. The French critic Edmond de Goncourt said it was as beautiful as the flesh of a Correggio.[17] In such pictures Courbet was demonstrating, in his habitual blunt manner, the Romantic determination to make the most intimate subjects fit themes for art.

Soon the climate of realism spread beyond the borders of France. In 1866 a young Philadelphian, Thomas Eakins, came to Paris to study art. He worked under Gérôme, who was a professor at the École des Beaux-Arts, for several years. Gérôme was an arch-conservative and later in life a virulent opponent of the Impressionists. But his scrupulously detailed studies of Eastern characters and costumes and his mastery of conventional perspective were valuable to Eakins. Emotionally he learned more from his contact with the painting of Velázquez and Rembrandt and a long visit to Spain. Back in the States he eventually became Director of Instruction at the Pennsylvania Academy. Arguably the greatest American painter of the nineteenth century, his thoughtful, exploratory work did not gain easy acceptance in conventional East Coast society.

His powerful portrayal of an operation in progress was refused a place in the art building at the 1876 Centennial Exhibition in Phila-delphia. The blood on the hands of the surgeon, the prostrate body, and perhaps even more the dramatic intensity of the setting here and now in a hospital and not in some safe mythological never-never land, all made it too disturbing for genteel stomachs. A few years later at the age of thirty-nine Eakins painted another controversial masterpiece, *The Swimming Hole* [213]. Like all his best work it moves on many planes. He was a devotee of exercise and the outdoor life and the picture conveys the rustic freshness of the New World. Eakins has put his dog into the scene. He himself is seen swimming into the picture at the bottom right. The other men are all friends or students. There

213. Eakins, The Swimming Hole, *1883.*

is a lounging ease in their stance that recalls the bonhomie of a man's domain, that of the frontier.

At the same time the postures deliberately echo classical poses. The composition is as carefully organized in a pyramidical triangle as *The Raft of the Medusa*. There is another thing: despite the varied movements underway, not one figure reveals so much as a flash of genitals. This arranged omission brings a curious tension to the apparent naturalism. Polite society was then, as now, profoundly afraid of the open manifestation of the male body. Three years after painting *The Swimming Hole*, Eakins was dismissed from his post at the Academy. The official reason was for removing a loin cloth from a nude model to demonstrate musculature and bone structure to his life class. In his later career he concentrated on portraiture.

Ironically, the year before his dismissal the University of Pennsylvania was involved in one of the largest recordings of the human body ever attempted. Dozens of members of the university—professors, athletes, and ordinary students, housewives and children and professional dancers—were photographed from many angles by batteries of cameras, dancing, wrestling, and performing every sort of action—in the nude. Moreover the photographs were published worldwide, projected as slides and lectured about, without a flicker of protest. It was in the sacred name of scientific research; hence it was not only acceptable but a valuable service to the advance of American knowledge for one virtuous young woman to strip and throw a bucket of water over a friend who was equally naked [214]. The energy and precision of the athletes, the fun and spontaneity of the children, seem as fresh today as a hundred years ago. Nakedness takes away the quaintness that bustles and elastic-sided boots would give, and makes the cheerful young people appear only a day or two from our time.

That they were recorded is due to the persistence of an ingenious eccentric, who was born Edward Muggeridge in Kingston upon Thames, England. By the time he was a photographer on the West Coast in the sixties he had transformed himself into Eadweard Muybridge. Weird he might have been, but he was certainly technically clever. For Leland Stanford, a former governor of California and breeder of pedigree horses, Muybridge perfected a system of relating a battery of twenty-four cameras to trip wires that would be triggered by a passing horse. By this method he proved in the 1870s that quadrupeds did not run

214. Muybridge, Woman Emptying Bucket of Water on Seated Companion, *1884–85.*

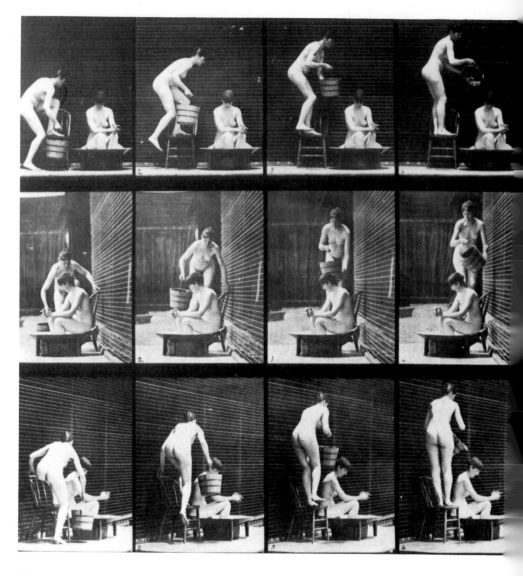

like rockinghorses, but with legs placed alternately. Eakins corresponded with him from 1879. The diving figure in *The Swimming Hole* was probably influenced by photography. When the university decided to implement Muybridge's plans to record the human figure in motion, Eakins was made a member of the supervising commission. It was an ambitious project. Special housing was built and forty-eight cameras were employed for a year, taking over a hundred thousand photographs. By mounting his pictures on a revolving plate synchronized with another with slits in it, Muybridge could project a flickering image that appeared to move.

His contemporary, the sculptor Auguste Rodin, also wanted to show movement in progress. From his middle years in the 1890s he developed a style of drawing that sought to capture the immediate thrust of action [215]. Looking fixedly at the model, who would be dancing or posturing at will in the studio, his hand would complete, sight unseen, a rapid pencil sketch of her contours. (No doubt he would have agreed with Delacroix, who told a would-be pupil, that if on seeing a man jump out of a fourth-floor window he could not complete a sketch of him before he reached the ground, he had better give up.) Later Rodin would tidy up the outline and, selecting the best of the many sketches he would have made in one session, would trace them onto new sheets of paper. On this simplified form he would apply a terra-cotta or sienna wash to give volume [216]. Occasionally, he cut out the figures and regrouped them in a way that anticipated by over twenty years the techniques of collage that were developed by the surrealists [217].

Rodin, largely for his own pleasure, and to give himself potential postures for future development as sculpture, was bringing drawing from its nineteenth-century mold toward methods that would be further

215. Rodin, female nude dancing, ca. 1900.

exploited by Egon Schiele and Gustav Klimt in Vienna in the next decade. Rodin treated the model realistically and chose to portray her in the sprawl of unspecific action. Often the model played up to the presence of the draftsman. This brought the viewer into the erotic interlock of artist and model [218]; a dynamic connection at the turn of the century when decorum was officially expected to reign even in the studio. Rodin was recording with a sophisticated but ultimately spontaneous sleight of hand his own reactions to the youthful flesh that was cavorting in front of him. He was a lifelong voyeur. His friend and biographer Judith Cladel reported how, after scrutinizing and analyzing at length the form of a reclining model, he turned and murmured: "What a joy is my ceaseless study of the human flower! How fortunate that in my profession I am able to love and also speak of my love!"[18]

So shortsighted that he was rejected for active service in the Franco-Prussian war, he habitually worked very close to his model. He was

216. Rodin, dancing figure, ca. 1900–5.

217. Rodin, montage sheet with two cut-out figures, ca. 1900–5.

accustomed to feeling the live body as he did the growing form under his fingers. When Isadora Duncan took him to her Paris studio and danced for him, "He ran his hands over my neck, breast, stroked my arms and ran his hands over my hips, my bare legs and feet. He began to knead my whole body as if it were clay, while from him emanated heat that scorched and melted me."[19]

At this stage of his fame there were often several models lounging nude or seminude in his studio. The natural postures and movements they fell into were triggers for a rapid sketch or working in clay. (He carried small bits of clay around with him so that he could continue modeling even while eating.) Like all the Romantics, he was anxious to record the spontaneous expression of the body when under the impulse of strong emotions. But, from Géricault to Eakins, nineteenth-century artists found it difficult to depart from the powerful inheritance of classical gesture. This gave their compositions a formal rhetoric they were trying to avoid. The presence of the unposed bodies allowed Rodin in his sketches to approach the novel plasticity of the body that was to be exploited with even greater freedom in modern art by Klimt and Schiele and Matisse and Picasso. Undoubtedly, Rodin's models played up to the sculptor's known propensity for the erotic pose. But in this also Rodin gave a foretaste of modern art, where the emphasis in portraying the nude has usually fallen on the sensual and sexual.

Rodin was entranced by the fluid grace of a Cambodian dance group which came to France in 1905. A few years later Nijinsky made an even greater impact. His performance with the Diaghilev ballet of *L'Après-midi d'un faune* created a furore. He was called indecent, "with vile movements of erotic bestiality and gestures of unmitigated lewdness."[20] Rodin was one of those who rushed into print in his defense. "During the last twenty years," he wrote, "dancing seems to have set for itself the task of making us love the beauty of the body, movement and gesture . . . we admire Loïe Fuller, Isadora Duncan and Nijinsky because they have recovered once more the freedom of instinct and discovered again the soul of tradition, founded on respect and love of nature."[21] Such aims were close to Rodin's own for sculpture.

Nijinsky came to thank Rodin for the letter and stayed to pose. According to his wife, he spent many hours posing naked. A major sculpture never materialized, but Rodin, now seventy-two, produced a brilliant small study in plaster [219]. Different angles show how he has

218. Rodin, model reclining and lifting chemise, ca. 1898.

captured the complex character of the dancer with his Mongolian features, half angel, half ape, and the coiled energy which electrified all who saw it, and gave the illusion that Nijinsky could pause in the air in midleap.

Rodin sought in his work an equally impossible feat: the illusion of movement in a static form. In drawing, the watercolor wash overlying the pencil lines suggested the fluid nature of the human body, continually modifying its posture in minor ways even when at rest. Three-dimensional sculpture allowed the possibility of suggesting successive actions in a form seen from different viewpoints. This sort of dynamic contrapposto naturally lent itself to figures as roughly modeled as the Nijinsky; but Rodin was able to create the illusion of the continually changing reactions of life in sculpture that was much more highly finished. There was no calm, even in death, wrote his admirer and one-time secretary, the German poet Rilke; "for in decay, which is also movement, even what was dead was still subordinated to life. In Nature there was only movement; and an art that wished to give a conscientious and credible interpretation of life, might not take for its ideal a calm which was nonexistent."[22]

219. Rodin, Nijinsky, *1912.*

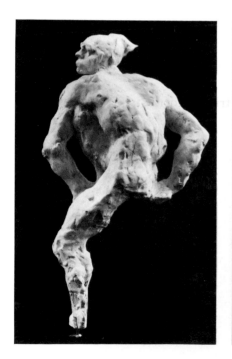

Rodin's very first life-size standing figure [220], begun in 1875, was so vital that it immediately created a controversy—something that was never far from Rodin's work from then on. He was already thirty-five, and a relatively unknown mason working on decorative figures for public buildings in Brussels, when he began making a sculpture that he hoped to enter for the Paris Salon. It was to be a tribute to the suffering of the French people in the recent disastrous war with Prussia. His own mother had died as a result of privations endured during the siege of Paris. Its title was to be *The Vanquished*.

Rodin worked for eighteen months. Originally the figure carried a spear. By removing it and changing the title to the less specific *Age of Bronze*, Rodin added to its profundity. Now the figure seemed to be awakening from the sleep of war, teetering on the brink of a racking decision. Some thought it reflected the pain of being reborn into life, others that it was hovering on the brink of suicide.

Providing a work with such ambiguity put Rodin ahead of his time. The twentieth-century viewer is accustomed to drawing such multiple conclusions; in the 1870s it was a not particularly welcome novelty.

220. Rodin, The Age of Bronze, *1876.*

Critics thought it pretentious. They queried the half-closed eyes and up-raised hand, and sneered at it as a sleepwalker.

However, there was general agreement as to the quality of the modeling: "very beautiful and extraordinarily original."[23] The posture recalls that of Michelangelo's *Dying Slave*, but Rodin's figure is slighter and finished with even greater realism. Such unprecedented perfection led to the rumor that the figure had been directly cast from the living model. Naturally Rodin denied it, but the questions persisted. The model offered to come to Paris and stand in the nude next to his statue. That would have settled the matter, but the offer was not taken up. Nor did the Salon jury even bother to open the crates of evidence Rodin sent them. He found himself condemned for the most galling reason: it simply was not believed that a relatively unknown sculptor in his late thirties could have produced by his own hands such a brilliant work.

It was three years before the slowly accumulating support of fellow artists led to the acceptance of *The Age of Bronze* at the Salon. With hindsight we can see it reveals qualities that persisted throughout Rodin's career: breathtaking technical virtuosity; an almost too rich mixture of theatricality, pathos, and eroticism; and an underlying banality in choice of theme. It was bought by the state and shortly afterward Rodin got the major commission of his life. He was to produce a monumental sculptured doorway for a proposed new Museum of Decorative Arts. (He said he would cover it with small-sized figures so that people could not accuse him of casting from living models again.) He chose the theme from Dante, and set to work.

The Gates of Hell became for him what the Pope's Tomb was for Michelangelo. Off and on Rodin worked on the *Gates* for thirty years. They were never cast in his lifetime. The museum was never built. Years after his death in 1917 the *Gates* were cast. Close study suggests they could never have been brought to make the climacteric impact for which he hoped. In the end the scale is too small and the rectilinear doorways too limiting to suggest adequately the broad cataract of tempestuous humanity that he wanted. Brilliantly though he handles changes of size and depth of dimension between different groups, the loss of ability to pass behind the figures destroys the amazing changes of perspective he was able to create in the round.

The extent of this loss can be seen in the figure of a crouching woman, called *The Danaïd*, originally intended for *The Gates* but removed by Rodin. She is a symbol of hopelessness, being condemned to draw water in the underworld with leaking vessels. Water flows like her hair onto the uncut marble into which she seems to be subsiding when seen from the viewpoint near her head. Walking around her to the right [221], the rough stone rises like a range of mountains over

221. *Rodin,* The Danaïd, *1888.*

222. *Rodin,* The Danaïd, *1888.*

which she hovers, a mourning Earth Mother, vast as thunderclouds. From the far side she returns to human scale, her raised behind and bent legs suggesting the effort with which she is dragging herself from the stone [222].

The chief sculptural value of *The Gates* was in providing the incentive for Rodin to create countless small studies such as this. The spawn of his creativity appears immense when viewed in his studio at Meudon. There, deserted, stand many hundreds of his original plaster casts. Frozen in gesture, their white limbs rise like ghosts waiting for the master's return. There are the various early attempts at portraying Balzac. *The Monument to Balzac* had been commissioned by a French literary body, the Société des Gens de Lettres. Difficulties began almost immediately. The society's representatives were dismayed by what they saw of the work in progress, and appalled by the end result. Rodin's method was to sculpt a naked figure which he then intended to cloak with a bronze cast of Balzac's dressing gown. In the Meudon studio are a number of the bulbous forms through which Rodin sought to perfect his conception of Balzac's massively energetic body. One study shows a headless man holding his erect penis [223]. This was the version incorporated in the final monument. The head came from a separate portrait bust that Rodin modeled from an early daguerreotype of the writer.

A storm of catcalls greeted the unveiling. The dressing gown was said to make the figure as shapeless as a snowman. Rodin knew that if he had hit it with a hammer the draperies would have broken off, revealing the naked figure beneath, and a pose more shocking than the critics could guess. The dressing gown accurately represented the long sleepless hours Balzac habitually spent writing. It was also a defiant cloak against an uncomprehending world; and it masked the prime and secret source of individual creativity, sexual energy.

Equally provocative in their time were many of Rodin's tributes to Venus. Whether fragmented, headless with legs asprawl, full of lusty vigor, or sinuously twisting without arms [224], the sad wraith of a northern muse, the plaster shards at Meudon seem a direct link to the mind of the sculptor. These silent witnesses vividly brought to mind the words of Rilke: "None of the drama of Life remained unexplored by this earnest, concentrated worker, who had never sought subjects nor desired anything which lay beyond the range of his own ever-

223. *Rodin, nude study for* Balzac, *1893.*

maturing technique: all the depths of nights of Love were revealed to him, all the dark, passionate and sorrowful spaciousness in which, as in a world still heroic, clothing was unknown, in which faces were blotted out and the human body came into its own."[24]

No wonder the illusiveness of inspiration was an important theme

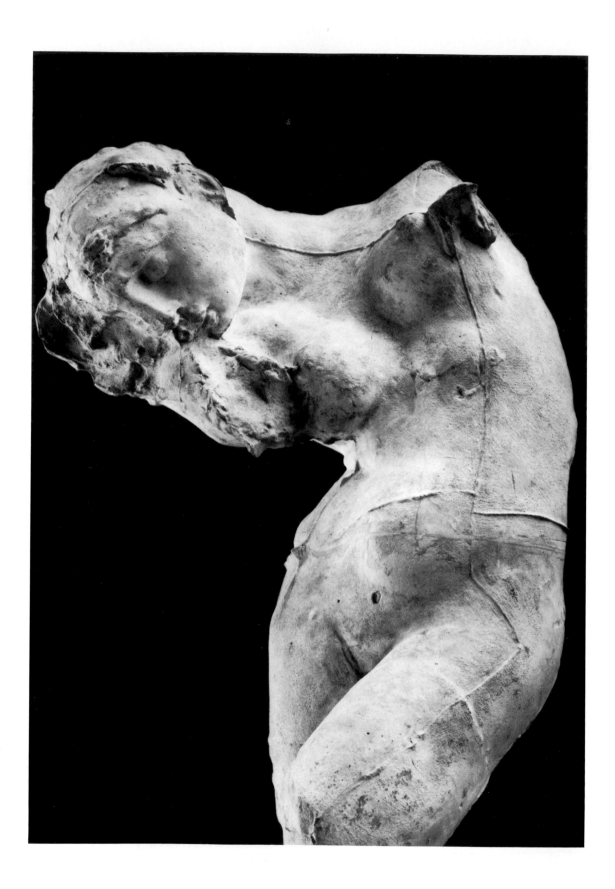

for Rodin. An artist who arrived at decision slowly, who worked all the time, trying out alternative approaches, combining elements from different attempts, he made many personifications of the creative muse. Always female, she often languished under the pale cast of thought. Sometimes she withdrew into herself, unyielding to the poet's embrace [225]. Like a frog who will not turn into a princess for him, she is

224. *Rodin,* Meditation Without Arms, *1883–84.*

225. *Rodin,* I Am Beautiful, *1880.*

about to leap out of his arms. He struggles to hold her aloft, but she turns her ungiving face away. But elsewhere she is shown not only whispering in the ear of her creator, but also sexually caressing him. Like the *Balzac*, another confirmation of how closely Rodin linked artistic creation with sexual libido.

Rodin with his obscure beginnings, his determination to equal Michelangelo, his career full of enduring labor and continuous controversy, his projection of his own passions in his work, his beautiful and faithful model-mistress, who after fifty years he marries in the last fortnight of her life, his countless affairs and scandals and extraordinary

226. Rodin, Christ and the Magdalene, *1894.*

personal presence that make him a legend in his own lifetime, famous among those who knew nothing of art—in all this he is the quintessential Romantic artist.

The Romantic Movement began that severance of the innovative artist from the masses which has gone on ever since. By insisting on the artist's own feelings being the ultimate criterion, the Romantic also severed himself from a common ground with future generations. Each new generation in turn would have to rely on its own intuitions "to perceive something unseen before," in Wordsworth's phrase.

The contemporary artist must depend not on the received judgments of established taste but on his own inspiration. Undoubtedly inspiration is a wayward gift. Meanwhile the artist must labor on. His task could be a tragic burden. Rodin did not hesitate to compare it with that of the Savior. This group [226] was variously titled *Christ and the Magdalene, Prometheus and the Oceanid,* and *The Genius and Pity.* Like Wordsworth he is linking the artist with the prophets and fire-bringers. But he seems also to be suggesting that the burden of the stone to which he is nailed is too great for him to carry. His human inspiration, the Magdalene, cannot free him from his destiny. She can only offer him the consolation of her body. His suffering head lies along her supportive arm, while her own head bows sorrowfully over his weak body, "like a flame tormented by the wind."[25] We are back with pathos again. The gestures of the martyred men and women we encountered on *The Raft of the Medusa* and *The Death of Sardanapalus* are reborn, but the plight of these successors is even more directly that of the artist.

9

A SUM OF DESTRUCTIONS

In every culture there seems an art form that is uniquely appropriate to it. The Greek temple, with its symmetry of pillars and smooth marble torsos, perfectly expresses the rational classical mind, just as the illuminated manuscript, with its labyrinth of abstract patterns turning into monsters and occasionally allowing a glimpse of a doleful human form, catches the obsessive, fearful world of the Dark Ages. In the twentieth century the characteristic medium must be the moving image on film and its electronic successors on television and video.

For art, and particularly the art that involves the body, this century has been a period of unprecedented excess. Never before have artists had such liberty to experiment. Equally, never before have artists—along with all other members of the human race—been so persecuted, uprooted, censored, and slain. License and order have been continually at war. These two principles are the essential ingredients of film. The flow of moving shadows in film is like the projection of a dream, soothing and soporific. Yet the cascade of images is constantly interrupted by the discipline of the director. Violent changes of angle, of movement, sudden close-ups, grasp our attention and emotions. We are subjected to visions of the world that we have not chosen and to which we can only passively contribute by watching. This in itself is one of the most striking characteristics of the twentieth century: everything is closer to us, everything impinges on us more nearly.

Art has reflected these changes and, in some cases, anticipated them. Like society as a whole, artists have indulged in an orgy of destruction. None of the sacred cows of the past have been allowed to escape slaughter. And even more than with the Romantics of the nineteenth century, artists' own lives have been involved with their creativity.

227. Picasso, Les Demoiselles d'Avignon, *1907.*

Their personal activity, their own most private feelings, are frequently the subject of their art. For all these reasons film, with its excesses and elisions, would be the best medium in which to portray the vicissitudes of the body's image in the first fifty years of the century. It would need to be a film that drew on the visual innovations artists themselves employed so brilliantly. The ideal director would have been Luis Buñuel, the erst-while colleague of Salvador Dali and one of the few undisputed geniuses of the cinema.

Buñuel was a member of the surrealist group of artists when they were at their most potent, in the early thirties. In temperament, he seems an appropriate interpreter of the time. A man who could write that the destructive impulse in him was stronger than the creative urge—that "the idea of burning down a museum, for instance, has always seemed more enticing than the opening of a cultural centre or the inauguration of a new hospital"[1]—speaks with the authentic voice of the first half of the century.

For long periods the whole world seems to have been affected by collective madness, a craziness that is revealed in his own way by the individual artist also. But little of this was apparent when 1900 dawned. Europe was the center of an ever-expanding world of knowledge and power and in the very center of Europe was Vienna. The Emperor Franz Josef ruled a city that swung from the majestic buildings on the great curved boulevard of the Ringstrasse, to the circle of the Prater Wheel that rose over the pleasure gardens, to the spinning of uniforms and perfumed silks to the endless waltz.

Der Reigen (La Ronde) was the play of the year. Schnitzler's version of casual avaricious sex was too close to the truth and it had to be taken off the stage. Hypocrisy oiled the wheels of Empire. Yet there were "tragic faces, hunger and hatred" despite the Austro-Hungarians having what was described as "the best bureaucracy in Europe."[2] While the coffeehouses clacked to the latest gossip, Dr. Freud was about to publish *The Interpretation of Dreams*. But the immediate scandal was over Vienna's greatest artist, Gustav Klimt. The year before, he had dared to exhibit a painting five foot high of a female nude. There was nothing particularly odd about that, especially as Klimt portrayed her in his flat, decorated style as a sort of Symbolist icon. But as well as the long hair, threaded with flowers and flowing down to her breasts, there was another patch of golden down between her legs. It seems extraor-

228. *Klimt,* Danae, *ca. 1907.*

dinary that the pubic bush had seldom been explicitly portrayed in an oil painting meant for public showing before. It caused a sensation, as Klimt knew it would. He called it *Nuda Veritas*. The nude holds up a mirror to the recoiling audience. Above her he wrote an inscription from Schiller: "If thou canst not please all men by thine actions and by thine art, then please the few; it is bad to please the many." It certainly did not please the police, who confiscated it.

This did not deter Klimt. Dark-bearded and broad of face, he was the darling of the ladies of Viennese society. There was usually a naked

229. Schiele, Reclining Girl, *1910.*

model wandering around his studio. But his figures never occupy a real space. There are no horizons in his pictures. These glamorous women come to us embedded in gold, and bright stones and enameling, like Celtic jewels or Byzantine mosaics. The subtle tones of flesh seem softer and more vulnerable when surrounded by the adamantine glint of mineral. In his most famous painting, *Danae* [228], precious metals actually invade the woman. She lies back on the edge of the bed, her legs lifted as if ready for the entry of the god. Jupiter's appreciation of her charms spurts over her in a golden shower. Titian and many other artists had painted versions of this erotic fairy tale but none so overtly linking sex and money.

Danae's look of voluptuous rapture was echoed in a drawing that Klimt did in the same year. It was to illustrate an edition of Lucian's *Dialogues*, but appears a straightforward study of a woman masturbating. Such poses are common in pornographic magazines today. In 1907, the era of bustles and stays, it was extremely shocking. The social acceptance of widespread prostitution and the brief encounters of the *séparées* (the private rooms provided by many restaurants) did not prevent masturbation from being an unmentionable subject. Moreover, it was considered morally and physically debilitating.

Nevertheless, Klimt's young protégé, Egon Schiele, made an even more explicit attack on the subject [229]. Schiele was only twenty, and the model was clearly younger. Her innocent, languorous expression and pubescent body are a disturbing contrast to the bony, urgent fingers. Schiele had an extraordinary gift for magnifying the repellent aspects of physical obsession. Klimt was said "to have confused the act of painting with the immediacy of amorous delight."[3] He habitually slept with his models and his pictures shine with sensual pleasure. Schiele's have the beady-eyed anguish of lust [230]. In this view in front of a mirror we are in the position of the artist, glowering away from the gyrating behind of the girl, who regards her made-up face with cool satisfaction. Pose, hat, and stockings are reminiscent of Cranach [178], but here there is no titivating wisp of veil. That tuft of hair, both fore and aft, jeers at the artist condemned to get on with his drawing.

Schiele does not romanticize his subjects. They are frequently angular and skinny, their blotched, imperfect flesh sagging into wrinkles [231]. But they are also intensely desired. They were thin, according to

230. Schiele, Self-Portrait with Nude Model in Front of a Mirror, *1910.*

Schiele, because they were poor, like him, and often hungry. He had all the self-pity of the narcissist. His self-portraits suggest an energy that is driving him to despair. He wrote: "I believe that man must suffer from sexual torture as long as he is capable of sexual feeling."[4]

He penned those words in prison. Staying with his seventeen-year-old mistress in a small country town had not prevented him from inviting in an number of schoolgirls and persuading them to undress. The police were called, and when they found erotic drawings pinned to the walls, Schiele was charged with seducing a minor. He got off relatively lightly, though the judge burned one of his pictures in court. Schiele's obsessions, his cruel and nervy eroticism, make him seem modern, whereas Klimt's warm, uncomplicated sensuality puts him back in the halcyon years before the First World War. The hint of perversity is attractive to us, not repellant. "Have adults forgotten how . . . sexually stimulated and excited they were themselves as children,"

Schiele asked his biographer, Arthur Roessler.[5] Perhaps he had a premonition that he would not have long to experiment. He and his wife were to die within three days of each other in the influenza epidemic in 1918. It had already carried off Klimt.

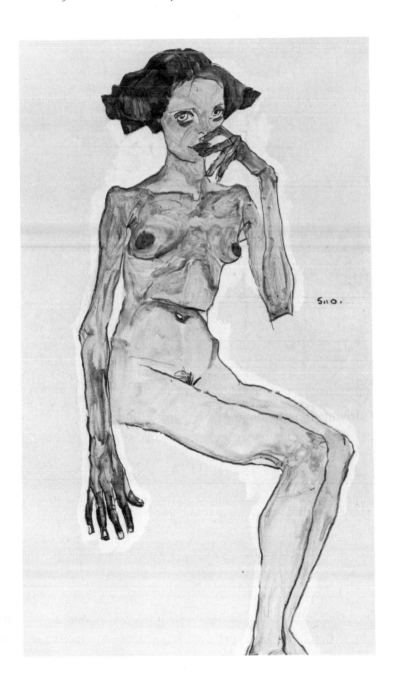

231. Schiele, Seated Young Girl, *1910.*

In prewar Vienna, many had felt intimations of disaster. The city seemed to be dancing itself to doom. Schnitzler wrote at the time that they were aware "the end of their world is near."[6] Death, madness, and visions of atavistic violence were common [232]. Surrounded with a gross materialism, it seemed morally justifiable to will such a society's downfall. Europe was widely regarded as played out, though intellectual and creative life had never been at a higher pitch.

Some intrepid souls had already left. One was the aspiring stock-broker turned artist, Paul Gauguin. His images of the South Seas have

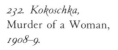

232. Kokoschka, Murder of a Woman, *1908–9.*

233. Gauguin, Two Tahitian Women, 1899.

retained their exotic power. Yet there is something comforting, almost domestic, in these beautiful girls [233].

Gauguin made his long journey seeking for a primitive renewal of energy. But the pictures he painted are as decorative and charming as a tapestry. The brilliant colors blend melodiously as they do in the rain forests of Oceania. They have the sweet, undulating rhythm of Polynesian chants. The songs of the South Seas are often mesmeric in their repetitions, like the distant murmur of the surf on the reef [234].

234. Gauguin, Fatata
Te Miti, *1892.*

How sweet it were, hearing the downward stream,
With half-shut eyes ever to seem
Falling asleep in a half-dream!
To dream and dream, like yonder amber light,
Which will not leave the myrrh-bush on the height;
To hear each other's whisper'd speech;
Eating the Lotos day by day,
To watch the crisping ripples on the beach,
And tender curving lines of creamy spray:
To lend our hearts and spirits wholly
To the influence of mild-minded melancholy . . .[7]

The tropical islands Gauguin longed for were only a dream. If they
had ever existed, Western diseases, and Western bureaucracy, had

obliterated them well before his time. He had hoped to find something like the island of Dr. Moreau. In H. G. Wells's story, men were turned back into wild animals. Instead, Gauguin found wooden horses revolving in a children's merry-go-round in the center of Papeete.

He continued to long for his enchanted island. He planned to move to one which was "still nearly cannibal. I believe that there, this completely wild element, this total spark, will give me before I die one last spark of enthusiasm, which will rejuvenate my imagination,"[8]

That total wild spark was not lit in the South Seas. Despite Gauguin's attempt to restructure a lost primitive culture in his canvases, every exquisite curve and nuance of color speaks of a refined European sensibility. Though his small wooden carvings mimick a much greater degree of savagery, in general he could not achieve that liberation from the heritage of Western art that he had sought. That step was taken by a far more ruthless and iconoclastic talent.

Pablo Picasso was a youthful prodigy. When not quite fourteen he applied to the School of Fine Arts at Barcelona. Much under age, he was allowed to skip the early classes and take the entry examination at the advanced level. A month was the given time. He completed the drawings in a day. Quite early Picasso wrote on a painting *yo el rey* (I am the King).

Outstanding abilities of hand and eye do not provide the artist with the subject he should paint nor the manner in which he ought to carry it out. So we see the youthful Picasso trying on style after style with the same speed with which he went from broad-brimmed bohemian headgear, to top hat, to cloth cap [235]. He was by no means the dashing sophisticate this drawing suggests. For a time he shared the top hat, and even a bed, with another aspiring creator, Max Jacob, a Jewish poet from Brittany. He had the bed at night while Picasso painted. Picasso slept during the day when Jacob was out earning their keep.

They were often hungry, and Picasso's pictures frequently show the thin, suffering poor. Yet they seem mannered and sentimental rather than deeply felt. Picasso's early trips to Paris did not bring him the immediate success a child genius would expect. Details in some of his sketches of brothel scenes suggest he may have acquired a venereal disease. Fear of the ultimate consequences might account for several pictures of blind men. His first Spanish companion in Paris, a fellow

artist, committed suicide over a girl they both knew. Two years later, Picasso painted a large picture, *La Vie*, giving the central figure the features of his dead friend. The early drawings show this figure was originally himself [236]. A naked girl is leaning lovingly against him. He is pointing out to her a picture of an apparently anguished couple. It could be an allegory on the wages of sin.

235. *Picasso,* Picasso in a Top Hat, *1901.*

236. *Picasso, study for* La Vie, *1903.*

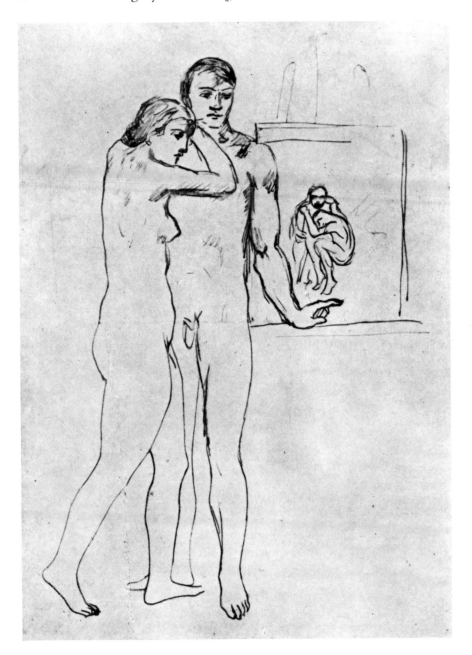

Throughout his long life Picasso's images of women fluctuate between making them the source of pleasure or the omnivorous predator. Often they are both at once. Picasso was an instinctive creator, and the whole process of his work is closely involved with the impulses of his sexual life. The waning of physical interest would be accompanied in his art with the darkening of themes, allegories on death and loss. The start of a new affair would signal the re-creation of vitality, often in a fresh direction.

His first long relationship began when he was not quite twenty-three. Fernande Olivier was living in the same ramshackle warren of artists' studios as he was. She was six months younger and some inches taller. He celebrated their union with the first of the pictures in which the artist broodingly contemplates his muse—a series that continued all his life with the different women with whom he became involved.

Many writers have remarked that an awareness of tragic isolation is essentially Spanish. Yet so far Picasso had not been able to find a unique and lasting style to express his profoundest feelings. In 1906 he took Fernande on a journey of rediscovery to his native land. They traveled by mule along the rugged slopes of the Pyrenees. Picasso wanted to empty himself, in Gertrude Stein's phrase, of the gentle fantasies of circus life he had been painting. Here in the mountains his art acquired a new grandeur. He had often painted the narcissistic Fernande at her toilet before, but never with such a monumental assurance [237].

Classical balance, maintaining an equipoise between the sensuous and the serene, is hard to achieve in the modern world. Back in Paris in the autumn of 1906 Picasso's style shifted toward more radical simplicities. A number of influences were at work on him. Through the years of Picasso's apprenticeship in Paris, one artist's reputation had grown continuously. Paul Cézanne had endured years of relative obscurity painting in the south of France. But in his last decade (he died in October 1906) more and more of his work was on display in Paris. Artists, in particular, came to recognize his unique attainment. For Picasso it was the attraction of the opposite.

Cézanne's painting of massively limbed bathers [238] lacked any of the facile accomplishment that was at Picasso's fingertips. For someone who since childhood drew with the ease of Raphael, it was the unrelenting effort, the unfinished roughness with which Cézanne struggled to grasp the, for him, unfamiliar volumes of the human figure, that was compelling. Cézanne's unswerving determination to make an enduring monumental art out of the simplest subjects—apples, his studio, a small mountain nearby—had an irresistible appeal to Picasso, who was able to leap chameleon-like from one style to another. The bathers were unlike any other image in Western art up to their time. These women, heavy as a circle of prehistoric dolmen, weathered and distorted as stones, rising like materializations of earth itself, shed every fragment of the classical tradition which had girded the aspirations of artists for two thousand years. There was nothing pretty or pleasing about them;

237. Picasso, La Toilette, *1906.*

238. *Cézanne,* Les Grandes Baigneuses, *1894–1905.*

and Picasso admired them because he had found it difficult to discard the innate grace that came with his superlative skill.

Why should he, and other young artists at the beginning of the century, wish to destroy their birthright, the heritage of past art? Partly this went back to the Romantic urge to express feelings more truthfully, to break through conventions that had become hackneyed. Then there was the dissatisfaction of thinking creative people with the gross materialism of this last golden age of imperial ventures and industrial exploitation and *Belle Époque* hedonism. The urge to *épater le bourgeois,* to question accepted standards, has continued to be a strong motivation in art throughout the century and has had its counterpart in the self-destructiveness of society itself.

For Picasso the immediate problem was to lose his facile ease and strike deeper. One way might be through the discipline of an ancient European style that was archaic rather than classical. Picasso had seen the exhibition of early Iberian sculpture at the Louvre and soon acquired an example. He had probably seen the posthumous exhibitions of

Gauguin's work put on in Paris in 1903 and on a larger scale in 1906. He would have been impressed by the rough energy of Gauguin's printed drawings with their scenes of haunting—and haunted— exoticism. Then there was the naïve primitivism demonstrated by Picasso's friend Henri Rousseau. As his nickname Le Douanier suggested he worked in the French customs service, and was a self-taught artist. His views of tropical forests were largely drawn from his visits to botanical gardens. But his imagination peopled them with the spectral menace of a dream [239]. Picasso admired his simplicity, akin to the untutored but penetrating eye of the child. In an extraordinary self-portrait [240], Picasso combined these concepts. Standing on the brink of the crucial struggle of his artistic development, he stripped himself down to naked childhood.

"It is as though he were not primitivizing art but primitivizing his own self . . . the age of the artist is now made strangely ungraspable, as though he could be adolescent, or younger, or quite out of time and without age."[9] Eternal youth was a popular theme at the time. Like

239. Rousseau, The Dream, *1910.*

Peter Pan Picasso hoped that he too would fly into the teeth of convention, yet capture the attention of his audience.

There was another spur to his ambition. Visiting his friends the American brother and sister Leo and Gertrude Stein, he saw a large painting Leo had just acquired. *La Joie de Vivre* [241] had been greeted with derision when it had been exhibited at the Salon des Indépendants that summer. It was unlike anything its creator, Henri Matisse, had painted before. A painting that deliberately evoked a mythical Golden

240. Picasso, Young Nude Boy, *1906.*

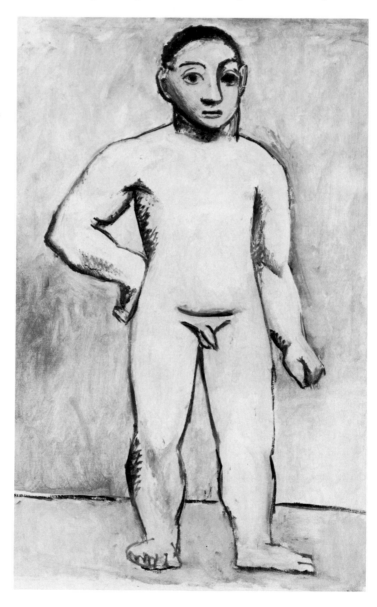

Age of lovemaking, ritual dancing, and pipe-playing goatherds seemed dangerously close to a return to the sort of classical theme that had been cheapened by the Salon painters of the previous century. But Matisse had painted it in a nonrealistic, decorative style that reminded its critics of wallpaper and multicolored shop fronts. Whatever else, it represented exactly the sort of radical step into the new that Picasso wanted to take. Matisse at thirty-seven was twelve years older than the Spaniard, and was already the central figure among a group of the more advanced artists. When they first met at the Steins, Matisse with his imposing beard and heavy spectacles, and his mastery of language, quite outshone Picasso, the young foreigner.

Like Picasso, Matisse was searching in his own way for a fresh purity of painting. He wrote at this time, "if I put a black dot on a sheet of paper the dot will be visible no matter how far I stand away from it—it is a clear notation; but beside this dot I place another one, and then a third. Already there is confusion . . ."[10] The pressure for

241. Matisse, La Joie de Vivre, 1905–6.

simplification carried him in 1906 to create a lithograph of a nude which is a boneless rhythm of curves. Yet whatever the distortions or abstractions, Matisse, the Frenchman, looks for a resolution that will satisfy and reconcile. Picasso, the Spaniard, seeks primarily to shock and disrupt.

For both, the nude remained the principal interest. If a new style was to evolve, it was the human body which would have to demonstrate the changes and bear the brunt of the attack. Toward the end of 1906, Picasso painted several versions of two nudes. At first they resembled in style the pictures he had painted of Fernande in Spain during the summer. They grew increasingly heavy and lumpish [242]—primitive, but in an archaic European sense. These figures look rooted to the earth by their weight; the opposite of the graceful linear abstractions with which Matisse had peopled his bucolic paradise. Significantly, one is opening a curtain. They appear to be beckoning us inside. What lies within?

Picasso had difficulty in deciding. He returned to his old preoccupation, the wages of sin. Several sketches show a sailor surrounded by naked whores in a brothel. When he began on the painting itself in May 1907 all anecdotal elements had gone. Only the women remain [227]. Standing before the ocher, blue, and white drapes that bulge oppressively on every side, they stare directly at us. They welcome us, without joy, into their clutches. What clutches! The women on the left, with their angular bodies and crude heads, would be enough to make any pleasure-seeker run a mile. They are clearly the sisters of the couple beside the curtain, stylistically related to Picasso's interest in Iberian sculpture. But the ghouls on the right could confront us only in a nightmare. If Matisse's new vision encompasses a reassuring return to an ancient hedonistic world, Picasso's tells us, with characteristic Spanish passion, that entering it is going to be a painful readjustment in which we shall have to jettison all we hold dear.

It is the disjunction between the two styles in which the women are painted that gives the picture much of its uneasy force. Almost certainly Picasso repainted the two on the right after a visit to the Museum of Historic Sculpture. Their brutish masks, derived from Central African carvings, bring an unexpected menace to the scene. But primeval fetishes are only the tools for Picasso's own violence. All revolutions have to be fueled by hatred and aggression. Picasso found

his in his feelings for women. He continued to view them with lust, fascination, disgust, fear, and anger into his nineties.

By letting in these visitants from the Dark Continent he was also tacitly admitting the degeneration of traditional Western forms. Seeking primitive vitality, he was putting the ax to the complex structure that had stemmed from Greece and Rome, had been rebuilt in the Renaissance, and had sheltered European culture ever since. It was a process of dismemberment that was to continue throughout his lifetime. Primitive art was only the first of numerous weapons by which the Old Order was to be decimated. Of course these masks and figures from Gabon and the New Hebrides were not used as they were intended as cult objects in religious ritual, but, like the barbarian mercenaries in Ancient Rome, were employed as agents of destruction.

The painting (it was not called *Les Demoiselles d'Avignon* for many years) was not an instantaneous triumph. Picasso did not attempt to exhibit it. He simply stopped working on it and invited his friends around to his studio. Eighty years later, the picture remains powerfully disturbing. To the first visitors it was incomprehensible. Matisse thought angrily it was an attempt to ridicule the whole modern movement (and probably himself in particular). Another painter, Georges Braque, said it was as though they were supposed to exchange their usual diet for the paraffin of a fire-eater. The censure was so general that someone remarked: "One day we shall find Pablo has hanged himself behind his great canvas."[11]

From the position of their time they were not wrong. There was no precedent for the destruction of accepted values on this scale. The extraordinary thing was how quickly cultivated society capitulated. Picasso continued to paint postscripts to the *Demoiselles* in the same manner, his so-called African period. Before the end of the year Braque had overcome his doubts and was at work on a large nude which showed the influence of both Matisse and Picasso [243]. Braque continued the chunky, multifaceted style in landscapes of increasing abstraction. Matisse disdainfully said that he was "making little cubes."[12] Picasso and Braque became close friends, and by the end of 1909 their work was generally referred to as "Cubism."

The process of dismembering the body went on apace. By the spring of 1908 a standing nude by Picasso [244] had been reduced to a series

243. *Braque,* Large Nude, *1907–8.*

of planes within a still recognizably human shape. The colors at this time were predominantly tobacco browns and blues. From being oval masks the faces acquired more flat contrary surfaces, as though chiseled from some adamantine wood. Colors became even more restricted—

244. *Picasso,* Standing Nude, *1908.*

graduations of gray and fawn. Appearances were increasingly demolished so that the form resembled a fragment of rock crystal more than a person. By 1910, even this mineral solidarity had been disintegrated [245]. This nude woman might be a pack of cards, supported on an armature like a standard folding lamp. All relationship to humanity was scoured away. The body was segmented into separated fragments, viewed from different angles. As the art dealer Daniel-Henry Kahnweiler said, Picasso "had taken the great step, he had pierced the closed form."[13] Apollinaire, his friend and supporter, wrote that Picasso had assassinated anatomy "with the science and technique of a great surgeon.[14]

Other scientists were preparing the way for even more radical dissection. By an almost eerie synchronism of history, the years when Picasso, and others, were cutting art adrift from its Renaissance roots

245. *Picasso,* Nude Woman, *1910.*

were the very ones when Einstein developed the theories that broke the grip of Newton's laws on the physical world. In 1911 Rutherford demonstrated the molecular structure of the atom. Like nuclear fission, the fragmentation of the body was too potent a weapon to stay in a few hands. Eager practitioners sprang up far from Paris. United in iconoclastic fervor, these artists came under various banners: Vorticism in England, Primitivism in Germany, Futurism in Italy.

The young artists who called themselves the Futurists were in love with speed and all the manifestations of the mechanical age which they sensed was dawning. They celebrated it, in a characteristically twentieth-century way, by propaganda: an endless stream of bellicose manifestos.

They adopted the techniques of Cubism and allied them with the findings of multiple-exposure photography. The Futurists felt that Picasso by taking the object apart analytically had failed to experience it in action. They studied the motorcar "in order to be able to portray the essential force-lines of speed."[15] They promised to destroy museums, libraries, and academies of every kind and to fight feminism. They longed ardently for the ultimate hygiene of war. "Art and war are the great manifestations of sexuality; lust is their flower. We must strip lust of all the sentimental veils that disfigure it. Sentiment is a creature of fashion, lust is eternal. Lust triumphs, because it is the joyous exaltation that drives one beyond oneself, the delight in possession and domination, the headiest and surest intoxication of conquest."[16] Not surprisingly, they approved of night clubs, those temples to the elevation of masculine desire. Gino Severini's painting of the Bal Tabarin [246] has more kicks than most can-cans. Through the tossing, sequin-speckled skirts of the dancers, we can glimpse the whirl of hurrying waiters, overflowing glasses, laughing spectators, a jaundiced stage-door Johnny, and the object of his gaze descending from the ceiling on a castrating pair of giant scissors.

The Futurists were ecstatic over all forms of violence. "We will glorify war," they trumpeted, "militarism, patriotism, the destructive gesture of freedom-bringers, beautiful ideas worth dying for, and scorn for women."[17] The war to end war was one of those beautiful ideas, but its reality was closer to the *Apocalyptic Vision* of a German, Ludwig Meidner [247], whose premonitions drove him to a frenzy of prophetic paintings in 1912–13. In these two years Meidner, a thoughtful and not

very prolific artist who had lived in Paris, poured out an amazing forecast of the war that was to come. It is as though all the frantic rhythms of Futurism have shaken nature apart at the seams. Cities crumble, the earth explodes and writhes, catching naked humanity in its muddy coils.

In 1914 when the war came, the majority went to it eagerly; patriotic fervor, that almost universal subconscious urge to throw off the shackles

246. Severini, Dynamic Hieroglyphic of the Bal Tabarin, *1912.*

of the old worn-out centuries and systems of Europe that had brought the modern movements in art, led to a willing plunge into mass suicide, "like swimmers into cleanness leaping."[18]

In fact, one of the first things that struck troops fresh to the battlefield was the fearful stench of putrefaction. Continual artillery barrages kept disinterring the hastily disposed-of corpses. Every shell hole at Verdun had its ghastly stinking fragment of humanity. "Day after day the German heavies pounded the corpses . . . until they were quartered and requartered . . . Every square foot contained some decomposed piece of flesh: you found the dead embedded in the walls of trenches, heads, legs and half-bodies . . . Human entrails were to be seen dangling in the branches of a tree, and a torso without a head, without arms, without legs, stuck to the trunk of a tree, flattened and opened."[19] Here was the Analytic Cubism of reality.

The war involved the dragooning of mankind on an unprecedented scale. Not only were vast numbers killed; never had so many people grown accustomed to killing so many. In this it was a forecast of worse things to come. Huddled naked together under the watchful eye of uniformed authority, the young German soldiers having an enforced communal shower in Kirchner's painting of 1915 [248], strike an uneasy

248. Kirchner, Artillerymen in the Shower, 1915.

249. Dix, Souvenir of the Mirrored Halls in Brussels, *1920.*

resonance. Those sickly yellow forms packed close under the descending gaseous blue-green streams, the lounging jackboots—the painting is like a forecast of Auschwitz, even down to an open furnace door.

The First World War was the last all-male conflict. The maimed survivors returned to an indifferent world. In Germany their isolation, made more bitter by defeat, was limned in irony by social realists such as Otto Dix [249]. The fruits of sacrifice, as far as the common soldier was concerned, might be a pair of hobnailed boots and the memory of a few bottles of French champagne, a rose plucked from the hedgerows of Picardy, and the poxy embrace of a Belgian whore. The reflections of endless frowzy couplings, each different but all the same, echo around the painting like the mesmeric choruses in the cabaret songs of Brecht and Weill.

The desire to blot out the past and make a fresh start, disowning all the hypocrisy and cant that had led to the horrors of the war, was strong in artists. Out of a cabaret in Switzerland came Dada. It was defined by its monocled spokesman, Tristan Tzara, as an "art without bedroom slippers or parallels."[20] Dada was against the future. Its practitioners showed an appreciation of destruction that went so far as to provide an ax at an exhibition for the use of critical visitors. Tzara said progress could be defined as

Ideal, Ideal, Ideal
Knowledge, Knowledge, Knowledge
Boomboom, boomboom, boomboom[21]

Pretty soon Dada went boomboom itself, but its iconoclastic fervor continued to blow around the studios. One of its most talented exponents was a young German artist, Max Ernst. Brought up in a stuffily religious family, he told his father that he was Jesus when he was five years old. His father proceeded to paint him as the Christ child. Later the boredom of school in a convent, where the walls were embellished with the delicate bones and skulls of eleven thousand virgins who had given up their lives rather than their chastity led him to fantasize more bizarre presences. He had been a blond and curly-haired child, and perhaps his adult painting of a similar boy Jesus being chastised by his mother [250] is an unconscious act of self-punishment for his presumption in taking on that role himself. This painting was considered blasphemous

enough to get its place of exhibition closed in the 1920s. Later a priest pointed out to Ernst that it would have been even more sacrilegious if the lad had been whacked with his own fallen halo.

Observing the scene through the window are the piercing eyes of the artist, flanked by Paul Éluard and André Breton. The latter two were founder-members of surrealism, the most influential art movement between the wars. Almost all European artists were affected by it.

250. Ernst, The Virgin Spanking the Infant Jesus Before Three Witnesses, *1928.*

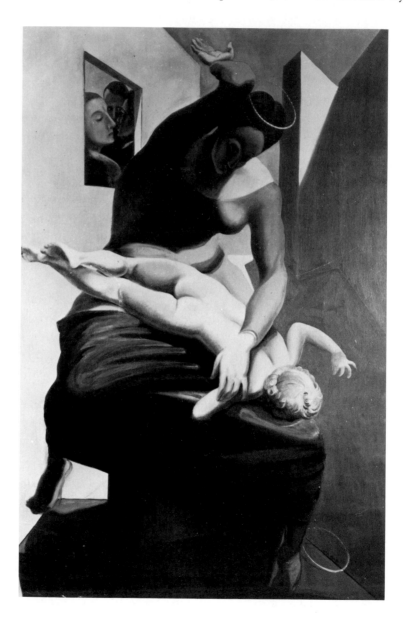

Reading the humorless, dense metaphysics of Breton makes this surprising, but surrealism was actually less a polemical platform than a bag containing most of the major preoccupations of the time. One was the desire to shock. Then there was the search for new insights. "We must remember that the idea of surrealism is directed merely to the total recovery of our psychic strength by a means which is no more than a vertiginous descent within us, the systematic illumination of hidden places and the progressive clouding of other areas, a perpetual excursion to absolutely forbidden territory," wrote Breton in his Second Manifesto.[22] How to plumb the depths? There were two principal methods: the recollection of dreams and their exploitation in art, and the use of semiautomatic forms of creation. Ernst drew on both. He was endlessly inventive. Primarily to him we owe built collage, where fragments of old prints are assembled to make a new image; frottage, produced by placing a paper or cloth over a rough surface and rubbing it with a pencil or brush; and dripping and spraying paint onto the canvas, a technique widely taken up by the American abstract expressionists after the war. The "novels without words," which he created by pasting together clippings from Victorian illustrations, are an imaginative *tour de force*.

Ernst also exploited the technique called decalcomania. Paint or ink applied to a surface is pressed against a further surface, which is then peeled off. In *The Robing of the Bride* [251] this process was used on the fanlike headdress on the right, and in the picture within a picture on the upper left. The painting as a whole seems to be an extension of the collage method which had produced the "novels." The addition of animal heads turned mundane engravings into scenes of nightmare danger. Here the feathered robes and masks both conceal and reveal their naked inmates, while the towering edifice in the center watches us with multiple eyes: a commanding pair glaring imperiously from either side of the beak; a slumberous pair in the gold mask above the breasts; and a single eye peering out anxiously from the feathers halfway between. Each figure seems to be in a different stage of metamorphosis from human to bird. Birds often appear to be harbingers of menace in Ernst's work. The revolting androgynous imp picking his/her nose on the tiled floor may relate the picture to an incident in 1906 when fifteen-year-old Ernst's pet cockatoo died. He had just found it when

251. Ernst, The Robing of the Bride, *1939.*

his father announced the birth of a sister. Ernst fainted, and "a series of mystical crises, fits of hysteria, exaltations and depressions followed."[23]

Looking for psychoanalytic explanations is usually legitimate with Surrealist artists. Seeking means to capture the transient, the submerged, the subversive, to portray what had never been seen in art and hardly imagined, it was natural that the Surrealists should be drawn to the theories of Freud and the study of psychopathology. Artists have always used configurations of form which have a compulsive attraction for them, but the Surrealists consciously sought means to dredge up their deepest obsessions. One way was the doodle, to do something and decide what it was afterward. Seldom since easel painting began can such a minimal notation as Joan Miró's bunch of curving lines [252] have been presented as a finished picture. Yet, like the prehistoric symbols on the walls of caves, these marks clearly suggest forms: in this case female forms. When, over the streaks and splashes of paint, a scribbled sentence is superimposed you have not only a title for the picture but a message about its content. *Oh! un de ces messieurs qui a fait tout ça* (Oh, One of Those Men Who's Done All That) suggests an overheard fragment of gossip. Overheard on the beach, in the street, in the theater? As with Ernst's collage novels, Miró leaves you to provide your own interpretation.

Like Picasso, Miró was a Spaniard, but his particular wit often makes his pictures seem lighter in vein. His intention was just as

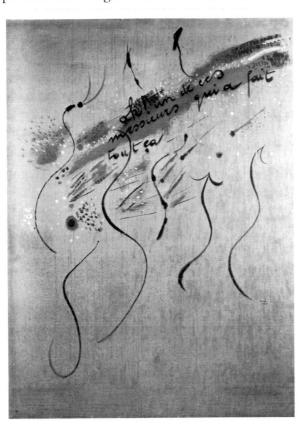

252. *Miró,* Oh! One of Those Men Who's Done All That, *1925.*

subversive though. His fragmented, notational style recalls the eye of an ironic and uninhibited infant. Children do not make logical connections between things and hence are less surprised by unordered events. Their view of things is undiluted by acquired conventions. Miró's pictures reflect this disturbing lack of a cohesive system; objects come in all sizes and unexpected shapes. They do not seem to respond to any known physical laws. It is said[24] that Einstein believed in a universe comprehensible to human reason, though why this should be so was the greatest mystery. Human reason, seeking order and system, is not necessarily able to encompass the infinitely more complex systems and different dimensions of a limitless universe. Humans tacitly recognize this in the acceptance of an element of luck in their lives— that is, of nonordered events that impinge on us memorably and often disastrously. Miró's forms accost us in this random and ambiguous way. His *Standing Woman* [253] is reduced to the crudest ovoids and yet

253. Miró, Standing Woman, *1937.*

254. Magritte, The Rape, *1934.*

exudes a truculent vitality. At first we tend to see the figure as immensely fat with a tiny head peering down at us from its surround of spiky hair. But it is possible to see this simply as a hairy topknot; the breasts then become eyes, the vestigial "arms" change to ears, and the rocklike form on which the woman appears to be poised becomes her body. Everything is always changing into something else in Surrealist art, as of course it is in a dream.

Freud tells us that dreams have their own logic and carry a personal message for us. What about art that has been made out of somebody else's inner compulsions? The Belgian artist René Magritte presents us with another shifting view of woman [254]. This grotesque masculine head is also a female body without a head. When we see that the title is *The Rape*, we assume that those bulging eyes belong to a male voyeur who mentally strips every attractive woman he meets. Then we notice that long feminine neck. Might not Magritte be suggesting that women who flaunt their attractions in men's faces are guilty of an act of mental rape on the poor, susceptible male? When he was thirteen Magritte's mother committed suicide by throwing herself into the River Sambre in the middle of the night. The next day the boy saw her body being brought back into the house, her head covered in a scarf. (Women with their faces concealed are a recurring theme in his pictures.) The long hair flows past the figure like water. The title suggests that his mother's self-inflicted injury to her own body was a form of rape; but perhaps another victim was the artist, who carried the memory of it in his head.

Magritte, like many Surrealists, produced titles that tease. In his comfortable bourgeois home in Belgium he had a reputation as a practical joker. His paintings often pose visual conundrums. *The Unattainable Woman* [255] stands naked, her hand clasping her bosom in a familiar gesture of modesty. She is outlined against a surface of stones. On this surface are a number of masculine hands. Quite separate,

255. Magritte, The Unattainable Woman, *1928.*

each severed at the wrist, they appear to be blindly searching for her. They increase our empathy with her gesture. One, palm upward, reminds us of the comfort of holding a warm human breast. The other hands are in fact pressing against rounded surfaces not dissimilar in shape and size to the female bosom. But they are only stones.

The Surrealist attitude toward love illustrates many of the contrary feelings that Freud encountered in his analysis of dreams. Witness this scene from Buñuel's film *Un Chien Andalou*.

A man pushes a woman against the wall of her room. They embrace feverishly. Their kisses are frantic. This is the "mad love" endorsed by the Surrealists. "Beauty will be convulsive or will not be at all," wrote Breton.[25] The man's hands seize the girl's breasts. Energetically his fingers knead their supple contours. The girl groans and sighs, while, squeezing and rubbing, the hands seem to be wearing away the tightly drawn wool of her jersey. It is as though the friction is making the fibers evaporate [256]. Now indeed he is holding naked breasts, splendid in the curves of their firm perfection. Firm? They are hard. They are the marble breasts of a statue.

256. Buñuel and Dali, still from film Un Chien Andalou, *1928.*

Breton explained that convulsive beauty, "would lose its whole meaning . . . if it were imagined as being in movement instead of in the exact expiration of this movement."[26] The work of art should present the same perfection, the same hardness, rigidity, regularity, and luster as a piece of crystal. But only in dreams can we imagine any pleasure in mingling with an adamantine lover. And only in art can we freeze such images.

Un Chien Andalou, one of the most brilliantly inventive films ever made, was created by two young Spaniards in 1928. Luis Buñuel and Salvador Dali had known each other since university days. Buñuel directed from the script Dali had written in a week. The famous image of the hand crawling with ants had come from one of Dali's dreams. He refined his art from his natural nervous hysteria. "I am living, controlled delirium . . . my genius resides in that double reality of my personality; the marriage at the highest level of critical intelligence and its irrational and dynamic opposite."[27] This he called his "paranoia." The French psychoanalyst Jacques Lacan had just made the term fashionable. It has been defined as a continuing systematic delirium of interpretation, which does not produce any lasting deterioration of the intellect. Dali believed it was general.

A frightened virgin at twenty-five, precociously clever, but racked with fits of nervous laughter, Dali spent a great deal of his time painting; "alone and naked in my bedroom, and it often happened that I would put my brush down so as to take my cock in the same hand and go from one pleasure to the other living through the same ecstacy."[28] The picture he was working on was *The Great Masturbator* [257]. The strange central shape is that of a massive rock at Cape Creus in northern Spain. Dali painted it several times. He was fascinated by its silent immobility confronting the turbulence of the waves. In the configuration of the stone Dali was able to see the "Great Masturbator" with "his huge nose, immense eyelids, a rock of strangeness the fascination of which still has the power of the Sphinx over me."[29] This bizarre phantom has hair but no mouth. Where it should be, crouches a giant grasshopper that is inseminating it. Since his childhood Dali had been fascinated and revolted by grasshoppers. Like rock, they have a rigid inflexible exterior. The thorax of this one is being eaten by a swarm of ants. Ants are also busily exploring a seam in the phantom. This shape manages

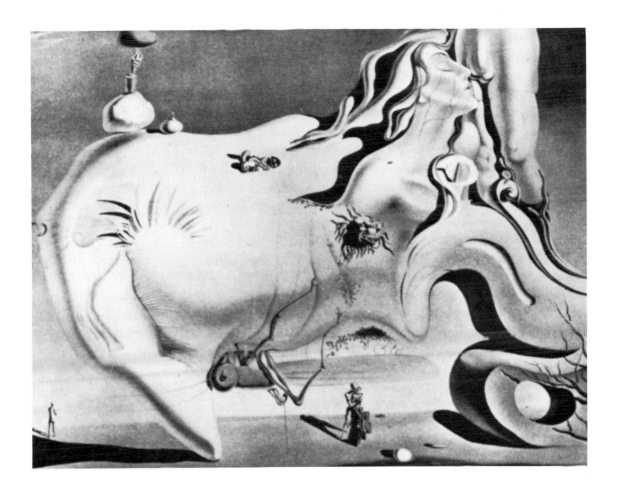

to be both hard and deliquescent at the same time, like a Camembert cheese that has run across a plate and then coagulated. Judging by the number of drooping surfaces, the Great Masturbator did not always have an easy task. But a woman's face is approaching that bundle of detumescent organs between the legs on the right.

In September 1929 Dali was painting in Cadaques, a fishing village in northern Spain, when he was visited by Magritte and Éluard and their wives. Paul Éluard, a poet and founder member of the surrealist movement, had only recently heard of Dali. *Un Chien Andalou*, his paintings, and wittily bizarre interpretations of his own eccentricities had given him an instant reputation. He in turn knew about Gala, Éluard's wife. At least ten years older than Dali, she had been in the movement since its inception and was thought clever, strong-willed,

257. Dali, The Great Masturbator, *1929.*

and promiscuous. Within days of this meeting they decided to stay together. And so they did, for the rest of their lives. It cannot always have been easy. In *The Great Masturbator* the male figure has no feet and has bloody scratches on his knees. The Mary Magdalene-like profile of Gala has below it a large flower, open, with its stamen confidently erect; but where the center of her body would be is the head of a lion. Surrounded by a hairy mane, its jaws are open to reveal large fangs and a powerful tongue. Dali has said that the lion's maw represents his fear that possession of a woman would lead to the revelation of his impotence.[30]

Gala was able to calm his anxieties and canalize them into fruitful work. She was his soul sister, his double, his lover, his business manager. Within a few years Dali became, and has remained, the best-known artist in the world after Picasso. He was on the cover of *Time* as early as 1936. His monstrous ego, his craftily organized craziness, his amazing, but often vulgar facility, the easily understood conventional styles in which he portrayed his unconventional subjects, his love of money, and his genius for publicity made him the ideal wild artist of the media age. None of this might have happened without Gala's steadying influence.

Marriage had the opposite effect on his fellow Spaniard Picasso. Unlike many of his friends Picasso took no part in the war. Designing costumes and backdrops for Diaghilev in Rome and London brought him into the top echelon of cultural society and a wife, Olga, who was a ballet dancer. In July to September 1918 when the last great battles were being fought on the Western Front, they were honeymooning in Biarritz at the home of a wealthy Chilean lady. Spain was neutral, so Picasso could not be blamed for not joining the orgy of destruction. Nevertheless it meant he had not directly experienced a trauma that had been the common lot of most of his contemporaries. Joining the international set was not a satisfactory substitute. Once more he was the brilliant outsider.

At nearly forty, in February 1921, he became a father for the first time. The domestic scene on the beach at Antibes [258] looks idyllic at first glance. However, the father appears remarkably youthful. Significantly, he has closed his eyes and turned his head away from his family. No wonder his son is poking him in the ear to get his attention. His mother puts out a heavy solicitous arm. She towers above the two

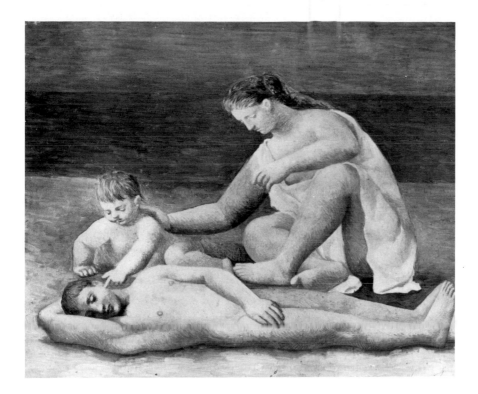

258. Picasso, Family at the Edge of the Sea, 1923.

males, bigger than both of them. The father's left hand seems placed less in a gesture of modesty than to protect his sex from his wife. Her attentive eye, grasping hand, and trampling foot all run down the central vertical axis of the picture immediately above his hidden organ. Such juxtapositions are rarely accidental in Picasso, one of the most autobiographical of painters.

He was bored with bourgeois conventions. Olga lived by them. Even his early loving portraits of her suggest a prim, unbending personality. He was soon doing other pictures much more ferocious. The elegant drawings of dancers that he had created in their first years together had led to massively classical bathers, pipe-playing men, and lumbering women. Just as before producing *Les Demoiselles d'Avignon* Picasso had become pregnant, so to speak, with heavy lumpish forms, [242] so these grossly conventional women metaphorically burst into the lean, virulent activity of *The Three Dancers* [259]. Outlined against the upright windows of a somber room with ugly formal wallpaper are three maenads unlike any seen on an antique frieze. If *Les Demoiselles* had led to the fragmentation of the body in Cubism, *The Three Dancers*

are a foretaste of new and even more savage excesses of distortion. Thus the ecstatic naked figure in the center has one eye which is only the line of the brow, while the other resembles the sexual orifice, which is not between her legs. The woman on the left throws herself backward so violently that, as in a multiple exposure, she appears to have at least four tossing breasts. She bares her teeth at us in a terrifying snarl; yet she also has in her forehead a profile of a calmly expectant crescent moon. This profile looks across the swirling figures to a face that is outlined in black against the window on the right. The whole painting is a knotted fist of compressed aggressive energy. Each serrated, contrary line is like a nail driven in hatred. In a famous interview Picasso said: "A picture used to be a sum of additions. In my case a picture is a sum of destructions."[31]

Picasso was expressing his rage and frustration at the whole monstrous regiment of women. He loved and feared them all his life, but now he was actually imprisoned by one. Divorce, under French law, would have demanded that he make impossible sacrifices in the ownership of his work; even the tools of his trade would have been deemed held in common with his wife. In one picture Picasso, reduced to a mere shadow, is literally being eaten up by a demon who manages to be absurd as well as all-devouring.

With time the Olga-monsters grow even more menacing [260]. Like Grendel's mother this giantess has just emerged from the watery depths, clacking her evil jaws, which are also two spiked fists. Her breasts have turned into well-filled punching gloves. Everything about the figure is hard, bony, and angular. With Lady Macbeth she would beseech the fates to take the milk from her woman's breasts for gall:

> *And fill me, from the crown to the toe, top-full*
> *Of direst cruelty!*[32]

Along with Olga's implacable gentility went a strong streak of jealousy. She continued to try to interfere in Picasso's affairs long after they eventually separated, and at the end of her life was still crazily grasping for his attention. She had plenty to make her jealous. In January 1927 Picasso picked up a seventeen-year-old schoolgirl on a Paris street. Within a week Marie-Thérèse Walter was his mistress. Her blond Scandinavian looks and youthfully lazy body generated the

259. Picasso, Three Dancers, *1925.*

260. Picasso, Seated Bather, *1929.*

most powerfully erotic creations of his life. No longer is it simply lust and aggression. Some sculptured heads, while clearly representing Marie-Thérèse, intermingle male and female sexuality into a magic totem of replete sensuality [37].

Several of the great series of paintings Picasso made of Marie-Thérèse in 1932 show her in front of a mirror. Her sleeping form is divided, but brought together like the reciprocal circles, the yin and yang, of Taoist philosophy [261]. Thus are the opposites, mental and physical, rational and sensual, male and female, dark and light, reconciled. Her dreaming head, wrapped in the memory of the body's pleasures, must have hoped it would be so with her and her fearsomely gifted and demanding lover.

If the 1920s had been for artists the decade of the child, with its rediscovery of childish pursuits—squiggles and rubbings and paper cutouts—and childish preoccupations—fantasies and dreams and nightmares—so the thirties might be characterized as belonging to youth. Youth, with its aspirations, idealism, and impetuosity: youth was in the

261. Picasso, The Mirror, *1932.*

air, bridging the continents in pioneering solo flights; youth was climbing mountains and holding great rallies. Youth was visible to itself as never before, dancing and singing across the silver screen. Youth could also be manipulated and assaulted. It was a common theme in European fiction at the time. Sexual experience should be pushed to the limits, so that it entered the territory of sacrilege, something that the surrealists with their antireligious fervor, regarded as a sacred duty.

Thus the young painter Balthus, when a new model presented herself at his Paris studio in 1933, leaped at her with a knife in his hand and tried to rip off her blouse. Fifteen years old and well brought up, she was horrified. He proceeded to record her reactions. He was an assiduous draftsman, who returned again and again to favorite themes. Many involve adolescent girls in scenes of brooding eroticism. In *The Guitar Lesson* of 1934 a child is thrown over the knee of a mature woman, who seems about to carry out some form of sexual initiation. The young victim lies back like a mesmerized rabbit, already half opened up. The preliminary drawings make clear it was the supine widespread posture which fascinated Balthus. Such a provocative subject ensured that the picture was shown in a private room when Balthus had his first exhibition in Paris in 1934; it was not included in his major retrospective at the Metropolitan Museum in 1984; and its present owner prohibited its reproduction in this book.

We can see a somewhat similar abandoned pose in *The Nude with a Cat* [262] which Balthus painted fifteen years later. Her sensuously playful gesture toward the feline and her decorously raised right leg make the model appear less helpless than the girl in *The Guitar Lesson*. Yet, despite the golden light from the window with which Balthus caresses her skin, the object of her languid gaze seems dangerously large and irritable for a family playmate.

Balthus frequently introduces such notes of menace into his claustrophobic interiors. *Cathy Dressing* [263] is based on an incident in *Wuthering Heights*. In Emily Brontë's novel Heathcliff finds Cathy dressed in a silk gown ready to receive her suitor, Edgar Linton. This scene of hidden Victorian jealousies is turned into a provocative striptease. Cathy flaunts her body brazenly in front of the glowering Heathcliff, who is transformed from the Romantic spirit of nature into the Oxford bags and bow tie fashionable for a man-about-town in the 1930s. Indeed he is a portrait of the artist and Cathy is his future wife, Antoinette de

Watteville. But there is nothing straightforwardly sensuous about this meeting; both protagonists seem wrapped in a private mood of smoldering anger and controlled erotic violence.

262. *Balthus,* The Nude with a Cat, *1949.*

An ironic acceptance in his art of sadomasochism and of sexual attraction as an ultimate form of alienation makes Balthus (who was born of Polish parents Balthasar Klossowski) an important minor figure of this disaffected decade. The writer Antonin Artaud, who was a friend of the painter's, defined a picture by Balthus as an invitation to lovemaking that had something cruel and dangerous in it. Artaud himself was looking for an art that took risks. He and Balthus were involved in creating a theater that would involve famous historical and mythological figures performing extraordinary deeds. The Theatre of Cruelty did not, in fact, materialize. No matter, it was already by this

263. Balthus, Cathy Dressing, *1933.*

time, 1935, being laid down, on an infinitely vaster scale, in Germany. Nazi propaganda films triumphantly marshaled the gullible human will as never before. Artists since the beginning of the century had evoked the power of primitive gods and destructive emotions to reenergize their work; Hitler, a failed artist, managed it on a national scale. Once let out, these forces were hard to put back in the box. They were brewing and seething throughout the thirties. They affected all the arts in most parts of the West.

As early as 1928, Picasso had created a new analogy for the human form: a series of drawings of creatures made of stone, and bones and bits of flotsam washed up on the Normandy shore [264]. Perhaps it was a way of adequately disguising the voluptuous presence of his schoolgirl lover from the awareness of his jealous wife. Perhaps it was just another example of his extraordinary fecund eye, which could turn anything he picked up into a fresh aesthetic experience. At the time he said he thought of them as a series of monuments. Monuments to what? Looking back at them across the gulf of such Nazi slaughter grounds as Babi Yar and those other valleys of bones which were shortly to rift humanity they seem prophetic.

In 1936, that other perversely brilliant Spaniard, Dali, produced his own premonition of disaster [265]. Hollow centered, a collection of rotting bones and grappling hands, propped precariously on what might be an outside lavatory, it is a fearsome image of self-destruction. Dali, a master of twitchy self-love and loathing, catches vividly the incom-

264. Picasso, Design for a Monument, *1928.*

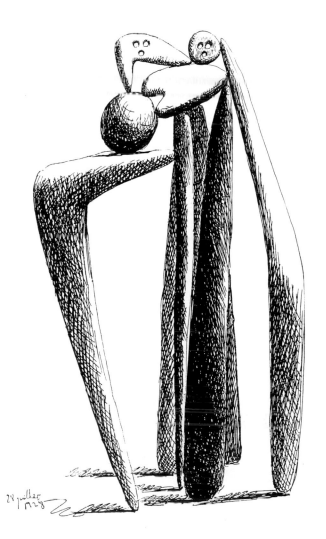

prehension, frustration, anger, and pain that the individual feels when the times are out of joint. His protagonist grimaces blindly at the sky. His arms grow from his hip. One hand squeezes a red inflamed breast; the other scrabbles out impotently on the earth. One leg looms lopsidedly out of a shoulder. A foot, apparently severed, presses upward against the creature's buttocks. Despite its provocative title, *Soft Construction with Boiled Beans*, and Dali's usual obsession with coprology, demonstrated by the shiny great turd that drapes unwholesomely over a thigh, the figure has a dreadful relevance.

Dali's own views on politics ran counter to those of many artists of the time. He favored Franco. He endorsed Hitler. When his fellow surrealists protested, he declared in his defense that his paintings were a transmission of dreams which, according to the surrealists' own manifesto, must under no circumstances be censured or controlled.

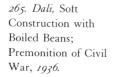

265. Dali, Soft Construction with Boiled Beans; Premonition of Civil War, *1936.*

What if he dreamed of Hitler? He had every right to paint his own visions! Breton, who had with difficulty swallowed Dali's preoccupation with shit, gagged on the Nazi dictator. Dali left the Surrealist movement.

The Surrealists had been right to recognize the prescience of their favorite author, Lautréamont. He had extolled a world of unbridled appetite. But when it happened it was not literature. The future was neither an enchanted playground nor a psychiatric clinic. As the thirties grew older the sense of approaching evil became more tangible. Few concretized it as accurately as an advertising agent turned artist, Hans Bellmer. A German opposed to the Nazis, with a sickly wife and a passion for his teenage cousin who lived with them, Bellmer released his feelings, which were always uncomfortably complex, by making dolls. Photographed, these sad waifs seem a forecast of the debauch of innocence that was to come [266]. Like the dolls, the human body was going to be dismembered, defiled, gassed, suffocated, starved, incinerated. Scenes as unreal as any surrealist dream became commonplace. They are unloading the trains at Auschwitz. Several men "are carrying a small girl with only one leg. They hold her by the arms and the one leg. Tears are running down her face and she whispers faintly: "Sir, it hurts, it hurts . . ." They throw her on the truck on top of the corpses. She will burn alive along with them."[33]

Torment has returned to earth much as it was imagined in medieval visions of Hell. Even this has been portrayed. Among the millions who passed through the Nazi camps were many artists. Some were able to record in ink, rust, blood, or soot what they saw [267]. The Polish communist who sketched the emaciated bodies of the new arrivals at Buchenwald wrote: "The first breaking of a human being depended on brutally stripping clothing off one's body, which began in the first hours of our arrival in the camp and ended with a pile of naked corpses near the crematorium."[34]

Making pictures was an affirmation of humanity; their possession could mean torture or death. The arbitrariness of such punishment was one of the ways to dehumanize the prisoner. The aim was to reduce him to the level of a terrified animal. The courage involved in the act of drawing the terrible scenes he witnessed was an assertion of his will to survive as a coherent individual.

It was the opposite of the impulses of the modern movements in art at the beginning of the century. Then artists had invoked primitive emotions, destructive violence. The artists were striving for more freedom and fresh styles of expression. Society was moved by broadly similar impulses. The exploitation of the human ego, its private fantasies and individual whims, carried art into new heights of self-assertion which were promptly dwarfed by the monstrous manias of Hitler and his fellow dictators.

In the contest between freedom and authority that has been raging throughout this century it was inevitable that the artist should assert his right to freedom and equally certain that he would lose. He has been like a child playing among the ruins caused by his adversary, the authority which actually created the scenes the artist only dared to imagine.

"Mankind which in Homer's time was an object of contemplation for the Olympian gods, now is one for itself. Its self-alienation has

266. Bellmer, The Doll, *1934.*

reached such a degree that it can experience its own destruction as an aesthetic pleasure of the first order."[35] Those prophetic words were written by the German critic Walter Benjamin in 1936, the year London began broadcasting the world's first television service. Half a century later we have all experienced their truth.

In 1945 the other major technological achievement of our time, in physics, ended the war with a bang that has reverberated ever since. It temporarily blasted the human figure off the fashionable easels of Western painters. Abstract expressionism metaphorically gave us a world swept clean of man. Yet humanity is a resilient mammal. He and she have started to pop up again, sometimes in mutant forms. The story of the body in art is not yet over.

267. Konieczny, New Arrivals at Buchenwald, *1945.*

10

SOMETHING RICH AND STRANGE

Her feet must have left their shadow on the dewy grass. Each bare toe deep imprinted, showing the pressure of her running. She was fleet and slender as befits a mountain nymph, daughter of a river. Like a flicker of late moonlight she fled through the gardens, her naked limbs pale as the sun rising through the Roman mists. To no avail. She could feel his hot breath on her shoulder, gathering strength, rising triumphantly to envelop her. Already her hair, flying backward in her speedy flight, was brushing the sun-god's cheek. The mighty Apollo was upon her. He loved her; but he was a hard male god, cold and rational, cruel despite his long infatuation and pursuit. She belonged to the old order, was a priestess of Mother Earth. As his strong arm went around her she cried out to Mother Earth and her plea was answered:

> Her limbs grew numb and heavy, her soft breasts
> Were closed with delicate bark, her hair was leaves,
> Her arms were branches, and her speedy feet
> Rooted and held, and her head became a tree top,
> Everything gone except her grace, her shining[1]

So the nature spirit, harried by skeptical reason, lapsed back into the tree from which gullible humanity had first summoned her. Yet the new god did not forget her. After all, he needed to command the allegiance from mankind that had been her due.

268. Bernini, Apollo and Daphne, *1622–25.*

Apollo loved her still. He placed his hand
Where he had hoped and felt the heart still beating
Under the bark; and he embraced the branches
As if they still were limbs, and kissed the wood,
And the wood shrank from his kisses, and the god
Exclaimed: "Since you can never be my bride,
My tree at least you shall be! Let the laurel
Adorn, henceforth, my hair, my lyre, my quiver:
Let Roman victors, in the long procession,
Wear laurel leaves for triumph and ovation.[2]

Changes in custom and belief can take centuries, or they can come with the speed of a confrontation on the road to Damascus. Such was the transformation of Daphne into the laurel. That breathless instant while she is still mouthing a call for help which has already been answered is the one Gianlorenzo Bernini chose to carve [268]. Daphne is poised between two existences. From the tips of her toes sprouting roots to her outstretched fingers bursting into leaf, she is already a part of the vegetable world. Yet her long hair is still a-twirl from the sudden twists of her head in response to the touch of Apollo's restraining hand. Bernini is said to have thought he never equaled that effect of lightness. In the inanimate marble he had to show the urgency of human flight burgeoning into rooted growth. Contrary impulses in one statue suggesting both the earlier surge and the future ebb; hard to achieve in the flexible, malleable clay modeling that leads to bronze; more difficult in the irreversible reductions of carving.

Bernini's statue represents a triple metamorphosis. The achievement of the artist turns stone into a paradigm for living flesh. Then there is the transmutation of Daphne in the story from human form to arboreal. Finally there is the immense modification of belief that the myth personifies; the relinquishing of the primitive animism which saw spirits in all the natural elements of woodland, mountain, and river that surrounded early man, for the ordered hierarchy of superior deities. Historically, this metaphysical change must have followed the development of society into cities. Where and how this first occurred we do not know, except that it must have been in the millennia of the neolithic revolution when humanity turned in the temperate zones from hunting and gathering to herding and planting. It was the greatest change mankind has encompassed until modern times.

Now we feel ourselves to be embarked on another revolutionary journey. The impetus signaled in the Renaissance, crucially energized by the industrial and social upheavals of the last two hundred years, is whisking us along at an ever-increasing tempo. Technology is changing the texture of our lives from decade to decade. It is as though the two million years that climaxed in the cave paintings witnessed the infancy of man and woman when he and she took their first tottering steps, naked in a hostile world. From the building of Çatal Hüyük to the destruction of Hiroshima was a childhood full of discoveries, the playing out of many fairy tales, tantrums, and dreams, the learning of a host of skills. Now technology has presented us with a key to our own vehicle; like the adolescent allowed to drive the family car, for the first time we are in charge of our own destiny, able to destroy ourselves if we do not behave in a mature manner.

As we all know, adolescence is a dangerous period. The physical changes in our bodies are often mirrored by crucial developments in personality. Along with these hormonal modifications our view of everything undergoes a subtle metamorphosis. Nothing is as it was. Nor in our heart of hearts do we have any certainty that we shall be able to handle the adult future. Trying to decipher what it might bring, we feel like the children we were yesterday. We wish we could return to the parental protection that at least gave us a spurious comfort. Yet there is an excitement at the thought of total immersion in a new and, perforce, more responsible life. We cannot imagine what rewards, what fresh sensations and experiences, will engulf us.

> *Of his bones are coral made;*
> *Those are pearls that were his eyes;*
> *Nothing of him that doth fade,*
> *But doth suffer a sea-change*
> *Into something rich and strange.*[3]

Metamorphosis, the transformation of a character's personality and appearances, was a common theme in the plays of Shakespeare, and with other writers and artists of the Renaissance. In Bernini's statue,

Daphne calls forth a change in her nature under the stress of an immediate threat. It is not surprising that in a much more universally threatening environment modern artists have also sought to portray the human body in various new guises and metaphors. In earlier periods they were able to draw on generally accepted beliefs and a common artistic vocabulary to illustrate them. The first half of the century demolished much of the old order, and left artists to find their individual way. The painters and sculptors in this chapter do not adhere to groups or movements (though sometimes different individuals have been labeled with a particular fashionable "ism"). They have evolved their own interpretation of the human predicament, and they have done it for most of this period against the tide of fashion, which for the thirty years after the Second World War ran strongly for various forms of abstract art.

The image of the body has been banished before in times of great change, particularly under the pressure of new and masculine-oriented religions, Muslim and Protestant. The twentieth century move to abstraction was not overtly religious, though its supporters claimed to be purifying art by removing the worn-out images of earlier times. To many this seemed the logical conclusion of the iconoclastic impulses of the first half of the century.

The dominance of paint and feeling over form and content was first established in America. It coincided with the dropping of the atomic bomb and the emergence of the United States as the world's most powerful nation. Such a role was difficult for a republican democracy to play at a time when the old colonial powers of Europe were, more or less painfully, disentangling themselves from their former possessions. American ambivalence at stepping into the vacuum thus created was perfectly portrayed in the vast canvases of abstract expressionism. Paint was often handled with unprecedented violence but the gestures were in a void [269]. On the walls of museums and public buildings these grandiose paintings proclaimed the energy and power of the West, but tactfully omitted the context in which it might be unleashed.

To the masses of mankind the prime personification of America remains not a splatter of paint but the moving pictures of its celluloid heroes. Even here, as the century draws toward its final decade, and the wide screen yields to the multifarious images of video, fairy tales and nightmares dominate, ambiguity proliferates. Like children's toys, muscle men can mutate into machines, robots have feelings, humanoids with interchangeable features abound.

Similar metamorphoses are visible in many of the works of those major artists who have continued to labor with the body. It is as though in this restless world, where universal values are no longer immediately apparent, a simple affirmation of humanity is not usually sufficient. Like the pavement huckster, the artist's creation needs to juggle several appearances at once to hold the attention. In the last forty years artists have attempted this sleight-of-hand in various ways, pressing the body into some strange molds.

Nothing could be further from the lunging, breathless verisimilitude

269. De Kooning, Suburb in Havana, 1958

of Bernini than the motionless, attenuated female figures the Swiss artist Alberto Giacometti created in the 1940s to 1960s. Naked, their hands by their sides, standing stiffly erect, they seem at first sight sentinels or guardians of some secret [270]. They hold us with their gaze, which seems to contain an accusation. However we shift our position it follows us around the room. At the same time, like sentinels or guardians, they are not approachable. When we get near they keep their distance, holding us at bay with that level regard. If we get within

270. Giacometti,
Standing Woman I,
1960.

271. *Giacometti,* The Glade, *1950.*

arm's length they relapse into shafts of roughly worked bronze. The personality that held and returned our glance is inviolate, its essence beyond our grasp. If we do seize a figure it is only a stick of metal that we hold. It has none of the tactile resemblance to a human thigh or shoulder that gives poignance to Bernini's Daphne even while she is turning into a laurel.

Giacometti's women also have an affinity to trees. Their relatively broad bases seem like the spread of roots. One group is even called *The Forest.* Another is *The Glade* [271]. Giacometti grew up in a village in the Italian part of Switzerland. These figures remind us of pines grouped on a mountainside. Often such trees seem to have a human presence. Lonely yet dignified, below the crest of a high ridge, enduring the buffets of harsh weather, together yet apart in a way that deciduous trees, with their spreading welcoming branches, are not. Nor do conifers react to the seasons in the obvious way that leaf-shedding trees do. They endure till they die.

There is a terrible loneliness in Giacometti's figures. They seem to epitomize the alienation of the existential years that followed the end of the war. A philosophy evolved in its most fashionable form by Jean-Paul Sartre in occupied France, it naturally put responsibility for actions on the individual. In a defeated country, invested by a ruthless enemy, its citizens divided against themselves into those who favored resistance and those who collaborated, it was foolish to trust anyone. Nor was it easy to know what was right. Sartre universalized this predicament by saying that man is free to choose, but cannot know what will be the result of his decision. Yet, like the woman presented by the German commandant with the option of choosing which of her sons was to be executed and which spared, there is no opting out of making a choice. If she had made no choice both would have died. In life, not to choose is itself a choice and will have equally inevitable, but unforeseeable consequences. Hence the absurdity of liberty.

For Sartre, hell is other people. We cannot stop them impinging on our view of the world and modifying it. Giacometti's women seem to be guarding their space from us. We have all experienced that uncomfortable sensation of entering a prohibited aura, when we have stepped unwittingly into a private conversation at a social gathering. The glances freeze us out, warn us that we are entering forbidden territory. "The fact of other people is uncontestable, and strikes one to the heart. I realise it in terms of *discomfort*—I am perpetually *in danger* from them."[4]

And in the war the danger was real. This girl [272] standing tense and naked with her hair flowing over her shoulders might not only be a judge but a victim. Giacometti's figures are monuments to the ultimate in human vulnerability and courage. They are distanced from us by the burial trench which they have just dug and on the edge of which they stand. The distance gives them anonymity; it is better for the executioner not to know his target. As human beings we are all implicated in the mass crimes of our time. Yet we are impotent to change them. Even our grief is useless. In the existentialist view we cannot take on the suffering of others. All we can feel is guilt at the sight of another's unhappiness.

Not that Giacometti viewed his work in such terms. Some of the figures are based on confrontations he had in brothels. Several groups represent the line of prostitutes on parade before a would-be customer. In one group [273] the women are standing on a base taller than themselves, which in turn is on a tall bronze stand. The effect is to make them seem infinitely distant. Of them Giacometti wrote: "Several naked women seen at the Sphinx while I was seated at the end of the room. The distance which separated us (the polished floor) and which

272. Giacometti, Standing Woman, *1959.*

seemed insurmountable in spite of my desire to cross it, impressed me as much as the women."[5] He made these notes for the critic David Sylvester, with whom I made a film about Giacometti in 1962. Over lunch one day, Giacometti remarked that whenever he saw a naked woman his impulse was to fall down and worship. Perhaps it is this that gives his female figures their inviolate, noumenal presence.

273. Giacometti, Four Figurines on a Tall Stand, *1950.*

He is the only artist I have filmed who has continued his work and his life absolutely regardless of the presence of foreign technicians. He had occupied the same small studio in the rue Hippolyte Maindron in Paris since 1927. Next to it across a courtyard was the bed/sitting-room in which he lived. During the day it was used as an office by his brother Diego, who looked after all his affairs. Giacometti rose toward noon, completed his ablutions, got some money from his brother, stuffed the notes loose in his pocket, and went around the corner to eat in a neighboring restaurant. Here he would meet friends, and invariably treat them. He had the open-handed generosity of someone now well-off, who had known many frugal years. He was sixty, a tousled, limping figure. His strong face still had something of his peasant ancestry about it, though riven with introspective cares.

Getting back to the studio soon after two o'clock, he would immediately start sculpting and continue virtually without stopping until the light failed in mid-evening (we were there in May). The studio, thick in clay dust, was cluttered with plaster casts, abandoned armatures, small maquettes, plastic bags of gray clay, buckets full of rags, and half-finished sculptures wrapped in cloth like Egyptian mummies. There was a strong smell, as Giacometti sometimes urinated into the buckets and then forgot to empty them. He was working from memory on several figures and a portrait bust. Unwinding the cloths, which had kept one of them damp and malleable, he revealed a thin upright form. To our untutored eyes, apart from being in soft clay it looked as complete as the two or three bronzes in the studio. Giacometti attacked it with rapid fingers, paring it down and simultaneously rebuilding it. His hands moved from top to base and quickly returned to the head. In two or three minutes it would be completely remade. He would turn the figure ninety degrees and address the profile. Once again the head would be reconstituted, only to suffer further reworking when returned to the frontal position. From time to time his hands flickered down the whole figure, plucking a bit from here, pushing up a curve there. He said he wished to make figures as rounded as Marilyn Monroe but under his fingers they grew thin. Very occasionally he would sit back on a stool smoking a cigarette and regarding what he had done intently. Then the obsessive restructuring would begin again. After a while and for no obvious reason he would return the figure to its damp cloths and start on the next. The same pattern of continual reworking was repeated.

Giacometti said his aim was merely to complete a likeness; something he had been struggling to do since 1935. Scale had always bothered him even earlier when he was creating imaginary structures under the influence of the surrealists. In working on figures from memory he found to his alarm that they got smaller and smaller. Sometimes they were only an inch high. "They became so minuscule that often with a final stroke of the knife they disappeared into dust."[6] After some years he got married, and began to make larger figures. To his surprise, "only when long and slender were they like."[7] But he never felt he had been able to render appearance truthfully enough. He actually saw people across the street as tiny; when close they filled the whole visual field. In this mutable world how could he create a stable presence? So he labored incessantly. It was Diego who decided when a figure was ready for casting.

In the evening Giacometti would wash and go out to eat. Usually at this time a tour of brothels followed. He would return with a girl. She would appear from the bedroom the next day like a sleepy young cat, wander around in silent surprise, and eventually disappear. These female visitants seemed separate from Giacometti's daytime preoccupations, but perhaps an acknowledgment of their presence emerged in his sculpture. Within their slender proportions a number of the figures are unexpectedly voluptuous [274]. Given Giacometti's obsession with the gaze, it is tempting to infer that the unstated motive of his quest was for a true contact with the other, something the existentialists said was impossible and which he clearly found difficult. The frenzied reworking of the upright clay suggests that the figures are monuments to male as well as female loneliness. Arboreal spirits, guardians of the secret, goddesses, symbols of the alienation of contemporary city life, victims, challenging but vulnerable, courageous but apart: whatever way we look at them these sticks of bronze seem epitaphs to our time.

Ambiguities reverberate through the work of another sculptor who concentrated on the female form, Henry Moore. He too was born in a small northern town. His father was a Yorkshire coal miner, a breed of men as proud and independent as Afghan tribesmen. They also have a strong sense of responsibility to the community. Henry Moore demonstrated all these qualities. In art, he drew ideas out of widely

274. Giacometti,
Standing Woman,
1957.

differing cultures, primitive and classical. Among individuals, Picasso was a powerful influence.

Moore collected natural objects, and made many drawings and sculptures inspired by them. "Although it is the human figure which interests me most deeply, I have always paid great attention to natural forms, such as bones, shells, and pebbles . . . There are universal shapes to which everyone is subconsciously conditioned and to which they can respond if their conscious does not shut them off."[8] Moore's sculpture makes us aware of these correspondences. The reclining woman is also a cave or a cliff or a hillside. He wanted sculpture that had "something

275. *Moore,* Drawing of Seated Figure, *1933.*

of the energy and power of great mountains."[9] Even a life drawing can suggest a weight and scale out of proportion to the model's true size [275]. The strongly outlined shins and feet are like the near foothills, the breasts are the central glacis already hazy with distance, while the far peak of the head looms shiftily through the drifting cloud.

Giacometti's drawings of the nude seem eaten into by the surrounding atmosphere (an impression increased by his habit of rubbing out and partially smearing the outlines). His sculptures are thin pylons still giving out a message through their eyes, but otherwise revealing no sign of life. Moore's figures sprawl across the landscape, dominating it by a rugged inner force [276]. At their grandest they have the inevitability of the earth's contours. Yet like the natural lie of the land, they constantly reveal new aspects, fresh relationships. Moore's figures do

276. Moore, Two-Piece Reclining Figure No. 1, *1959.*

not have the piercing tension of Giacometti's but they do have a majestic certainty that gives them great emotional strength.

Moore's temperament was an exceptional mixture of robust confidence and an almost feminine delicacy of perception, making it seem inevitable that he emphasized the harmonies rather than the discords of nature. Yet a power in his work is the way it encompasses contrary elements that break through, almost one feels against the grain of the sculptor's intentions. Walking slowly around his larger works can produce revelations as exciting as flying low past outcrops of rock along a craggy seacoast. Thus it is possible to see the two-piece reclining figure as some water spirit, surging upward like a kraken from the vasty deeps, her leg already thrown upward for an encompassing bound into another element; but from a different angle this rearing shape takes on an opposing character [277]. It becomes an enormous male

277. Moore, Two-Piece Reclining Figure No. 1, *1959.*

278. *Moore,* Reclining Figure, *1939.*

form rising to menace the feminine part, which seems to be falling away before it.

Male and female are often present together in Moore's work, or they are different aspects of the same figure. Perhaps it is this reconciling use of natural shapes to bind together contraries that gives the sculptures their universal appeal. In his early career, like Michelangelo and Bernini, he preferred carving in stone; he felt it was being more true to the material than modeling in clay or plaster and then casting the result in bronze. He also made some powerful carvings in wood. "Wood has to come from a living tree, to be alive in order to carve it. You use different tools and the way wood splits is different from stone as well."[10] One of the most impressive of his reclining figures came from a piece of elm he got in Canterbury before the war [278]. "It was for me my most 'opened out' wood carving—you can look from one end to the other through the series of tunnels."[11]

In figures such as this the eye travels through the shining smooth ovoids like a speleologist exploring a series of magic wooden caves. The whorls of the natural grain echo the rhythms of the carving. The

279. *Moore,* Reclining Figure, *1939.*

280. *Moore,* Reclining Mother and Child, *1960–61.*

281. *Moore,* Reclining Mother and Child, *1960–61.*

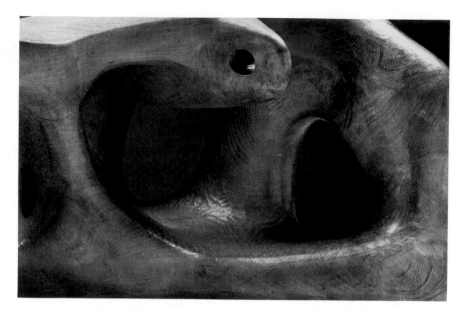

uterine connotation of the hollowed form is obvious but the effect is not at all sexual. Rather it is enveloping, a burrowing back into primal matter. In the midst of the figure is another; a lizard or snakelike shape rearing forward where a child's head might be [279]. Its suggestion is overwhelmingly masculine and alien despite the fact of it growing out of the reclining form. There is a sinewy tension here that belies the calm repose of the female. If such secondary figures are children, then they seem replete with the original sin in which we are all said to be born.

One of the most compelling of these dual forms was created in bronze over twenty years later than the elmwood figure [280]. Moore had come to think that to do nothing but carving was a restriction. The vision behind the work was what mattered, not the material. He called this piece *Reclining Mother and Child,* and indeed the larger shape laps around the smaller as the pelvis cups the womb. That analogy comes to mind because the smaller shape appears too primal to carry a fully human connotation. These flowing forms bring reminders of many animals: a seal and her pup, even a horse and foal lying down. It is a more opened-out figure than many, yet it seems brimming with contained significance. Every aspect yields a powerful nuance. "The child-form is powerfully ambiguous—at once explosively aggressive and a blunt huddled baby animal. The mother appears from the front to be nursing it, retaining it, from the back to be giving birth, expelling it."[12] [281]

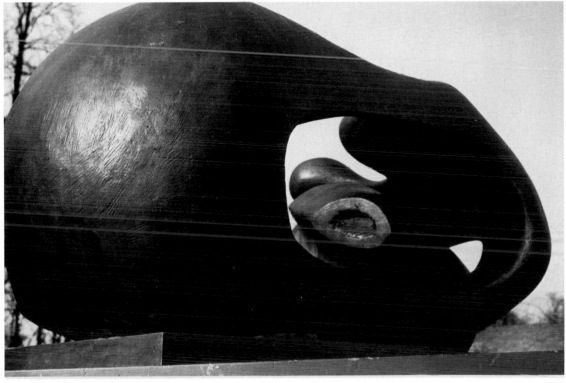

Pregnancy, the most radical metamorphosis the human body experiences until death, has seldom been commemorated until recent years and then, significantly, mostly by women artists. A painter who portrayed the gravid figure with exceptional candor was the American Alice Neel. One of her most perceptive studies is of her daughter-in-law [282]. She shows the taut smoothness of the swollen belly, like a giant orange, dominating body and psyche; the pressured ribs, engorged nipples, skinny arms, entwined legs, and flabby bottom, all waiting to play their part. Above the head of the couch and behind his wife is a portrait of Neel's son, the prospective father, a ghostly presence, absent but visible, not only on the wall but in her stomach. He broods over her as, wherever he might be, a husband tends to do during the last days of his wife's confinement. But she is not looking at him. Her eyes are abstracted; her mind drifting across the waters of her inner life.

Neel led a bohemian early life, losing two of her own children tragically, and moving through a number of turbulent relationships. She never lost her sympathy with those she painted. The exceptional

282. Neel, The Pregnant Woman, *1971.*

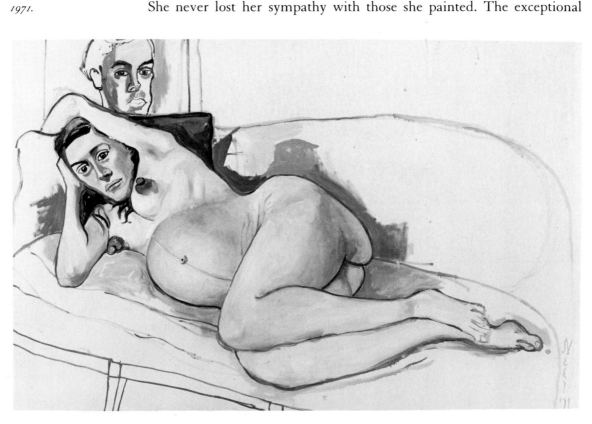

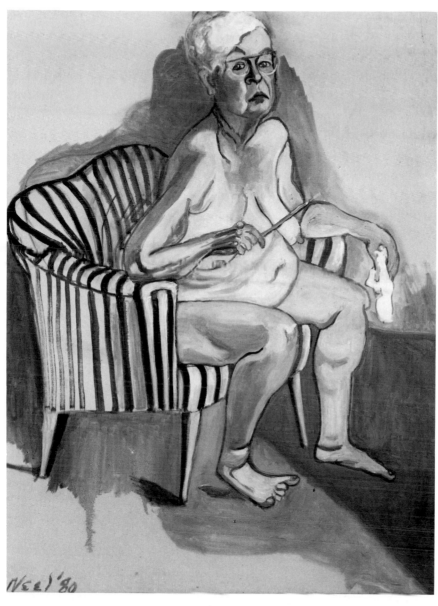

283. Neel, Self-Portrait, 1980.

sensitivity, which as a child made her cry over the story of Christ's wounds, allowed her to empathize with all her subjects irrespective of age or gender. We feel that Neel has understood what it costs to live inside that particular skin. In her final self-portrait [283] she put down the bent toes, the sagging lines of her own eighty-year-old body. It was painted in 1980, the year after she received a special award for outstanding achievement in art from the President, Jimmy Carter. She shows the

284 Kahlo, What the Water Gave Me, *1939.*

strength of will that gave her the courage to work so long unrecognized and against the tide of abstract fashion; but she does not conceal that she might be a bit of a tartar to live with.

Aging is a form of continual metamorphosis that we all have to undergo. Often its changes are wrought so imperceptibly that we are unable to pinpoint when they occurred. Not so with disasters, when the body is violently modified from without. When she was sixteen Frida Kahlo was traveling by bus across her native Mexico City when the vehicle collided with a street car. Her right leg, pelvis, and backbone were shattered. A steel rail skewered her at the level of the abdomen. Looking down on her, her companion (who was only bruised) saw that "Frida was totally nude. The collision had unfastened her clothes. Someone in the bus, probably a house painter, had been carrying a packet of powdered gold. This package broke, and the gold fell all over the bleeding body of Frida. When people saw her they cried, 'La bailarina, la bailarina!' With the gold on her red, bloody body, they thought she was a dancer."[13] Over thirty operations, bone grafts, resettings, clamps, and corsets led eventually at the age of forty-six, to the amputation of her leg, an operation she did not long survive.

Often having to paint from her bed, her life and art confined to the personal, to the portrayal, and transcendence, of her suffering, her experience seems an ironic metaphor for the historic role that masculine society has inflicted on women. She was able to marry a hero of her childhood, the mural painter of the Mexican Revolution, Diego Rivera. But she could not have a child. As well as several medically induced abortions she had a dangerous miscarriage.

Her imagination transformed tragic limitations into powerful fantasy [284]. Lying, soaking her poor torn limb in the bath, her fevered mind drifts from the smoking volcano of suffering, below which sits the skeleton of her lost child, to erotic dreams. Her floating body, the damaged parts concealed beneath the healing waters of forgetfulness, has a rope around its neck. One end is tied to the wrist of a lounging masculine figure. He lies on the sand, only dabbling his feet in the water and watching her with apparent indifference. He wears the mask of an Aztec idol, but his features resemble those of her husband. The other end of the rope, crawling with loathsome insects, is hitched around an iron rock and passes tautly to the waste outlet. Like the wheel of fate it draws her back toward her injured foot, strangling her between

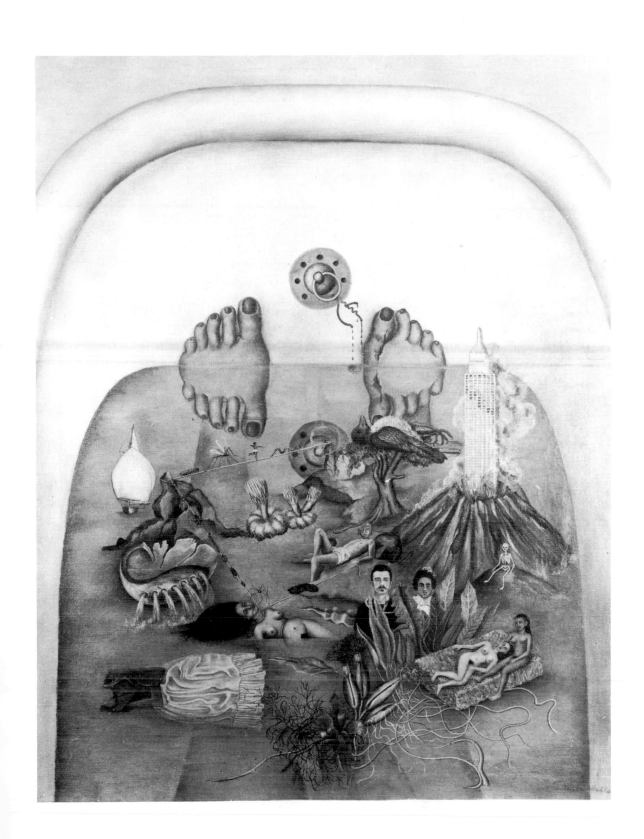

pain and desire. Below Diego, the faces of her parents, images of domestic rectitude, peer anxiously through the luxuriant leaves of Mexico. Their roots go down and mingle with the rose, fern strands, and barren seed pods of her own sexuality.

Kahlo, unawares, invented a style congruent to surrealism. The magic apparitions of her country's past and the potent spell of new political enchanters were pinned down by the inescapable truths of her injuries [285]. Below the mask, the body is irreparably fractured, held together by surgical dressings. Her backbone is a broken column. The nails in her flesh resemble the thorns in the Grünewald Christ [104]. Weeping, she looks at us with the implacable face of an Indian, unresigned but without hope. The hands which have shown her torment might also be holding her shroud. "Frida," wrote her husband, "is the only example in the history of art of an artist who tore open her chest and heart to reveal the biological truth of her feelings."[14] Never moving for long from the house in which she was born and died, she peopled the Mexico of her paintings with the phantoms of her inner life. Sometimes they acted on her; she remained as still as the child-self she often painted.

In her physical impassivity Kahlo may have anticipated a future trend in human society. For the first time in history, labor is no longer the ultimate manipulator of energy. Our dialogue is not with the four elements and the beasts of the fields but with machines. Unlike gentling a horse or fueling a steam engine, working with machines does not call for a coordination of muscle and brain. The dominance of mental responses, a rapid reaction to the control panel, is surely going to alter our physical being just as the turn from hunter to cultivator did. Delving the soil, man grew bulkier; chained to the computer console he will presumably evolve into a spindle-shanked brain-box.

No one has forecast this transition more imaginatively than the Chilean-born painter Matta. (He understandably abbreviated the resounding cadences of his birth-name, Roberto Matta Echaurren.) His figures have so effectively come to terms with solid-state technology that they seem part of the circuitry, plugging into each other like amorous vibrators [286]. Trained as an architect, he produced paintings, often very large, that seem to be housed in no known space. They have no horizon, but no ground either. Among streams of phosphorescent

285. Kahlo, The Broken Column, *1944.*

color, the electric hues of neon, the molten flow of incandescent space particles, robotic cardinals seem to be cogitating the eternal questions [287]. When he first began his attempts to relate the frontiers of science to the phenomena of his own imagination he accepted that it would be an endless task. All his pictures suggest a state of becoming. They often seem like possible blueprints for the future evolution of man. It may be a chaotic process but it lacks the mutant gloom of much modern science fiction. Man may change, but his energy and curiosity are inexhaustible. This could be said of Matta himself. Neat, twinkling, and spry in his seventies, he continued to map the transformations that we are invoking for ourselves.

Humor does not figure very largely in the story of the body in art, but the magical potential of sex and the power evoked by its symbols are among the first records humanity has left us. Matta seems to suggest

286. Matta,
Composition, *1945.*

that even the processes of reproduction may evolve [288], but sexual energy itself remains dominant. Erotic stimuli may be delivered by activating fields of force that break down the reflecting psychic barriers of inhibition but the human hand is still crucial. As it seems certain to be in the computer bank age. The image of the hand also takes us back to the dawn of art [20]. Without it, there would have been no art. We would have had no record of our earliest metamorphosis, the horned man of the cave painting [30]. The antlers throw a long shadow. Their tines are echoed in the antennae of the rutting man in Matta's painting. By donning his skin the shaman entered into the power of the animal. Equally, by taking on the attributes of the machine, Matta argues, man will learn to master its potential.

His parables on evolution involve the body assimilating to the mineral world of physics. To another witty commentator on human destiny, Louise Bourgeois, the appropriate analogies tend to be bio morphic. Like Matta's paintings her sculptures often involve the

287. Matta, The Prophetor, 1954.

interrelatedness of groups. One of the most provocative [289] is carved in marble, yet it has the adherent qualities of frog spawn, and seems a way of containing multiple eggs. However these objects could be tumescent males, poking out of their protective sheaths, or even a group of cloaked conspirators. An entirely characteristic irony clothes these amoebic shapes that might be jelly in the marmoreal grandeur of polished stone.

Bourgeois continually plays games with our expectations. No one dwelt so sharply on the discomfitures of sexuality. Resolutely French, despite her half-century in New York, she grew up in a self-consciously critical family with a charismatic and dominating father. Later she bore her American husband three sons. She needed to be independent, having a life surrounded by males.

Judging by her self-portrait [290], Bourgeois had a poor opinion of

288. Matta, The Glazer, *1944.*

289. Bourgeois, Cumul I, *1969.*

her own body. Hanging from a wire, only about two feet long, it resembles a cocoon or the nest of some small animal. "This is the way I experience my torso . . . somehow with a certain dissatisfaction and regret that one's own body is not as beautiful as one would like it to be. It doesn't seem to measure up by any standard of beauty."[15] She has created a number of other female forms. Overloaded with breasts and extra protuberances, they stand alone with wobbly difficulty [291]; an expression of woman's dissatisfaction with her inescapable biology.

However, Bourgeois is just as hard on men. *Fillette* [292], despite its feminine title, is unmistakably a mangy penis. Made in an unpleasantly textured latex, it is slung by the head from a meat hook and put on

290. Bourgeois, Torso Self-Portrait, *ca. 1963–64.*

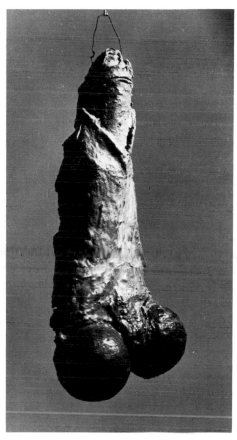

display like the executed criminals of olden times. Perhaps this is also a play on the expression "well hung."

Some of her most powerful pieces probe the ambiguities of male and female. The overlying soft shapes of *Trani Episode* [293] resemble breasts, with their nipple-like protuberances. The loose surface of the latex suggests the moveable skin on a flaccid penis. The ovoids snuggle together like dormant creatures who will soon be nuzzling their way into fresh mischief. Her sympathies were with human vulnerability and the need to come together to recoup energy. Despite its difficulties, the male-female partnership got her measured approval. It was a way of turning basic anxiety into manageable loneliness.

The postwar decades bred a new generation of affirmative women artists, confident enough to find their own paths rather than follow masculine preoccupations in art as previous creative women had tended

291. Bourgeois, Fragile Goddess, *ca. 1970.*

292. Bourgeois, Filette, *1968.*

293. Bourgeois, Trani Episode, *ca. 1971–72.*

to do. Some painted men as men had always painted women, as objects of desire. Some, such as the English sculptor, Elisabeth Frink, showed man in a more flattering light than men themselves were usually prepared to do, in this self-critical era.

To put yourself in the position of the opposite sex is a metamorphosis that many lovers have toyed with in their imagination. Frink is unusual in that she apotheosizes the male in the lonely eminence of power. Her seated man [294] might be a law-giver, a political leader, a general. Such figures of authority have seldom been looked at kindly by Western artists in recent years. Frink has emphasized the essential humanity that we would hope to find in our judge. Under her hands he has the maturity that comes with survival. His posture conveys the easy acceptance of responsibility; but his care-worn features and alert gaze imply a compassion generated by past suffering. For Frink nudity suggests the essential vulnerability of the male. "Power has been put on man whether he likes it or not."[16]

The mixture of toughness and tenderness with which she has invested her recent figures suggests the context of Third World rulers, where periods of power often follow years of exile or ferocious imprisonment, rather than the more tranquil politics of democracy. Only the cataclysm of total war brought life and death into common experience in Europe. As a child growing up in the Second World War, Frink lived in East Anglia. There were many airfields nearby and she remembers the return of damaged planes; an unforgettable sight, the bombers limping across the North Sea, their burning fuselages ebbing and flaming in the wind—the very torches of war. She has made a number of powerful images of falling birdmen [295]. Her figures, winged and helmeted, but otherwise naked, convey the

294. Frink, Seated Man, *1984.*

helpless inertia of failing strength, the tragic unanimity of youthful warriors.

This flaccid abandonment to the elements is something that Frink's birdmen share with the clay sculpture of Mary Frank. Frank's life-size figures are fragile by nature. Large flanges of clay support each other without any additional armature, like monstrous pancakes. Firing, at very high temperatures, produces a hard but brittle surface, heavy but delicate. The hollow shards, already partially dismembered, are a reminder of the transience of earthly beauty.

The Woman with Outstretched Arms [296] seems a female Icarus,

295. Frink, Falling Birdman, *ca. 1952.*

returned to earth like the fallen leaves. Like them, she is sinking back into the soil, to become the sustenance for fresh life. Dissolving into the elements, she embraces the metamorphosis with welcoming arms. But her head, thrown back like a lover's, mourns for the light on which her eyes are closing. The year this was sculpted Frank's only daughter was killed in an air crash, aged twenty-one.

296. *Frank,* Woman with Outstretched Arms, *1975.*

Frank had studied dance under Martha Graham when she first came as a child to New York from London early in the war. Perhaps it was the same temperamental affinity that had drawn her to ballet that made her emphasize the importance of gesture in her sculpture. Handling the very large thin surfaces of clay, she had to be deft and quick. The ballet dancer, responding to the momentary changes of music and fellow dancers, echoes the way her arms and fingers reacted to the urgent demands of the clay. The dancer heightens our emotions rather than giving us a precise psychological portrait. Traditionally, either by makeup or mask, his gestures are generalized.

Similarly Mary Frank's sculptured forms, voluptuously reclining, seem elemental deities rather than individuals. Is the lover one or two? Is it the earth itself, which embraces her, turning her limbs like Daphne's into branches or water, stroking her pelvis with feathery fronds? Two faces are pressed together, but perhaps they are aspects of the same face [297]. Several critics have said it is Mary Frank's own strong-boned features which grace her figures. She maintains this is not so.[17] She is haunted by a face that seems to her to come from the earliest times: the primordial face. This was the supernal beauty of the god, assumed by his masked human protagonist in the seasonal rites of renewal.

The performing arts, particularly dance, give us an inkling of the magic ritual used to evoke. Ritual summoned forth and contained the most powerful metamorphosis the human frame could encompass: the transfiguration of the group. It is something that over the centuries we have gradually lost, though in performances of music and theater, we can still occasionally feel, far off, the touch of its consoling strength. Ritual is the way of disciplining and universalizing emotion and so is the parent of all the arts; just as philosophy, the disciplining and universalizing of thought, gave birth to all the sciences. Reason and emotion should work hand in hand, but Apollo has been an overweening partner, undermining where he should support.

Modern art, by going back to primitive or ancient prototypes has sought to liberate the vitality originally evoked by ritual and the cult objects created for it. The use of such potent imagery has lent the art of this century its raw iconoclastic energy, but it has turned out to be Midas' gold. Once the shock effect has worn off, the artist has to try on a new mask. Ritual does not deal with the particular, but we, the audience, were able to relate it to our own experience because it sprang from a common ground of belief. Without that common ground generalized art, such as that of Moore and Giacometti and others we have been discussing, can seem empty in the way that a Madonna and Child on the walls of a medieval cathedral does not.

How to mine again that ancient gold? One who tried was Henri Matisse. An unlikely champion, trained as a lawyer, with that ingrained fastidious good taste of the French, Matisse was a worried man who always found drawing hard work. He labored, he said, for a lifetime in order to make the difficult seem easy. In the early years of the century, when Parisian critics labeled him *Fauve*, he was reaching for a new simplicity in expressing the human form. "We are moving towards serenity by simplification of ideas and means. Our only object is wholeness. We must learn, perhaps relearn, to express ourselves by means of line. Plastic art will inspire the most direct emotion possible by the simplest means . . . three colours for a big panel of *La Danse*; blue for the sky, pink for the bodies, green for the hill."[18]

In fact in 1909 when he came to paint *The Dance* [298] he reworked the figures a hard brick red. They dominate the picture, pressing the

297. Frank, Lovers, *1974.*

edges of the very large canvas (more than eight feet high and over twelve feet across). Their postures are said to be based on a fishermen's dance, the *sardana*, which Matisse had witnessed on a beach in the South of France. But the poses, the contrapuntal twist of the figure on the left, which gives the circle much of its tension, hark back to the ecstatic energy of the maenads [80]. Hanging on the staircase of Shchukin's palace in prerevolutionary Moscow, it must have been as disturbing as a visit from Rasputin. Perhaps Matisse himself felt some incongruity in his naked stompers presiding over an eighteenth-century staircase down which paraded the tiaras, bustles, and decorations of the overdressed, overrich, and overfed. At any rate, much later he recalled his 1911 visit to Moscow somewhat sourly: it had seemed like a huge Asian village.

Within a few years he had retreated from extreme modernism to a hotel room in Nice. Here he painted the ideal holiday of the middle-aged Frenchman; a pretty room with a view of the south, modest luxuries and a sensuous young companion [300]. For many years, through his fifties, Matisse lived the daydream. But of course the

298. Matisse, The Dance, *1909.*

succession of girls he dressed and undressed in the wisps of lace and silk that he designed for them were there only as models. The palm tree outside the window was on the promenade of a comfortable European resort far from the torrid zone. When he actually went to Tahiti he found it superb but boring. What he really enjoyed was working.

"My purpose," he stated, "is to render my emotion. This state of soul is created by the objects which surround me and which react in me: from the horizon to myself, myself included. For very often I put myself in the picture, and I am aware of what exists behind me. I express as naturally the space and the objects which are situated there as if I had only the sea and sky in front of me; that is to say, the simplest thing in the world. This is to make it understood that the

299. Matisse, The Artist and His Model, *1919.*

unity realized in my picture, however complex it may be, is not difficult for me to obtain, because it comes to me naturally."[19] He was a monstrous egotist. It was his interest in self that allowed him to work so pitilessly hard; his models complained that they never had a day off. Perhaps his legal training helped him to study his own work and to learn from it. He was able to watch its progress as analytically as he included himself in it; an enigmatic figure, beady-eyed behind the protective beard and glasses.

No artist in modern times has had a more accurate control over the effects of his paintings and known more precisely how to achieve them. He believed in color's therapeutic power. Visiting a sick friend he would leave behind a painting to radiate its healing glow. Illness caused his own final metamorphosis at seventy-one. Two serious operations made it difficult for him to continue painting. He had his assistants color expanses of paper with gouache. These areas of radiant blue, emerald, violet, and orange-red he attacked personally with a pair of scissors, visualizing with brilliant skill the balance of shape and color when they were gummed together. He called it "drawing with scissors."[20]

It was a liberated extension of the more laborious process by which he had assembled the materials for his paintings in his rooms in Nice

300. Matisse, The Swimming Pool, *1952.*

twenty years before. Then he had brought together oriental cushions, patterned silks, carved screens, vases of flowers, and reflecting mirrors against which he had posed his model in the gauzy pantaloons and turbans he had invented for her. Now there was no need for all these props to his imagination. He drew straight out of his head the free shapes that the flat areas of gouache suggested. These *papiers découpés* brought an unexpected brilliance to the end of his career, and an influence that has been long-lasting. It was an extraordinary metamorphosis for a painter who had been written off by the avant-garde as finished in the 1920s. Late in life he found a whole fresh field of creation, a summation of all his earlier endeavors. Ailing but triumphant he wrote: "cutting into living colour reminds me of the sculptor's direct carving."[21]

His divers leaping into *The Swimming Pool* [300] achieve the ecstatic lightness that he had sought in *La Danse*. Stripped of all individual character they are pure patterns of pleasure. Here is the body without the connotation of biographical guilt and anxiety. So we experience it in our few moments when mind, spirit, and physique come together in an effortless harmony. Such moments are not a blind hedonism. Matisse believed all art worthy of the name was religious. "Be it a

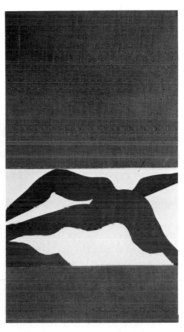

creation of lines, or colour: if it is not religious, it doesn't exist."[22]

By religion he meant the love of creation in all its manifestations. And the first work of creation he knew was himself. He had a need to express himself as profoundly as he could. This could be in many ways. He remembered that when he was painting *La Danse* he had been to the Moulin de la Galette. He had watched the dancing. "The dancers hold each other by the hand, they run across the room, and they wind around the people who are standing around . . . it is all extremely gay."[23] While he was painting he was singing to himself the tune he had heard at the Moulin de la Galette. There was a close connection between the pure emotion of music and color. "Look at these blue women [301] . . . These are paper cut-outs and this is the arabesque. The arabesque is musically organized. It has its own timbre."[24]

301. Matisse, The Hair, *1952.*

So she dances across our pages for the last time: the body as an end in itself. She has the joy of movement that the child expresses, that Matisse must have empathized with from his sick bed. "Arms, legs all the lines act like parts of an orchestra, a register, movements, different pitches . . ."[25] Thus the spectator's imagination is freed from all limits. This lightness of leaping, the purity of line and color, brings a feeling of release, of obstacles cleared. To express the deepest feelings, to break down the barriers in which we hem the body, has always been the intention of the artist. Art helps reconcile us with ourselves.

Matisse believed his role was to provide calm. He himself had the need for peace. He had spent a lifetime driven by self-criticism and unease. Out of it he had created a vision of tranquility; a repose that he had not found himself, until perhaps his final years. He had been prepared to sacrifice himself, and others, to his vision. His son remembered him as a selfish father. Matisse said that his drawings and his canvases were his real children.

But what if he had labored all those years without talent? Then the verdict of history would have been harsh: a lifetime's effort lost in the sands of time. At the end of his long career, the first master of oil paints, Titian, painted a picture that memorably showed the fate of the presumptuous [302]. In legend, Marsyas was a satyr and a follower of the great goddess Cybele. He found a magic flute and became famous for playing it at her festivals. Jealous, Apollo, the god of music, challenged him to a contest, flute against lyre. The Muses were unable to judge between them until Apollo ordained they should both sing and play at the same time. This was easy enough for the string player, but impossible for Marsyas with his flute. The victorious god extracted a cruel punishment. Marsyas was to be flayed alive.

The ruthless god of reason, who caused the beautiful Daphne to gain an extra skin of bark, ensured that the satyr should lose his. In Titian's painting the metamorphosis is already under way. Suspended by his feet from a tree, which accentuates his furry beast legs, Marsyas hangs head downward. His youthfully handsome face is racked by fear and pain. He is still conscious, though a small dog is already lapping up his blood. Another is being held back by a deformed child, while an old man watches the scene sorrowfully. The executioners are revealed in a ghastly fitful light absorbed in their task. Only Apollo glows with a baneful radiance. Transported by the beauty of his own music, he is unconcerned by the fate he has decreed for his rustic rival.

The overpowering mastery and magnificence of Titian's paint adds its own comment to the pitiless judgment of art. Only the successful survive. No one knew that better than Titian, who was in his eighties when he produced this very large picture. He had shown himself the master of every form of painting. In his last decades, like Matisse, he evolved a new and freer handling of material; a brilliant use of color to suggest mood that brings to mind Delacroix, and almost anticipates the Impressionists in its broken rendering of form. He would use his fingers to dab in an accent or heighten a surface. "He laid in his pictures," wrote his assistant, "with a mass of colour which served as a ground work for what he wanted to express."[26]

In this picture what he is expressing is as complex as Shakespeare's attitude to King Lear. Out of the clotted undergrowth, dense as a primeval forest, the executioners emerge like embodiments of evil to prey on the body of the vanquished. Just so is time eating into the body of the painter. As Lear does, Titian evokes the stormy grief-seized light—a darkness visible—yet challenges it to do its worst. The fate of Marsyas is metaphorically the fate of all failed artists—extinction. Each new creative challenge is a risk. There were many criticisms of Titian's late style at the time. It was generally thought to show a waning of his powers. Now the exigencies of fashion have caused us to value especially these later canvases as a prophetic demonstration of painterly freedom.

We cannot say what the future will make of the vagrant shapes that we have held up as a mirror of ourselves toward the end of the twentieth century. Perhaps like Marsyas they will be found wanting. There are no longer any generally accepted criteria with which we can judge them.

It is probable that whatever images will be selected by future historians to represent our era will reveal a common element: the characteristic stance of Western man and woman in this period of transition. The upright forms of Giacometti, the reclining figures of Henry Moore, the images of suffering and endurance of Frida Kahlo and Elisabeth Frink, the ironic shapes of Louise Bourgeois, all share an aspect of lonely self-reliance that is the human condition in our time. Only the frenetic identification with the galvanic pulsations of the cybernetic world of Matta or the pure hedonism of Matisse's cutouts

302. Titian, The Punishment of Marsyas, *1570.*

seem to escape the tension of the individual. In the immense proliferation of the human image that has accompanied the age of communication we can see moment by moment all around us similar, but impure, evocations to surrender to the mindless pursuit of pleasure, greed, and power. Yet in the midst of plenty the thoughtful person is alone; waiting, like Giacometti's standing women, for the turn of the hinge that will carry us into the next manifestation of the human destiny.

AFTERWORD

The earliest links in the chain that led to this book were forged over fifty years ago when my father first took me, a sickly twelve-year-old, around the British Museum. I was just beginning to emerge from a childhood of almost continuous ill-health, including four years prone on my back in a spinal chair. By and large, the healthy body is accepted by the young without thought, its performances and potential part and parcel of the gift of life; the ailing body is constantly in mind. I was only too aware of my own weedy inefficiency. What a contrast to the splendid forms of classical art! They were a heart-warming affirmation of a perfection I would never achieve but which I felt instinctively should be striven toward. The sight of all this beauty of male and female did not depress me: rather, it gave a stability and focus to my nascent fantasies, and confirmed me in their rectitude. If artists could imagine such perfection, it was all right for me to dream of it in my long hours of enforced idleness.

Years later, as a young man in the late forties I spent my demobilization leave visiting the United States. My first day in New York I went to the Museum of Modern Art and was astounded by the brilliance and daring of *Les Demoiselles d'Avignon* and the other early Picassos. After six years of the drabness and discipline of World War II they seemed to proclaim man's unconquerable iconoclastic energy. Two years later I passed the summer vacation from Edinburgh University in Italy. Florence and Rome led me inevitably to fall under the lifelong spell of Michelangelo.

Art has continued to feed me vicariously ever since. In middle life I descended for the first time into the desert tombs of the Old Kingdom nobles at Sakkara in Egypt. There I saw carved in reliefs on the walls, the everyday activities of peasant life that spoke clearly across five thousand years of the enduring continuity of human aspirations. A more recent personal discovery, the erotic temple figures of India, were a reminder of the physical delights that blossom afresh for every generation. The imagery of art clothes our imagination and gives us the vocabulary to express the drama of our own lives. Poor art facilitates a stunted understanding; great art adds to the stature of our feelings. Supreme artists like Rembrandt have increased sympathy and toleration for the idiosyncrasies of human nature. Rembrandt did not dismiss or minimize the body's imperfections, indeed he could look at them with something approaching a fascinated horror; yet in the end he accepted each unique being with love. Such insight and imagination seem a major cause for our continuing faith in mankind's future; as Goethe remarked about Michelangelo: "No-one who has not seen the Sistine Chapel can have a clear idea of what a human being can achieve."[1]

Yet the mention of Michelangelo is a reminder of the powerful contrary feeling that the image of the body can arouse. Even the most acclaimed artist in Christendom suffered censorship in his own time and the controversy over his painting of the Last Judgment in the Sistine is still active as I write, more than four hundred years later. In most societies the portrayal of the body remains hedged with conventional prohibitions, and in some, the Muslim countries, it is totally barred.

We think this an anachronism related to the prescriptions of a particular religion, but the public reaction to many exhibitions of modern art involving the explicit portrayal of the naked human form shows that it has universal affinities. For centuries it has been accepted that male artists could portray women as objects of desire. When women artists began to paint men in the same way they were often the subject of scandal, and occasionally of censorship. Initial rebuffs made Alice Neel unwilling to exhibit for nearly three decades. A major London show in 1980 of Women's Images of Men created unprecedented media coverage, much of it hostile and abusive. As the organizers of the exhibition pointed out: "As long as the artists showed compassion, sympathy and tenderness towards their subject they were praised, for these qualities were seen as a reflection of their femininity. It was when they displayed "unfeminine" qualities that the critics—female as well as male—found it hard to cope . . . Marina Vaizey (of *The Sunday*

Times) was not alone in seeing "a forest of penises" although relatively few works displayed the offending parts and none gave them more than their natural proportions would allow."[2]

Through recorded history man has held the power in society, creating the rigid, unyieldy systems that give pretext for our mutual aggressions, and the majority of the art works that embellish them. As woman enters her rightful estate in art as in other professions, it is inevitable that man will be portrayed in a more objective and critical manner than in the past. Such new objectivity could be salutary, though it is to be hoped that women will contribute more open and less dogmatic attitudes, and a new impetus to art. A regenerative force is needed. We seem to be in a hiatus of creativity. The movements of modern art that rocketed through the early twentieth century have lost steam. They gave us many new marvels but we should not regret them; they were fueled by a monstrous egoism that we can no longer afford, in the narrowing resources of a rapidly overcrowding world. If art is a yardstick of cultural trends, and in some sense a forecast of impending change, then the present pause in creativity may signify the lull before the nuclear storm, or more hopefully the pregnant interim preceeding a new metamorphosis of human society. In either event we shall need all the hope and inspiration that art can give.

Should art be able to return to its ancient role and reassert the dignity, courage, and genius of man, the human form is likely to be the vehicle for such expression. Nothing approaches the resonance of ourselves. It remains for future men and women to find ways to reflect our image meaningfully and anew. They will not go far wrong if they begin with Rilke's bold aspiration:

> *I have faith in all those things that are not yet said*
> *I want to set free my most holy feelings.*
> *What no one has dared to want*
> *Will be for me impossible to refuse.*[3]

ACKNOWLEDGMENTS

The idea of actually writing the book began to form in my mind through meetings I had with Kenneth Clark at the very end of his life. To him I owe a profound debt as mentor and friend through hours of illuminating conversation that spread across sixteen years and three continents. I have been fortunate that my profession has brought me in close working contact with many creative minds. In particular I have been influenced in my attitudes to art by my collaborations at various times with John Berger, Sir William Coldstream, Professor Leopold Ettlinger, Sir Lawrence Gowing, Robert Hughes, and David Sylvester. In the early stages of planning, I was lucky to have the suggestions of Lilly Rivlin on contemporary American women artists (and often introductions to them). My son Adrian Gill, contributed many useful ideas, not least a drawing that helped clarify my early conception of the cover photograph. I owe thanks to all those other artists who discussed their work with me both in England and the United States, and to the many friends and scholars who at one time or another I consulted: Father Cyril Barrett, Louise Bourgeois, Colin Clark, Betty Dodson, Nigel Evans, Mary Frank, Dame Elisabeth Frink, Carlos Fuentes, Roberta Graham, Germaine Greer, Murray Grigor, Eunice Golden, Mandy Havers, Michael Jones, Mary Ann Kenyon, Michael Leonard, Juanita McNeely, Robert Mapplethorpe, Elaine Schemilt, Joan Semmel, Sylvia Sleigh, Anita Steckel, Peter Webb. Errors and omissions are my responsibility and no fault of theirs.

The illegibility of my handwritten manuscripts was transformed on electric typewriter and word processor by the patient labors of Melanie Clark, Debbie Hall, and Janet Patterson. A special mention should go to Gail Buchicchio, who played among many roles that of the unflagging liaison in countless cross-Atlantic calls. To them many thanks, as well as to Lucy Sisman for her fruitful designs for the original layout of the book and the initial culling of the illustrations. The team who labored to make it all fit together at Doubleday was ably headed by Marysarah Quinn, who created the final design. Which brings me to the active motivator of the whole enterprise, the person whose enthusiasm, critical perceptiveness, and vigorous support sustained me over five years and numerous rewrites: my peerless editor, Nan A. Talese. It was a fortunate evening for me when I found myself sitting next to this deceptively gentle dynamo at a New York dinner party early in 1984.

Finally, to my wife Georgina and daughter Chloe, I owe recompense for all those days when I would lapse into reverie in the middle of an important conversation—and all those nights when, struck by what appeared an inspirational thought at 5 A.M., I would leap out of bed to record it. The fact that we are still together is a tribute to their tolerance, faith, and love, which I can only strive to return.

NOTES

CHAPTER 1: IDEAL BEAUTY

1. The Book of Genesis, Bible, King James Version.
2. Clark, *The Nude*.
3. Stokes, *Reflections on the Nude*.
4. Ibid.
5. All direct quotes from the author's conversations with Robert Mapplethorpe, September, October, December 1985.
6. Macmurray, *Reason and Emotion*.
7. Plato, *The Symposium*.
8. Clark, *The Nude*.
9. Quoted in Wilson, *Edward Weston: Nudes*.
10. Ibid.
11. Quoted in Barr, *Picasso: Fifty Years of His Art*.
12. Direct quote from the author's interview with Sylvia Sleigh, November 1984.
13. Ibid.
14. Ibid.

CHAPTER 2: ENERGY AND FERTILITY

1. Quoted in Guinea, *Altamira*.
2. C. Hontze, quoted in Giedion, *The Eternal Present*.
3. Dylan Thomas, "Ballad of the Long-Legged Bait."
4. Leroi-Gourhan, *Treasures of Prehistoric Art*.
5. Ibid.
6. Ibid.
7. Ibid.
8. Berger, *Success and Failure of Picasso*.
9. Clark, *The Nude*.
10. Giedion, *The Eternal Present*.
11. BBC interview with Willem de Kooning by David Sylvester, published in *Location*, Spring 1963.

CHAPTER 3: MEN LIKE GODS

1. Herodotus, *The Histories*.
2. Engels, *The Origin of the Family*.
3. Quoted in De Rachewiltz, *Black Eros*.
4. Egyptian *Book of the Dead*, Chapter XVII, as translated in De Rachewiltz, *Black Eros*.
5. Herodotus, *The Histories*.
6. Quoted in De Rachewiltz, *Black Eros*.
7. Reported by Strabo, the Greek geographer, in the first century B.C. Quoted in Tannahill, *Sex in History*.
8. Tannahill, *Sex in History*.
9. Quoted in Hawkes, *The First Great Civilisation*.

10. Percy Bysshe Shelley, *Ozymandias.*
11. Robert Southey, *The Battle of Blenheim.*
12. Quoted in Hawkes, *The First Great Civilisation.*

CHAPTER 4: THE PERFECTION OF PLEASURE
1. Miller, *The Colossus of Maroussi.*
2. Aeschylus, *The Oresteia.*
3. Tannahill, *Sex in History.*
4. Athenaeus. Quoted in Seltman, *Women in Antiquity.*
5. Fagles and Stanford, Introduction to Aeschylus, *The Oresteia.*
6. Quoted in Seltman, *Women in Antiquity.*
7. *Oxford Book of Greek Verse in Translation* (translated by Maurice Bowra).
8. Meyer, *Sexual Life in Ancient India.*
9. Chaudhuri, *Hinduism.*
10. *Krishna Jaurna Khanda.* Quoted in Chaudhuri, *Hinduism.*
11. Crighton, *The Floating World.*
12. Tenth-century Japanese poem (translated by Arthur Waley), in Japanese Poetry: The Uta.

CHAPTER 5: PILGRIMAGE THROUGH PAIN
1. Tacitus, *The Annals of Imperial Rome.*
2. Canetti, *Crowds and Power.*
3. Ibid.
4. Quoted in Workman, *Persecution in the Early Church.*
5. Gibbon, *Decline and Fall of the Roman Empire.*
6. Suetonius, *The Twelve Caesars.*
7. Bible, St. Paul, First Epistle to the Corinthians.
8. Quoted in Johnson, *A History of Christianity.*
9. Ibid.
10. Quoted in Huxley, *Music at Night.*
11. Quoted in Gascoigne, *The Christians.*
12. Dante, *The Divine Comedy, Inferno,* Canto III.
13. Andrew Marvell, "To His Coy Mistress."
14. Huysmans, *Grünewald.*
15. Geoffrey Chaucer, *The Canterbury Tales, The Wife of Bath's Prologue.*
16. William Blake, "Infant Joy."
17. Geoffrey Chaucer, *Balade de bon conseyl.*

CHAPTER 6: THE WAGES OF FAME
1. Samuel Rogers, "Italy."
2. Alberti, *On Painting.*
3. Ibid.
4. Antonio Manetti, *Life of Brunelleschi.* Quoted in Bennett and Wilkins, *Donatello.*
5. Vasari, *The Lives of the Artists.*
6. Gombrich, *Norm and Form.*
7. Ibid.
8. Vasari, *The Lives of the Artists.*
9. Clark, *The Nude.*
10. Alberti, *On Painting.*
11. Ibid.

12. Ibid.
13. Ibid.
14. Vasari, *The Lives of the Artists*.
15. Ibid.
16. Bennett and Wilkins, *Donatello*.
17. Ibid.
18. A suggestion by Anita Moskowitz. Quoted in Bennett and Wikins, *Donatello*.
19. Clark, *The Art of Humanism*.
20. Ibid.
21. Alberti, *On Painting*.
22. Ibid.
23. Quoted in Clark, *The Nude*.
24. Wölfflin, *Classic Art*.
25. Christopher Marlowe, *Tamburlaine*.
26. Vasari, *The Lives of the Artists*.
27. Quoted in Wilde, *Michelangelo*.
28. Mark Twain, *The Innocents Abroad*.
29. As translated by Linda Murray in Murray, *Michelangelo*.
30. Vasari, *The Lives of the Artists*.
31. Quoted in Murray, *Michelangelo*.
32. Vasari, *The Lives of the Artists*.
33. Marsilio Ficino. Quoted in Wilde, *Michelangelo*.
34. Hartt, *Michelangelo*.
35. Vasari, *The Lives of the Artist*.
36. Murray, *Michelangelo*.
37. Hartt, *Michelangelo*.
38. Murray, *Michelangelo*.
39. Quoted in Shearman, *Mannerism*.
40. Vasari, *The Lives of the Artists*.

CHAPTER 7: THE HUMAN CONDITION

1. Vasari, *The Lives of the Artists*.
2. Leonardo da Vinci, *Notebooks*.
3. Vasari, *The Lives of the Artists*.
4. Leonardo da Vinci, *Notebooks*.
5. Ibid.
6. Ibid.
7. I am indebted to Mary D. Garrard's account in *Feminism and Art History*.
8. Quoted in Greer, *The Obstacle Race*.
9. Fromentin, *The Masters of Past Time*.
10. Bible, St. Luke's Gospel.
11. Bible, Second Book of Samuel.
12. John Donne, "The Extasy."
13. Casanova, *History of My Life*.
14. Original commentary on the "Prado" manuscript (translated by Hilda Harris). Goya, *Los Caprichos*.
15. Ibid.

CHAPTER 8: PATHOS OR PORNOGRAPHY?

1. William Wordsworth, *The Prelude*.
2. His first biographer, C. Clement. Quoted in Eitner, *Géricault*.

3. Delacroix, *The Journal of Eugene Delacroix*.
4. Ibid.
5. Ibid.
6. From Delacroix's note in the 1827 Salon catalogue.
7. Quoted in Huyghe, *Delacroix*.
8. Baudelaire, *The Painter of Modern Life*.
9. Ibid.
10. Quoted in Wilmerding, *American Art*.
11. Ibid.
12. Critical comment quoted in Rewald, *The History of Impressionism*.
13. Ibid.
14. Ibid.
15. Delacroix, *The Journal of Eugene Delacroix*.
16. Clark, *The Nude*.
17. Edmond de Goncourt. Quoted in Webb, *The Erotic Arts*.
18. Judith Cladel. Quoted in Sutton, *Triumphant Satyr*.
19. Isadora Duncan. Quoted in Sutton, *Triumphant Satyr*.
20. *Le Figaro*. Quoted in Descharnes and Chabrun, *Auguste Rodin*.
21. Letter in *Le Matin*. Quoted in Sutton, *Triumphant Satyr*.
22. Rilke, *Rodin and Other Prose Pieces*.
23. Quoted in Elson, ed. *Rodin Rediscovered*.
24. Rilke, *Rodin and Other Prose Pieces*.
25. Rilke, *Rodin and Other Prose Pieces*.

CHAPTER 9: A SUM OF DESTRUCTIONS

1. Buñuel, *My Last Sigh*.
2. Vergo, *Vienna 1900*.
3. Cassou, *The Concise Encyclopedia of Symbolism*.
4. Quoted in Whitford, *Egon Schiele*.
5. Ibid.
6. Ibid.
7. Tennyson, "Song of the Lotos-Eaters.
8. Gauguin, *Intimate Journals*.
9. Hilton, *Picasso's Picassos*.
10. Matisse, *Notes of a Painter*. Quoted in Gowing, *Matisse*.
11. Penrose, *Picasso*.
12. Rubin, ed., *Pablo Picasso*.
13. Quoted in Penrose, *Picasso*.
14. Quoted in Barr, *Picasso*.
15. Futurist quotation from Apollonio, ed., *Futurist Manifestos*.
16. Ibid.
17. Ibid.
18. Rupert Brooke, *War Sonnets*.
19. Horne, *The Price of Glory*.
20. Quoted in Jean. *The History of Surrealist Painting*.
21. Ibid.
22. Quoted in Passeron, *Surrealism*.
23. Jean, *The History of Surrealist Painting*.
24. Berlin, *Personal Impressions*.
25. Breton, *What is Surrealism?*
26. Ibid.

27. Parinaud, *The Unspeakable Confessions of Salvador Dali*.
28. Ibid.
29. Ibid.
30. Ibid.
31. From a conversation between Picasso and Christian Zervos. Quoted in Barr, *Picasso*.
32. William Shakespeare, *Macbeth*.
33. Borowski,*This Way for the Gas, Ladies and Gentlemen*.
34. Karol Konieczny. Quoted in Blatter and Milton, *Art of the Holocaust*.
35. Benjamin, *Illuminations*.

CHAPTER 10: SOMETHING RICH AND STRANGE

1. Ovid, *Metamorphoses* (translated by Humphries).
2. Ibid.
3. William Shakespeare, *The Tempest*.
4. Sartre, *Being and Nothingness*.
5. Quoted in Sylvester, *Alberto Giacometti*.
6. Ibid.
7. Ibid.
8. Moore. In film *Henry Moore*, BBC, 1951 (Directed by John Read).
9. Moore. Quoted in Sylvester, *Henry Moore*.
10. Moore and Hedgecoe, *Henry Moore*.
11. Moore and Levine, *Henry Moore Wood Sculpture*.
12. Sylvester, *Henry Moore*.
13. Quoted in Herrera, *Frida*.
14. Quoted in Mulvey and Wollen, *Frida Kahlo and Tina Modotti*.
15. Quoted in Wye, *Louise Bourgeois*.
16. From the author's interview with Dame Elisabeth Frink, December 1984.
17. From the author's interview with Mary Frank, November 1984.
18. Quoted in Gowing, *Matisse*.
19. Flam, *Matisse on Art*.
20. Ibid.
21. Ibid.
22. Ibid.
23. Ibid.
24. Ibid.
25. Ibid.
26. Murray and Murray, *A Dictionary of Art and Artists*.

AFTERWORD

1. Quoted in Goldscheider, *The Paintings of Michelangelo*.
2. Kent and Morreau, *Women's Images of Men*.
3. Rainer Maria Rilke, from *Das Stundenbuch (A Book for the House of Prayer)* (translated by Robert Bly).

The author gratefully acknowledges permission to quote from the following:

Collected Peoms by Dylan Thomas. J. M. Dent and Sons Ltd. and the Trustees for the Copyright of Dylan Thomas. Copyright © 1952.

Women in Antiquity, translated by Charles Seltman. Thames & Hudson Ltd. Copyright © 1956.

The Oxford Book of Greek Verse in Translation, edited by T. F. Higham and C. M. Bowra. Oxford University Press. Copyright 1938.

Hinduism, by N. C. Chaudhuri. Chatto & Windus (U.K.) and Oxford University Press (U.S.A.). Copyright © 1979.

The 'Uta from *Japanese Poetry*, by Arthur Waley. An East-West Center Book, University of Hawaii Press. Copyright © 1976.

A Choice of Chaucer's Verse, selected by Nevill Coghill. Faber and Faber Limited Publishers. Copyright © 1972.

Leon Battista Alberti on Painting, translated by John R. Spencer. Yale University Press. Copyright © 1966.

Selected Poems of Rainer Maria Rilke, translated from the German by Robert Bly. Harper & Row, Publishers, Inc. Copyright © 1981 by Robert Bly.

Metamorphoses, by Ovid (translated by Rolfe Humphries). Indiana University Press. Copyright © 1955.

BIBLIOGRAPHY

Many of the books listed have been published in different languages and editions; I have invariably given the version and publication date of the edition I consulted.

AESCHYLUS. *The Oreteia*. Translated by Robert Fagles. London: Penguin: 1984.

ALBERTI, LEON BATTISTA. *On Painting*. Translated by John R. Spencer. New Haven. Yale University Press, 1966.

ALDRED, CYRIL. *Egypt to the End of the Old Kingdom*. London: Thames & Hudson, 1974.

ALEXANDRIAN, SARANE. *L'Art Surrealiste*. Paris: Fernand Hazen Editeur, 1969.

ALKIM, U, BAHADIR. *The Ancient Civilisation of Anatolia*. London: Barrie & Rockliff, 1969.

ANAND, MULK RAJ. *Kama Kala*. Geneva: Nagel, 1963.

APOLLONIO, UMBRO, ED. *Futurist Manifestos*. London: Thames & Hudson, 1973.

AUGUSTINE, ST. *The City of God*. Translated by Henry Bettenson. London: Penguin, 1972.

AYRTON, MICHAEL, AND HENRY MOORE. *Giovanni Pisano Sculptor*. London: Thames & Hudson, 1969.

BARR, ALFRED H. *Picasso: Fifty Years of His Art*. New York: Museum of Modern Art, 1946.

BARRACLOUGH, GEOFFREY, ED. *The Times Atlas of World History*. London: Times Books, 1978.

BARRET, ANDRÉ. *Fontainebleau, le miroir des dames*. Paris: Laffont, 1984.

BAUDELAIRE, CHARLES. *The Painter of Modern Life*. Translated by Jonathan Mayne. London: Phaidon, 1964.

BAUMANN, HANS. *Lion Gate and Labyrinth*. Oxford: Oxford University Press, 1967.

BENAYOUN, ROBERT. *Erotique du Surrealisme*. Paris: J. J. Pauvert, 1965.

BENJAMIN, WALTER. *Illuminations*. Translated by Harry Zohn. London: Fontana, 1973.

BENNETT, BONNIE A., AND DAVID G. WILKINS. *Donatello*. Oxford: Phaidon, 1984.

BENTLEY, RICHARD. *Erotic Art*. London: Quartet, 1984.

BERENGUER, MAGIN. *El Arte Prehistorico en la Caeva Tito Bustillo*. Leon, Spain: Editorial Everest S.A., 1985.

BERGER, JOHN. *Success and Failure of Picasso*. London: Penguin, 1965.

————. *Ways of Seeing*. London: Penguin, 1972.

BERLIN, ISAIAH. *Personal Impressions*. Oxford: Oxford University Press, 1982.

BERNARD, BRUCE. *The Bible and Its Painters*. London: Orbis, 1983.

BERTI, LUCIANO. *Florence*. Florence: Saverio Becocci, 1979.

BETTERTON, ROSEMARY, ED. *Looking On*. London: Pandora Press, 1987.

BILLARD, JULES B., ED. *Ancient Egypt*. London: The National Geographic Society, 1978.

BLATTER, JANET, AND SYBIL MILTON. *Art of the Holocaust*. London: Orbis, 1982.

BOARDMAN, JOHN. *Athenian Red Figure Vases: The Archaic Period*. London: Thames & Hudson, 1975.

————. *Greek Art*. London: Thames & Hudson, 1985.

BOAS, FRANZ. *Primitive Art*. New York: Dover Publications, 1955.

BOLLINGER, HANZ. *Picasso's Vollard Suite*. London: Thames & Hudson, 1956.

BOON, K. G. *Rembrandt: The Complete Etchings*. London: Thames & Hudson, 1963.

BORD, JANET, AND COLIN BORD. *Earth Rites*. London: Granada, 1982.

BOROWSKI, TADEUSZ. *This Way for the Gas, Ladies and Gentlemen*. Translated by Barbara Vedder. London: Penguin, 1976.

BOWRA, C. M. *The Greek Experience*. New York: Mentor Books, 1957.

BRETON, ANDRÉ. *What is Surrealism?* Edited by Franklin Rosemont. New York: Monad, 1978.

BROUDE, NORMA, AND MARY D. GARRARD, EDS. *Feminism and Art History*. New York: Harper & Row, 1982.

BUÑUEL, LUIS. *My Last Sigh*. Translated by Abigail Israel. New York: Knopf, 1983.

BURCKHARDT, JACOB. *The Civilisation of the Renaissance in Italy*. Translated by S. G. C. Middlemore. Vienna: Phaidon, 1937.

CAMPBELL, JOSEPH. *The Masks of God*. London: Penguin, 1982.

CAMUS, ALBERT. *The Rebel*. Translated by Anthony Bower. London: Penguin, 1962.

CANETTI, ELIAS. *Crowds and Power*. Translated by Carol Stewart. New York: Seabury Press, 1978.

CARMEAN, E. A., JR. *Picasso, the Saltimbanques*. Washington, D.C.: National Gallery of Art, 1980.

CASANOVA, GIACOMO. *History of My Life*. New York: Harcourt Brace, 1967.

CASSOU, JEAN. *The Concise Encyclopedia of Symbolism*. Translated by Susie Saunders. Ware, England: Omega Books, 1984.

CELLINI, BENVENUTO. *The Life*. Translated by Anne Macdonell. London: Everyman's Library, Dent, 1907.

CHATWIN, BRUCE. *Lady*. London: Blond and Briggs, 1983.

CHAUDHURI, NIRAD C. *Hinduism*. Oxford: Oxford University Press, 1979.

CHRISTIAN, JOHN. *Burne-Jones*. London: Arts Council, 1975.

CLARK, GRAHAME, AND STUART PIGGOTT. *Prehistoric Societies*. London: Hutchinson, 1965.

CLARK, GRAHAME, ET AL. *The Dawn of Civilisation*. London: Thames & Hudson, 1961.

CLARK, KENNETH. *The Art of Humanism*. London: John Murray, 1983.

———. *Civilisation*. London: John Murray, 1969.

———. *An Introduction to Rembrandt*. London: John Murray, 1978.

———. *Leonardo da Vinci*. London: Pelican, 1958.

———. *The Nude*. London: John Murray, 1956.

———. *Rembrandt and the Italian Renaissance*. London: John Murray, 1966.

———. *The Romantic Rebellion*. New York: Harper & Row, 1973.

COLE, SONIA. *The Neolithic Revolution*. London: British Museum, 1967.

CRIGHTON, R. A. *The Floating World*. London: H.M.S.O., 1973.

DAMASE, JACQUES. *Les Folies du Music Hall*. London: Spring Books, 1970.

DELACROIX, EUGENE. *The Journal of Eugene Delacroix*. Edited by Hubert Wellington. Translated by Lucy Norton. London: Phaidon, 1951.

DESCHARNES, ROBERT, AND JEAN-FRANÇOIS CHABRUN. *Auguste Rodin*. New York: Park Lane, 1967.

DÜRER, ALBRECHT. *The Human Figure*. New York: Dover Publications, 1972.

DURRELL, LAWRENCE. *The Greek Islands*. London: Faber & Faber, 1978.

EISLER, GEORG. *Naked to Nude*. London: Thames & Hudson, 1977.

EITNER, LORENZ E. A. *Gericault*. London: Orbis, 1983.

ELSON, ALBERT E., ED. *Rodin Rediscovered*. Washington, D.C.: National Gallery of Art, 1981.

ENGELS, FREDERICK. *The Origin of the Family, Private Property and the State*. London: Lawrence and Wishart, 1972.

ERNST, MAX. *Une Semaine de Bonte*. New York: Dover Publications, 1976.

ETTLINGER, L. D., AND HELEN S. ETTLINGER. *Botticelli*. London: Thames & Hudson, 1976.

EURIPIDES. *The Bacchae*. Translated by Philip Vellacott. London: Penguin, 1972.

EVANS, PRITCHARD E. E. *The Position of Women in Primitive Societies*. London: Faber, 1966.

EVERY, GEORGE. *The Mass*. London: Gill and Macmillan, 1978.

FASOLA, UMBERTO M. *Peter and Paul in Rome*. Rome: Vision, 1980.

FASOLO, UGO. *Titian*. Translated by Patrick Creagh. Florence: Constable, 1980.

FELD, CHARLES. *Picasso, His Recent Drawings, 1966–68*. London: Pall Mall Press, 1969.

FLAM, JACK D. *Matisse on Art*. Oxford: Phaidon, 1984.

FOULQUIE, PAUL. *Existentialism*. Translated by Kathleen Raine. London: Dennis Dobson, 1948.

FREUD, SIGMUND. *Leonardo da Vinci*. Translated by Alan Tyson. London: Ark Paperbacks, 1984.

FRIEDLANDER, MAX J., AND JAKOB ROSENBERG. *The Paintings of Lucas Cranach*. London: Sotheby Parke Burnet, 1978.

FROMENTIN, EUGENE. *The Masters of Past Time.*. London: Dent, 1913.

GARRONE, CARDINAL GABRIEL-MARIE, ED. *The Vatican and Christian Rome*. Rome: Libreria Editrice Vaticana, 1975.

GASCOIGNE, BAMBER. *The Christians*. London: Cape, 1977.

GASSIER, PIERRE. *Goya, A Witness of His Times*. Translated by Helga Harrison. London: Alpine Fine Arts, 1985.

GAUGH, HARRY F. *Willem de Kooning*. New York: Abbeyville Press, 1983.

GAUGUIN, PAUL. *Intimate Journals*. Translated by Van Wyck Brooks. Bloomington: Indiana University Press, 1968.

GENNEP, ARNOLD, VAN. *The Rites of Passage*. London: Routledge & Kegan Paul, 1977.

GIANNELLI, GIULIO, ED. *The World of Ancient Rome*. London: MacDonald, 1967.

GIBBON, EDWARD. *Decline and Fall of the Roman Empire, abridged*. London: Penguin, 1963.

GIEDION, S. *The Eternal Present*. Oxford: Oxford University Press, 1962.

GOLDSCHEIDER, LUDWIG. *The Paintings of Michelangelo*. London: Phaidon, 1948.

GOMBRICH, E. H. *Meditations of a Hobby Horse*. London: Phaidon, 1963.

———. *Norm and Form*. London: Phaidon, 1966.

———. *Symbolic Images*. Oxford: Phaidon, 1972.

GOWING, LAWRENCE. *Matisse*. London: Thames & Hudson, 1979.

GOYA, FRANCISCO. *Los Caprichos*. Commentary translated by Hilda Harris. New York: Dover Publications, 1969.

GRAVES, ROBERT. *The Greek Myths*. London: Penguin, 1983.

———. Introduction to *New Larousse Encyclopedia of Mythology*. London: Hamlyn, 1981.

———. *The White Goddess*. London: Faber & Faber, 1981.

GREER GERMAINE. *The Obstacle Race*. London: Picador, 1979.

GRIGSON, GEOFFREY. *The Romantics*. London: Routledge, 1942.

GUINEA, DR. MIGUEL ANGEL GARCIA. *Altamira*. Translated by Lynn Polak. Madrid: Silex, 1979.

HALL-DUNCAN, NANCY. *Photographic Surrealism*. Cleveland: New Gallery, 1979.

HALLIWELL, LESLIE. *Halliwell's Filmgoer's Companion, 6th Edition.* London: Paladin, 1979.

HARDING, JAMES. *Artistes Pompiers.* London: Academy, 1979.

HARTT, FREDERICK. *Michelangelo.* New York: Abrams, 1964.

HAUSER, ARNOLD. *Mannerism: The Crisis of the Renaissance and the Origin of Modern Art.* London: Routledge, 1965.

———. *The Social History of Art.* London: Routledge, 1962.

HAWKES, JACQUETTA. *The First Great Civilisation.* London: Hutchinson, 1973.

HERODOTUS. *The Histories.* Translated by Aubrey de Sélincourt. London: Penguin, 1954.

HERRERA, HAYDEN. *Frida: A Biography of Frida Kahlo.* New York: Harper Colophon Books, 1983.

———. *Mary Frank.* Purchase, N.Y.: Neuberger Museum, 1978.

HIBBARD, HOWARD. *Bernini.* London: Pelican, 1965.

HIGHAM, CHARLES. *Life in the Old Stone Age.* Cambridge: Cambridge University Press, 1979.

HILLS, PATRICIA. *Alice Neel.* New York: Abrams, 1983.

HILTON, TIMOTHY. *Picasso's Picassos.* London: Arts Council, 1981.

HOLME, BRIAN. *The Art of Advertising.* London: Peerage Books, 1982.

HONOUR, HUGH. *Romanticism.* London: Penguin, 1984.

HORNE, ALISTAIR. *The Price of Glory: Verdun 1916.* London: Macmillan, 1962.

HUDSON, LIAM. *Bodies of Knowledge.* London: Weidenfeld & Nicolson, 1982.

HUGHES, ROBERT. *The Shock of the New.* London: BBC, 1980.

HUIZINGA, J. *The Waning of the Middle Ages.* Translated by F. Hopman. London: Penguin, 1979.

HUXLEY, ALDOUS. *Music at Night.* London: Penguin, 1950.

HUYGHE, RENÉ. *Delacroix.* Translated by Jonathan Griffin. London: Thames & Hudson, 1963.

HUYSMANS, J. K. *Grünewald.* London: Phaidon, 1976.

IONS, VERONICA. *Egyptian Mythology.* London: Hamlyn, 1982.

JEAN, MARCEL. *The History of Surrealist Painting.* Translated by Simon Watson Taylor. London: Weidenfeld & Nicolson, 1950.

JOACHIMIDES, CHRISTOS M., NORMAN ROSENTHAL, AND WIELAND SCHMIED, ED. *German Art in the 20th Century.* London: Royal Academy of Arts, 1985.

JOHNS, CATHERINE. *Sex or Symbol.* London: Colonnade Books, 1982.

JOHNSON, PAUL. *A History of Christianity.* London: Weidenfeld & Nicholson, 1976.

KENT, SARAH. *Elisabeth Frink.* London: Royal Academy of Arts, 1985.

———, AND J. MORREAU. *Women's Images of Men.* London: Writers and Readers, 1985.

KHANDALAVALA, KARL. *The Bhagavata Purana in Kangra Painting.* India: Lalit Kala Academi, 1974.

KLINGENDER, FRANCIS D. *Art and the Industrial Revolution.* London: Evelyn Adams & Mackay, 1968.

LACKNER, STEPHAN. *Beckmann.* New York: Abrams, 1977.

LAURTREAMONT, COMTE D. E. *Maldoror.* Translated by Alexis Lykiard. London: Allison and Busby, 1983.

LEONARDO DA VINCI. *Notebooks.* Edited by Irma A. Richter. Oxford: Worlds Classics, 1952.

LEROI-GOURHAN, ANDRÉ. *The Dawn of European Art.* Translated by Sara Champion. Cambridge: Cambridge University Press, 1982.

————. *Treasures of Prehistoric Art.* Translated by Norbert Guterman. New York: Abrams, 1968.

LEVEY, MICHAEL. *Early Renaissance.* London: Penguin, 1967.

————. *High Renaissance.* London: Penguin, 1975.

LORD, JAMES. *Giacometti.* London: Faber & Faber, 1986.

LUCIE-SMITH, EDWARD. *Art in the Seventies.* Oxford: Phaidon, 1980.

————. *The Body, Images of the Nude.* London: Thames & Hudson, 1981.

————. *Eroticism in Western Art.* London: Thames & Hudson, 1972.

————. *The Male Nude.* Oxford: Phaidon, 1985.

MACHIAVELLI, NICOLO. *The Prince.* London: Routledge, 1893.

MACMURRAY, JOHN. *Reason and Emotion.* London: Faber & Faber, 1947.

MALCOLM, JANET. *Diana and Nikon.* Boston: David R. Godine, 1980.

McCULLY, MARILYN. *A Picasso Anthology.* London: Arts Council, 1981.

McLEOD, MALCOLM, AND JOHN MACK. *Ethnic Sculpture.* London: British Museum, 1985.

MANNIX, DANIEL P. *Those About to Die.* London: Panther, 1971.

MELLAART, JAMES. *Earliest Civilisations of the Near East.* London: Thames & Hudson, 1965.

————. *The Neolithic of the Near East.* London: Thames & Hudson, 1975.

MEYER, JOHANN. *Sexual Life in Ancient India.* London: Routledge & Kegan Paul, 1952.

MICHELL, DR. GEORGE, AND DR. LINDA LEACH, EDS. *In the Image of Man.* London: Arts Council, 1982.

MILLER, HENRY. *The Colossus of Maroussi.* London: Penguin, 1964.

MINISTRY OF CULTURE, U.A.R. *A Guide to the Egyptian Museum.* Cairo: Government Printing Office, 1968.

MOORE, HENRY, AND JOHN HEDGECOE. *Henry Moore.* London: Ebury Press, 1986.

————, AND GEMMA LEVINE. *Henry Moore Wood Sculpture.* London: Sidgwick & Jackson, 1983.

MORGAN, STUART. *Robert Mapplethorpe 1970–1983*. London: ICA, 1983.

MULVEY, LAURA, AND PETER WOLLEN. *Frida Kahlo and Tina Modotti*. London: Whitechapel Art Gallery, 1982.

MUNRO, ELEANOR. *Originals: American Women Artists*. New York: Simon and Schuster, 1979.

MURDOCH, IRIS. *Sartre*. London: Collins Fontana Library, 1967.

MURRAY, LINDA. *Michelangelo*. London: Thames & Hudson, 1984.

MURRAY, PETER, AND LINDA MURRAY. *A Dictionary of Art and Artists*. London: Penguin, 1959.

MUYBRIDGE, EADWEARD. *The Human Figure in Motion*. New York: Dover Publications, 1955.

NARAIN, L. A. *Khajuraho*. New Delhi: Roli Books International, 1982.

NIETZSCHE, FRIEDRICH. *Beyond Good and Evil*. Translated by R. J. Hollingdale. London: Penguin, 1973.

———. *Twilight of the Idols and the Anti-Christ*. Translated by R. J. Hollingdale. London: Penguin, 1968.

O'KEEFFE, GEORGIA. *Georgia O'Keeffe*. New York: Viking, 1976.

ORTO, LUISA FRANCHI DELL'. *Ancient Rome*. Translated by Carol Wasserman. London: Summerfield Press, 1982.

OSTEN, GERT VON DER, AND HORST VEY OSTEN. *Painting and Sculpture in Germany and the Netherlands: 1500–1600*. London: Penguin, 1969.

OVENDEN, GRAHAM. *Nymphets & Fairies*. London: Academy, 1976.

PALMER, L. R. *A New Guide to the Palace of Knossos*. London: Faber & Faber, 1966.

PANOFSKY, ERWIN. *Renaissance and Renascences in Western Art*. London: Paladin, 1970.

PARINAUD, ANDRÉ. *The Unspeakable Confessions of Salvador Dali*. Translated by Harold J. Salonson. London: Quartet Books, 1977.

PASSERON, RENÉ. *Surrealism*. Translated by John Griffiths. Ware, England: Omega Books, 1984.

PEARSALL, RONALD. *Tell Me, Pretty Maiden*. Exeter, England: Webb & Bower, 1981.

———. *The Worm in the Bud*. London: Penguin, 1969.

PEDRETTI, CARLO. *Leonardo*. London: Thames & Hudson, 1973.

PENROSE, ROLAND. *Picasso: His Life and Work*. London: Granada, 1981.

———. *Portrait of Picasso*. London: Thames & Hudson, 1981.

———. *Picasso Sculpture*. London: Arts Council, 1967.

PLATO. *The Last Days of Socrates*. Translated by Hugh Tredennick. London: Penguin, 1954.

———. *The Symposium*. Translated by Walter Hamilton. London: Penguin, 1951.

POPE-HENNESSY, JOHN. *Essays on Italian Sculpture*. London: Phaidon, 1968.

POPHAM, A. E. *The Drawings of Leonardo da Vinci*. London: Cape, 1964.

POWELL, T. G. E. *Prehistoric Art*. London: Thames & Hudson, 1966.

PRITCHETT, V. S. *The Spanish Temper*. London: Hogarth Press, 1984.

RACHEWILTZ, BORIS DE. *Black Eros*. Translated by Peter Whigham. London: Allen & Unwin, 1968.

RAWSON, PHILIP. *The Art of Tantra*. London: Thames & Hudson, 1973.

———. *Indian Asia*. Oxford: Phaidon, 1977.

READ, JOHN. *Portrait of an Artist: Henry Moore*. London: Whizzard Press, 1979.

REWALD, JOHN. *The History of Impressionism*. London: Secker & Warburg, 1973.

REWALD, SABINE. *Balthus*. New York: Metropolitan Museum and Abrams, 1984.

RHODE, ERIC. *A History of the Cinema*. New York: Da Capo Paperback, 1985.

RICHTER, GISELA. *A Handbood of Greek Art*. London: Phaidon, 1959.

RILKE, RAINER MARIA. *Rodin and Other Prose Pieces*. Translated by G. Craig Houston. London: Quartet Books, 1986.

ROMER, JOHN. *Romer's Egypt*. London: Michael Joseph, 1982.

ROSEN, CHARLES, AND HENRI ZERNER. *Romanticism and Realism*. London: Faber & Faber, 1984.

ROWLANDS, JOHN. *Bosch, The Garden of Earthly Delights*. Oxford: Phaidon, 1979.

RUBIN, WILLIAM, ED. *Pablo Picasso*. New York: Museum of Modern Art, 1980.

SARTRE, JEAN-PAUL. *Being and Nothingness*. Translated by H. E. Barnes. London: Methuen 1957.

———. *Nausea*. London: Hamish Hamilton, 1962.

SCHIFF, GERT, *Picasso: The Last Years 1963–1973*. New York: George Braziller, 1983.

SCHIFF, GERT, ET AL. *Henry Fuseli*. London: Tate Gallery, 1975.

SCHNEEDE, UWE M. *Surrealism*. New York: Abrams, 1973.

SELTMAN, CHARLES. *Women in Antiquity*. London: Pan Books, 1956.

SHEARMAN, JOHN. *Mannerism*. London: Penguin, 1967.

SIEVEKING, ANN. *The Cave Artists*. London: Thames & Hudson, 1979.

SITWELL, OSBERT. *Left Hand, Right Hand*. London: Macmillan, 1945–50.

SPALDING, FRANCES. *Magnificent Dreams*. Oxford: Phaidon, 1978.

STEEGMULLER, FRANCIS, ED. AND TRANS. *Flaubert in Egypt*. London: Michael Haag, 1983.

STEIN, GERTRUDE. *Picasso*. New York: Dover Publications, 1984.

STEINBERG, LEO. *The Sexuality of Christ in Renaissance Art and in Modern Oblivion*. New York: Pantheon Books, 1983.

STEVENS, MARY ANN, ED. *The Orientalists. Delacroix to Mattisse*. Washington, D.C.: National Gallery of Art, 1984.

STIERLIN, HENRI. *The Cultural History of the Pharaohs*. Translated by Erica Abrams. Geneva: Agence Internationale d'Edition, 1983.

STOKES, ADRIAN. *Greek Culture and the Ego*. London: Tavistock Publications, 1958.

———. *Reflections on the Nude*. London: Tavistock Publications, 1967.

———. *Stones of Rimini*. New York: Schocken Books, 1969.

SUETONIUS. *The Twelve Caesars*. Translated by Robert Graves. London: Penguin, 1979.

SUTTON, DENYS. *Triumphant Satyr*. London: Country Life, 1966.

SWADDLING, JUDITH. *The Ancient Olympic Games*. London: British Museum, 1980.

SYLVESTER, DAVID. *Alberto Giacometti*. London: Arts Council, 1965.

———. *Henry Moore*. London. Arts Council, 1968

———. *Interviews with Francis Bacon*. London: Thames & Hudson, 1980.

TACITUS. *The Annals of Imperial Rome*. Translated by Michael Grant. London: Penguin, 1956.

TALESE, GAY. *Thy Neighbour's Wife*. London: Collins, 1980.

TANNAHILL, REAY. *Sex in History*. London: Abacus, 1981.

TAYLOR, JEREMY. *Holy Living and Dying*. London: Bohn, 1851.

TEMIZER, RACI. *Museum of Anatolian Civilizations*. Ankara, Turkey: Ankara Turizmi, 1981.

TWAIN, MARK. *The Innocents Abroad*. New York: Bantam Books, 1964.

VANDIER, JACQUES. *Les Antiquités Egyptiennes au Musée du Louvre*. Paris: Édit de Musées Nationaux, 1973.

VASARI, GEORGIO. *The Lives of the Artists*. Translated by George Bull. London: Penguin, 1965.

VERGO, PETER. *Vienna, 1900*. Edinburgh: H.M.S.O., 1983.

VERMEULE, EMILY. *Greece in the Bronze Age*. Chicago: University of Chicago, 1972.

VOLOPONI, PAOLO. *Masaccio*. Milan: Rizzoli, 1981.

WALKER, JOHN. *National Gallery of Art,* Washington, D.C. New York: Abrams, 1984.

WARNER, MARINA. *Alone of All Her Sex*. New York: Knopf, 1976.

WATSON, FRANCIS. *A Concise History of India*. London: Thames & Hudson, 1974.

WEBB, PETER. *The Erotic Arts*. London: Secker and Warburg, 1975.

WEITZMANN, KURT, AND MARGARET ENGLISH FRAZER. *Age of Spirituality*. New York: Metropolitan Museum of Art, 1977.

WHITELEY, JON. *Ingres*. London: Oresko Books, 1977.

WHITFORD, FRANK. *Egon Schiele*. London: Thames & Hudson, 1981.

WILDE, JOHANNES. *Michelangelo*. Oxford: Oxford University Press, 1978.

WILLIAMS, GWYN A. *Goya and the Impossible Revolution*. London: Penguin, 1984.

WILMERDING, JOHN. *American Art*. London: Pelican, 1976.

WILSON, CHARIS. *Edward Weston: Nudes*. New York: Aperture, 1977.

WIND, EDGAR. *Pagan Mysteries in the Renaissance*. London: Faber & Faber, 1968.

WITTKOWER, RUDOLF. *Bernini*. London: Phaidon, 1955.

WOLFFLIN, HEINRICH. *Classic Art*. Translated by Peter Murray and Linda Murray. London: Phaidon, 1959.

————. *Renaissance and Baroque*. Translated by Katherine Simon. London: Fontana, 1964.

WORKMAN, HERBERT B. *Persecution in the Early Church*. Oxford: Oxford University Press, 1980.

WYE, DEBORAH. *Louise Bourgeois*. New York: Museum of Modern Art, 1982.

YOUNG, WAYLAND. *Eros Denied*. London: Corgi Books, 1968.

PICTURE CREDITS

All illustrations are of paintings unless otherwise specified. Credits for reproduction belong to the holding gallery or museum unless another source is given.

CHAPTER I:

1. Mapplethorpe, *Lisa Lyon,* 1983. Photograph. Robert Mapplethorpe.

2. Mapplethorpe, *Lisa Lyon,* 1983. Photograph. Robert Mapplethorpe.

3. Graeco-Roman, *The Three Graces,* ca. first century. Marble relief. Cliché des Musées Nationaux, Paris.

4. Rodin, *The Three Shades,* 1881. Bronze. Musée Rodin, Paris.

5. Greek, *Standing Youth (The Kritios Boy),* ca. 480 B.C. Marble. Acropolis Museum, Athens. Newsweek Books.

6. Greek, *Warriors,* ca. 460 B.C. Bronze. Reggio Museum. Art Resource.

7. Hagesandros, Polydoros, and Athanodoros of Rhodes, *Laocöon and His Sons,* ca. 175–150 B.C. Marble. Vatican Museum, Rome. Lauros-Giraudon/Art Resource.

8. Greek, *Poseidon* (or *Zeus*), ca. 460 B.C. Bronze. National Museum, Athens. Bildarchiv Foto Marburg/Art Resource.

9. Mapplethorpe, *Lisa Lyon,* 1983. Photograph. Robert Mapplethorpe.

10. Mapplethorpe, *Untitled,* 1981. Photograph. Robert Mapplethorpe.

11. Correggio, *The Three Graces,* ca. 1518. Fresco, Camera di San Paulo, Parma. Art Resource.

12. Mapplethorpe, Polaroid, 1985. Photograph. Robert Mapplethorpe.

13. Greek, *A Winner Gets His Ribbons,* ca. 500–475 B.C. Vase painting. Reproduced by courtesy of the Trustees of the British Museum, London.

14. Weston, *Charis Wilson,* 1936. Photograph. Center for Creative Photography, Arizona Board of Regents, 1981.

15. Picasso, *The Sculptor and His Model,* 1933. Etching from Picasso's Vollard Suite. Art Resource. © ARS, New York/SPADEM, 1989.

16. Picasso, *Nude in an Armchair,* 1929. Musée Picasso, Paris. Lauros-Giraudon/Art Resource. © ARS, New York/SPADEM, 1989.

17. Picasso, *Reclining Nude and Head of Man,* 1972. Ink wash. Museum of Contemporary Art, Caracas. © ARS, New York/SPADEM, 1989.

18. Sleigh, *Double Image: Paul Rosano,* 1974. Photo credit: Geoffrey Clements.

19. Egypt, Middle Kingdom, *Unity of the Two Lands,* ca. 2000 B.C. Stone relief on the throne of Sen Wosret I at Lisht. Hirmer Fotoarchiv.

CHAPTER 2:

20. Paleolithic, left hand of a cave painter, ca. 15,000 B.C. Pigment on stone, cave of El Castillo. From S. Giedon, The Eternal Present: The Beginnings of Art, Bollinger Series 35, Vol. 6/1. Copyright © 1962 National Gallery of Art. Reprinted with permission of Princeton University Press.

21. Sautuola, drawing of Altamira cave painting, 1880. From *Altamira.* The New York Public Library.

22. Plaque on the *Pioneer 10* spacecraft, 1972. Engraving on aluminium. National Aeronautics and Space Administration.

23. Paleolithic, vulva incised on stone, ca. 27,000 B.C., from La Ferrassie, Dordogne. Les Eyzies Museum. From S. Giedon, The Eternal Present: The Beginnings of Art, Bollinger Series 35, Vol. 6/1. Copyright © 1962 National Gallery of Art. Reprinted with permission of Princeton University Press.

24. Paleolithic, double phallus on branched head of a pierced staff, ca. 12,000 B.C. Engraving on deer horn from the Gorge d'Enfer, Dordogne. St. Germain-en-Laye Museum. From *The Eternal Present: The Beginnings of Art* (National Gallery of Art). Photograph by Achille Wieder.

25. Phallic stalagmite. Natural stone. Cave of Le Combel, Pech-Merle, Lot. From S. Giedon, The Eternal Present: The Beginnings of Art, Bollinger Series 35, Vol. 6/1. Copyright © 1962 National Gallery of Art. Reprinted with permission of Princeton University Press.

26. Greek, herm, ca. 520 B.C. Carved marble pillar from Siphnos. National Museum, Athens. Bildarchiv Foto Marburg/Art Resource.

27. Plaster cast of carved reindeer antler, rolled out to show both sides, ca. 12,000 B.C. Carving from Lourthet, Hautes Pyrénées. Musée des Antiquités Nationales, Paris. Caisse Nationale des Monuments Historiques.

28. Paleolithic, carving of bison, ca. 12,000 B.C. Horn carving from La Madeleine, Dordogne. Musée des Antiquités Nationales, Paris.

29. Paleolithic, man with snout face, ca. 12,000 B.C., incised on stone. Grotto de la Marche, Vienna.

30. Paleolithic, antlered man, ca. 12,000 B.C. Painted and engraved. Cave of Les Trois Frères, Ariège.

31. Abbé Breuil, drawing of the antlered man. Musée de l'Homme, Paris.

32. A shaman of the Tungus tribe, 1705. Book engraving in *North and East Tartary* from the Houghton Library, Harvard University. From S. Giedon, The Eternal Present: The Beginnings of Art, Bollinger Series 35, Vol. 6/1. Copyright © 1962 National Gallery of Art. Reprinted with permission of Princeton University Press.

33. Paleolithic, masklike head, ca. 12,000 B.C. Engraved on cave wall, Altamira. From *The Eternal Present: The Beginnings of Art* (National Gallery of Art). Photograph by Achille Wieder.

34. African, Janus figure, nineteenth century. Carved in bone. From Zaire. Reproduced by courtesy of the Trustees of the British Museum, London.

35. The Lincoln Imp, thirteenth century. Stone carving. Lincoln Cathedral. Woodmansterne Picture Library.

36. Paleolithic, female statuette, ca. 22,000 B.C. Carved in mammoth ivory. Musée de l'Homme, Paris. Newsweek Books.

37. Picasso, *Head of a Woman*, 1931. Bronze. Musée Picasso, Paris.

38. Paleolithic, female statuette, ca. 20,000 B.C. Stone carving. Natural History Museum, Vienna. Laurie Platt Winfrey.

39. Mesolithic, hunters and ibex, ca. 7000 B.C. Rock painting, Spain. Newsweek Books.

40. Paleolithic, African rock engraving linking sexuality with hunting, incised on cave wall, Algeria. Frobenius-Institut.

41. African rock engraving of ritual intercourse, incised on cave wall, Fezzan, North Africa. Fabrizio Mori.

42. Giorgione, *Venus,* ca. 1500. Pinacoteca, Dresden.

43. Paleolithic, reclining female figure, ca. 12,000 B.C. Stone relief, cave of La Magdelaine, Tarn. From S. Giedon, The Eternal Present: The Beginnings of Art, Bollinger Series 35, Vol. 6/1. Copyright © 1962 National Gallery of Art. Reprinted with permission of Princeton University Press.

44. Michelangelo, *Captive,* ca. 1520. Marble, Accademia Florence. Newsweek Books.

45. Paleolithic, reclining female figure, ca. 12,000 B.C. Stone relief, cave of La Magdelaine, Tarn. From S. Giedon, The Eternal Present: The Beginnings of Art, Bollinger Series 35, Vol. 6/1. Copyright © 1962 National Gallery of Art. Reprinted with permission of Princeton University Press. Photograph by Achille Wieder.

46. Paleolithic, woman holding a horn, ca. 20,000 B.C. Stone relief from Laussel. Museum of Aquitaine, Bordeaux. From S. Giedon, The Eternal Present: The Beginnings of Art, Bollinger Series 35, Vol. 6/1. Copyright © 1962 National Gallery of Art. Reprinted with permission of Princeton University Press.

47. De Kooning, *Woman III,* 1951–52. Tehran Museum of Contemporary Art. The New York Public Library.

CHAPTER 3:

48. Archaic Period, *Palette of Narmer* (obverse), ca. 3000 B.C. Slate relief. Cairo Museum.

49. Old Kingdom, cowherder carrying a calf, ca. 2450 B.C. Stone relief, Tomb of Ti, Sakkara.

50. Old Kingdom, the steward Memy-Sabu and his wife, ca. 2500 B.C. Stone carving from Giza. The Metropolitan Museum of Art, New York.

51. Old Kingdom, a scribe (possibly Kai, a provincial governor), ca. 2500 B.C. Stone carving from Sakkara. Musée Louvre, Paris.

52. Archaic Period, *Palette of Narmer* (reverse), ca. 3000 B.C. Slate relief. Cairo Museum.

53. Old Kingdom, the goddess Hathor, ca. 2500. Stone relief, Temple of King Sahure, Sakkara. Werner Forman Archive.

54. New Kingdom, Hathor as a cow giving milk to the young Amenhotep II, ca. 1500 B.C. Painted limestone. Cairo Museum. Newsweek Books.

55. Old Kingdom, King Mykerinus between Hathor and local deity, ca. 2500 B.C. Slate from Giza. Cairo Museum.

56. Neolithic, Europe, man and woman, ca. 3600 B.C. Pottery figurines. National Museum of Antiquities, Bucharest. Art Resource.

57. Neolithic, Anatolia, fertility goddess, ca. 6000 B.C. Pottery figurine from Catal Hüyük. Museum of Anatolian Civilizations, Ankara.

58. Neolithic, Anatolia, bull, stag, and boar baiting, ca. 6000 B.C. Wall painting from Catal Hüyük. Museum of Anatolian Civilizations, Ankara.

59. Minoan Crete, bull leaping, ca. 1500 B.C. Fresco from the Palace of Knossos, Crete. Art Resource.

60. Modern drawing of Neolithic entwined figures, ca. 5400 B.C. Baked clay from Hacilar. Museum of Anatolian Civilizations, Ankara. From *Neolithic of the Near East.* The New York Public Library.

61. Late Period, Shu separating Geb and Nut, ca. 1000 B.C. Drawing on papyrus, Twenty-first Dynasty. Reproduced by courtesy of the Trustees of the British Museum, London.

62. Late Period, the goddess Nut, ca. 600 B.C. Carved inside lid of a stone sarcophagus, Twenty-sixth Dynasty. Reproduced by courtesy of the Trustees of the British Library, London.

63. Adrian Gill, ink and wash drawing of New Kingdom carved stone relief, Isis tending the dead Osiris, ca. 1300 B.C. Abydos.

64. Adrian Gill, ink and wash drawing of New Kingdom carved stone relief, conception of Horus, ca. 1300 B.C. Abydos.

65. Late Period, Isis with the infant Horus, ca. 300 B.C. Stone. Vatican Museums, Rome.

66. Old Kingdom, circumcision, ca. 2350 B.C. Stone relief, Sixth Dynasty. Cairo Museum. Giraudon/Art Resource.

67. New Kingdom, Isis and Nefus protect the djed column of Osiris, ca. 1360 B.C. Pectoral of Tutankhamen, Eighteenth Dynasty. Cairo Museum. Hirmer Fotoarchiv.

68. New Kingdom, dancing girls, ca. 1500 B.C. Wall painting, Eighteenth Dynasty. Reproduced by courtesy of the Trustees of the British Museum, London.

69. New Kingdom, Rameses III and a concubine, ca. 1190 B.C. Stone relief, Twentieth Dynasty. Temple of Medinet Habu. The New York Public Library.

70. New Kingdom, Nakht and his family on hunting trip, ca. 1410 B.C. Wall painting, Tomb of Nakht, Deir-el-Medina, Eighteenth Dynasty. Egyptian Expedition. The Metropolitan Museum of Art, New York.

71. New Kingdom, statue of Rameses II with a queen, ca. 1250 B.C. Stone. Abu Simbel. Nineteenth Dynasty. Hirmer Fotoarchiv.

72. Colossus of Rameses II, photograph of 1867. Laurie Platt Winfrey.

73. New Kingdom, Battle of Kadesh, 1294 B.C. Stone relief, Ramesseum. Nineteenth Dynasty, from *Cultural History of the Pharaohs*. (Agence International Edition, 1983, Henri Stierlin, Geneva.) The New York Public Library.

CHAPTER 4:

74. Indian, prince and dancing girl, tenth century. Stone temple carving, Khajuraho. Seth Joel-Wheeler Pictures.

75. Delos, Avenue of Priapus, third century B.C. Carved marble columns. From *Sex or Symbol* (Colonnade Books, 1982). The New York Public Library.

76. Michelangelo, *Noah's Drunkenness*, ca. 1510. Fresco, Sistine Chapel, Rome. Alinari Scala/Art Resource.

77. Greek, the Kleophrades Painter, *Dionysus and Revelers*, ca. 490 B.C. Vase painting. Wilhelm Collection, Basel. The New York Public Library.

78. Greek, Makron, *Maenad and Satyr,* ca. 480 B.C. Painting on cup. Staatliche Antikensammlungen, Munich.

79. Greek, Douris, *Reveling Satyrs,* ca. 485 B.C. Painting on wine cooler. Reproduced by courtesy of the Trustees of the British Museum, London.

80. Greek, after Scopas, *Maenad,* fourth century B.C. Marble. Skulturensammlung, Dresden. Bildarchiv Foto Marburg/Art Resource.

81. Greek, *Dancing Around a Model Phallus at a Festival,* fifth century B.C. Painting on cup, Villa Giulia, Rome.

82. Greek, Makron, *A Satyr-Player,* ca. 480 B.C. Painting on cup. Staatliche Antikensammlungen, Munich.

83. Greek, Epiktetos, musician and dancer, ca. 505 B.C. Painting on cup. British Museum, London. Bridgeman/Art Resource.

84. Roman, theatrical masks, first century B.C. Mosaic. Capitoline Museum, Rome. Art Resource.

85. Greek, the Dikaios Painter, *Lovers at a Symposium,* late sixth century B.C. Vase painting. Musées Royaux, Brussels.

86. Greek, the Brygos Painter, *Man with Young Boy,* ca. 490 B.C. Painting on cup. Ashmolean Museum, Oxford.

87. Greek, the Briseis Painter, *Man with Hetaerae,* ca. 485 B.C. Painting on cup, Ashmolean Museum, Oxford.

88. Greek, the Triptolemos Painter, *Lovemaking on a Bed,* ca. 470 B.C. Painting on cup. City Museum, Tarquinia. From *Sex or Symbol* (Colonnade Books, 1982). The New York Public Library.

89. Greek, the Shuvalov Painter, *Young Lovers,* late fifth century B.C. Painting on a jug. Antikenmuseum, Berlin, Staatliche Museen Preussischer Kulturbesitz.

90. Greek, Phintias, *Two Hetaerae,* ca. 510 B.C. Vase painting. Staatliche Antikensammlungen, Munich.

91. Indian, Markandesvara Temple, tenth century. Art Resource.

92. Indian, *Dancer Braiding Her Hair,* tenth century. Stone temple carving, Khajuraho. Jean-Louis Nou.

93. Indian, *Figures in Complex Embrace,* tenth century. Stone carving, Kandarya Temple, Khajuraho. Giraudon/Art Resource.

94. Indian, *Lovers.* Stone temple carving from central India, tenth century. Los Angeles County Museum of Art.

95. Indian, *Krishna Surprises the Gopis,* eighteenth century. Painting on cloth. By courtesy of the Board of Trustees of the Victoria and Albert Museum, London.

96. Indian, the Jain saint Bahubali, 981. Colossal stone carving at Sravana Belgola, Karnataka.

97. Indian, *The Sexual Posture Cakra Asana,* eighteenth century. Gouache on cloth. Ajit Mookerjee Collection. The New York Public Library.

98. Indian, *Prince and Lady Prolonging Intercourse with a Cup of Tea,* eighteenth century. Miniature painting. By courtesy of the Board of Trustees of the Victoria and Albert Museum, London.

99. Japanese, Harunobu, *Lovers by a Landscape Screen,* ca. 1768. Wood block print. By courtesy of the Board of Trustees of the Victoria and Albert Museum, London.

100. Japanese, Koryusai, *Lovers Behind a Folding Screen,* ca. 1770. Wood block print. By courtesy of the Board of Trustees of the Victoria and Albert Museum, London.

101. Japanese, Koryusai, *The Baths*, ca. 1770. Wood block print. By courtesy of the Board of Trustees of the Victoria and Albert Museum, London.

102. Japanese, Utamaro, frontispiece from *The Poem of the Pillow,* 1788. Wood block print. By courtesy of the Board of Trustees of the Victoria and Albert Museum, London.

103. Japanese, Utamaro, *Fishergirl Ravished by Water Spirits,* 1788. Wood block print. Reproduced by courtesy of the Trustees of the British Museum, London.

CHAPTER 5:

104. Grünewald, *Crucifixion* (detail), 1513–15, formerly altarpiece, Isenheim Monastery. Unterlinden Museum, Colmar. Giraudon/Art Resource.

105. Roman, *Christ the Sun Rising,* third century. Wall mosaic, Giullis Mausoleum, Vatican Necropolis. Vatican Museums. Newsweek Books.

106. Roman, *Leopard Attacking Condemned Man,* first century. Mosaic from Zliten Tripolitania. Instituto Archaeologico Germanico, Rome.

107. Roman, *The Farnese Bull,* third century. Marble. National Archeological Museum, Naples. Art Resource.

108. Roman, *Crucified Man,* second century(?). Graffito scratched on wall, Pozzuoli. Fasolo.

109. Bacon, *Three Studies for Figures at the Base of a Crucifixion,* 1944. The Tate Gallery, London.

110. Bacon, *Three Studies for a Crucifixion,* right-hand panel, 1962. Guggenheim Museum, New York. Newsweek Books.

111. Greek, Lysippos, *Herakles* (copy by the Athenian Glykon), fourth century B.C. Marble. National Museum, Naples. Bildarchiv Foto Marburg/Art Resource.

112. Roman, tintinnabulum, first century. Bronze. Rheinisches Landesmuseum, Trier.

113. Roman, Projecta's casket lid, ca. 380. Silver and silver gilt. Reproduced by courtesy of the Trustees of the British Museum, London.

114. Roman, Projecta's casket side, ca. 380. Silver and silver gilt. Reproduced by courtesy of the Trustees of the British Museum, London.

115. German, golden reliquary designed to contain Charlemagne's arm, fifteenth century. Cathedral Treasury, Aachen. Bildarchiv Foto Marburg/Art Resource.

116. German, *Adam and Eve Reproached by the Lord,* 1015. Bronze door panel, Hildesheim Cathedral.

117. German, *Expulsion from Paradise* (detail), 1015. Bronze door panel, Hildesheim Cathedral. Bildarchiv Foto Marburg/Art Resource.

118. English, *Adam and Eve Getting the Forbidden Fruit,* twelfth century. Wall painting, St. Botolph's Church, Hardham, Sussex. Royal Commission on the Historical Monuments of England.

119. French, *Woman Tormented by Lust,* twelfth century. Stone relief, Musée des Augustans, Toulouse. (From *Earth Rites,* Granada, 1982). The New York Public Library.

120. French, *Eve,* twelfth century. Stone, formerly in Autun Cathedral, now in Musée Relin. Giraudon/Art Resource.

121. Irish, female exhibitionist, twelfth century(?). National Museum of Ireland, Dublin.

122. Di Bartolo, *Hell: Punishment for Sinners,* 1393. Collegiate Church, San Gimignano. Art Resource.

123. Carpaccio, *St. George Slaying the Dragon* (detail), ca. 1500. Fresco, Chapel of St. George, Venice. Giraudon/Art Resource.

124. Baldung, *Death and the Woman,* ca. 1517. Oeffentliche Kunstsammling Basel, Kunstmuseum.

125. Grünewald, *Crucifixion,* 1513–15, formerly altarpiece, Isenheim Monastery. Unterlinden Museum Colmar. Giraudon/Art Resource.

126. Bourges Cathedral, *The Last Judgment,* thirteenth century. Stone relief on cathedral tympanum. Bildarchiv Foto Marburg/Art Resource.

127. Michelangelo, *Pietà,* 1498–99. Marble. St. Peter's, Rome.

128. Michelangelo, *Rondanini Pietà,* 1555–64. Marble. Civic Museum, Milan.

129. Michelangelo, *Resurrection,* ca. 1530s(?). Drawing. Royal Library, Windsor.

130. Michelangelo, *Risen Christ,* ca. 1530s(?). Drawing. Royal Library, Windsor. (All reproductions from the Royal Library, Windsor, by gracious permission of Her Majesty the Queen.)

CHAPTER 6:

131. Botticelli, *Birth of Venus* (detail), ca. 1480s. Uffizi, Florence. Alinari/Art Resource.

132. Donatello, *Judith and Holofernes,* ca. 1446–60. Bronze. Palazzo Vecchio, Florence.

133. Cellini, *Perseus,* ca. 1545–54. Bronze. Loggia dei Lanzi, Florence. Newsweek Books.

134. Giambologna, *Rape of the Sabine Women,* 1583. Marble. Loggia dei Lanzi, Florence. Scala/Art Resource.

135. Ammannati, *Fountain of Neptune, Nereid, and Triton,* 1563–75. Bronze. Piazza della Signoria, Florence. Newsweek Books.

136. Andrea Pisano, *Baptism of Christ,* 1330–36. Bronze door panel, Baptistry, Florence. Art Resource.

137. Ghiberti, *Abraham Sacrificing Isaac,* 1402. Bronze. Bargello, Florence. Newsweek Books.

138. Ghiberti, *The Creation of Eve,* ca. 1426. Bronze door panel, Baptistry, Florence. Alinari/Art Resource.

139. Raphael, drawing for *Disputa,* ca. 1510. Kunstinstitut, Frankfurt.

140. Vesalius, plate from *De Humani Corporis Fabrica,* 1543. Woodcut. British Library, London.

141. Masaccio, *Baptism of the Neophytes,* 1425–27. Fresco, Brancacci Chapel, Santa Maria del Carmine, Florence. Alinari-Scala/Art Resource.

142. Masaccio, *The Fall,* 1425–27. Fresco, Brancacci Chapel, Santa Maria del Carmine, Florence.

143. Donatello, *David,* ca. 1446–60. Bronze. Bargello, Florence. Newsweek Books.

144. Donatello, *Bust of San Rossore,* 1422–27. Bronze. Museo di San Matteo, Pisa. Art Resource.

145. Donatello, *David,* ca. 1446–60. Bronze. Bargello, Florence. Art Resource.

146. Donatello, *Atys-Amorino,* ca. 1440. Bronze. Bargello, Florence. Art Resource.

147. Andrea Della Robbia, *Boy with Bagpipes,* mid-fifteenth century. Terra-cotta. Victoria and Albert Museum, London.

148. Chimney piece, mid-fifteenth century. Palazzo Ducale, Urbino. Alinari/Art Resource.

149. Botticelli, *Birth of Venus*, ca. 1480s. Uffizi, Florence. Alinari/Art Resource.

150. Michelangelo, *David*, 1504. Marble. Accademia, Florence.

151. Michelangelo, *David*, 1504. Marble. Accademia, Florence.

152. Michelangelo, study for cartoon of the *Battle of Cascina*, ca. 1504–5. Drawing with chalk. Graphische Sammlung Albertina, Vienna.

153. Michelangelo, *God Dividing Light from Darkness*, 1511. Fresco, Sistine Chapel ceiling, the Vatican Museums, Rome. Art Resource.

154. Michelangelo, *The Creation of Adam*, 1511. Fresco, Sistine Chapel ceiling, the Vatican Museums, Rome.

155. Michelangelo, *nude figures*, ca. 1508–9. Fresco, Sistine Chapel ceiling, the Vatican Museums, Rome. Art Resource.

156. Michelangelo, *nude figure*, 1511. Fresco, Sistine Chapel ceiling, the Vatican Museums, Rome. Art Resource.

157. Michelangelo, *The Last Judgment*, 1536–41. Fresco, Sistine Chapel, the Vatican Museums, Rome. Art Resource.

158. Michelangelo, *Self-Portrait* (detail from *The Last Judgment*), ca. 1536–38. Fresco, Sistine Chapel, the Vatican Museums, Rome. Art Resource.

159. Michelangelo, *Prince of Hell* (detail from *The Last Judgment*), 1541. Fresco, Sistine Chapel, the Vatican Museums, Rome. Art Resource.

160. Titian, *Venus with the Organist*, ca. 1548. Prado, Madrid. Art Resource.

CHAPTER 7:

161. Dürer, *Self-Portrait* (naked), ca. 1503. Pen and brush, Schlossmuseum, Weimar. Kunstsammlungen zu Weimar.

162. Raphael, nude studies for the *Battle of Ostia*, 1515. Drawing with red chalk. Graphische Sammlung Albertina, Vienna.

163. Leonardo, standing nude man, ca. 1506–8. Pen and red chalk. Royal Library, Windsor.

164. Leonardo, anatomical studies of head and shoulders of a man, 1510. Pen and ink. Royal Library, Windsor.

165. Leonardo, studies of Madonna and Child with a cat, ca. 1478. Pen and black chalk. Reproduced by courtesy of the Trustees of the British Museum, London.

166. Leonardo, studies for kneeling Leda and horse for *Battle of Anghiari*, ca. 1503–4. Pen and black chalk. Royal Library, Windsor.

167. Copy after Michelangelo, *Leda and the Swan,* sixteenth century. Cartoon. Royal Academy of Arts, London.

168. Leonardo, a star of Bethlehem and other plants, ca. 1505–8. Pen and ink. Royal Library, Windsor.

169. Leonardo, study for Leda's coiffure, ca. 1508. Pen and ink. Royal Library, Windsor.

170. Cesare da Sesto, copy of Leonardo's *Leda and the Swan,* early sixteenth century. Wilton House, Wiltshire. The Bridgeman Art Library.

171. Leonardo, dissection of the principal organs of a woman, ca. 1508. Pen and ink and wash over black chalk. Royal Library, Windsor.

172. Leonardo, male and female organs of generation, ca. 1508. Pen and ink. Royal Library, Windsor.

173. Leonardo, drawing of an embryo in the womb, ca. 1510. Pen and ink. Royal Library, Windsor.

174. Leonardo, studies of infants, ca. 1510. Pen and black chalk. Royal Library, Windsor.

175. Leonardo, *Madonna and Child with St. Anne and St. John,* ca. 1510–11. Cartoon in charcoal and white. National Gallery, London.

176. Dürer, *The Women's Bath,* 1496. Pen and ink. Kunsthalle, Bremen.

177. Dürer, *Sea Monster Abducting a Woman,* ca. 1498. Engraving. Reproduced by courtesy of the Trustee of the British Museum, London.

178. Cranach, *Venus,* ca. 1530s. Kunstinstitut, Frankfurt.

179. Cranach, *The Judgment of Paris,* 1530. Staatliche Kunsthalle, Karlsruhe.

180. Verrio, Heaven Room, Burghley House, England, 1686–97. Stamford Lincolnshire. English Life Publications, Derby.

181. Tintoretto, *Susanna and the Elders,* ca. 1555. Kunsthistorisches Museum, Vienna.

182. Gentileschi, *Susanna and the Elders,* ca. 1610. Schloss Weissenstein, Pommersfelden.

183. Gentileschi, *Judith Decapitating Holofernes,* ca. 1614–20. Uffizi Gallery, Florence. Art Resource.

184. Rubens, *Rape of the Daughters of Leucippus,* ca. 1616–17. Alte Pinakothek, Munich.

185. Rubens, *Hélène Fourment in a Fur Robe,* ca. 1631. Kunsthistorisches Museum, Vienna.

186. Caravaggio, *Love Triumphant,* 1598–99. Berlin-Dahlem.

187. Barbizet (after Michelangelo), *Ganymede.* Engraving. Reproduced by courtesy of the Trustees of the British Museum, London.

188. Rembrandt, *The Rape of Ganymede,* 1635. Staatliche Kunstsammlungen, Dresden.

189. Rembrandt, *Diana at the Bath,* 1630. Etching. Rijksmuseum-Stichting, Amsterdam.

190. Rembrandt, *The Return of the Prodigal Son,* 1636. Etching. Rijksmuseum-Stichting, Amsterdam.

191. Rembrandt, *Bathsheba*, 1654. Musée Louvre, Paris.

192. Boucher, *The Setting of the Sun,* 1753. Reproduced by permission of the Trustees of the Wallace Collection, London.

193. Boucher, *Miss Morphy,* 1751. Alte Pinakothek, Munich.

194. Fuseli, *The Dane King Poisoned by His Brother,* 1771. Pen and ink and wash. Graphik-Sammlung (Eth), Zurich.

195. Goya, *Blow,* 1799. Aquatint plate from *Los Caprichos* (Editions Cercle d'Art, 1960). The New York Public Library.

196. Goya, *Bury Them and Keep Quiet,* ca. 1820. Engraving from *The Disasters of War.* The New York Public Library.

CHAPTER 8:

197. Géricault, *The Raft of the Medusa,* (detail), 1819. Musée Louvre, Paris. Art Resource.

198. David, *Leonidas at Thermopylae,* 1814. Musée Louvre. Art Resource.

199. Géricault, *The Raft of the Medusa,* 1819. Musée Louvre. Art Resource.

200. Géricault, study of dissected limbs, 1818–19. Musée Fabre, Montpellier.

201. Gros, sketch for *Bucephalus Vanquished by Alexander,* 1798. Ink and wash. Private Collection. The New York Public Library.

202. Vernet, *Mazeppa and the Wolves,* 1826. Préfecture Avignon.

203. Delacroix, *The Death of Sardanapalus,* 1827. Musée Louvre, Paris.

204. Gérôme, *The Slave Market,* n.d. Sterling and Francine Clark Art Institute, Williamstown, Massachusetts.

205. Powers, *The Greek Slave,* 1843. Marble. The Corcoran Gallery of Art, Washington, gift of William Wilson Corcoran.

206. Ingres, *Roger Freeing Angelica,* 1819. Musée Louvre, Paris.

207. Manet, *Déjeuner sur l'herbe,* 1863, Musée d'Orsay, Paris.

208. Cabanel, *The Birth of Venus*, 1862. The Pennsylvania Academy of the Fine Arts.

209. Manet, *Olympia*, 1863. Musée d'Orsay, Paris.

210. Courbet, *The Bathers*, 1853. Musée Fabre, Montpellier.

211. Courbet, *Sleep*, 1866. Petit Palais, Paris. Giraudon/Art Resource.

212. Courbet, *The Origin of the World*, 1866. Whereabouts unknown. Gemini Smith, Inc., La Jolla.

213. Eakins, *The Swimming Hole*, 1883. Collection of the Modern Art Museum of Fort Worth, Museum Purchase, the Friends of Art.

214. Muybridge, *Woman Emptying Bucket of Water on Seated Companion*, 1884–85. Photographs originally published in *Animal Locomotion*, 1887. George Eastman House, Rochester, New York.

215. Rodin, female nude dancing, ca. 1900. Pencil. Musée Rodin, Paris. © ARS, New York/ADAGP, 1989.

216. Rodin, dancing figure, ca. 1900–5. Pencil with watercolor wash. National Gallery of Art, Washington, Gift of Mrs. John W. Simpson.

217. Rodin, montage sheet with two cut-out figures, ca. 1900–5. Pencil with watercolor wash. Graphic Arts Collection, Princeton University.

218. Rodin, model reclining and lifting chemise, ca. 1898. Pencil. Musée Rodin, Paris. © ARS, New York/ADAGP, 1989.

219. Rodin, *Nijinsky*, 1912. Plaster. Musée Rodin, Paris. © ARS, New York/ADAGP, 1989.

220. Rodin, *The Age of Bronze*, 1876. Plaster. Musée Rodin, Paris. © ARS, New York/ADAGP, 1989

221. Rodin, *The Danaid*, 1888. Marble. Musée Rodin, Paris, J. E. Bulloz.

222. Rodin, *The Danaid*, 1888. Marble. Musée Rodin, Paris, J. E. Bulloz.

223. Rodin, nude study for *Balzac*, 1893. Plaster. Musée Rodin, Paris. © ARS, New York/ADAGP, 1989.

224. Rodin, *Meditation Without Arms*, 1883–84. Plaster. Musée Rodin, Paris. © ARS, New York/ADAGP, 1989.

225. Rodin, *I Am Beautiful*, 1880. Plaster. Musée Rodin, Paris. © ARS, New York/ADAGP, 1989.

226. Rodin, *Christ and the Magdalene*, 1894. Plaster. The Fine Arts Museums of San Francisco. Gift of Alma de Bretteville Spreckels.

CHAPTER 9:

227. Picasso, *Les Demoiselles d'Avignon,* 1907. The Museum of Modern Art, New York. © ARS, New York/SPADEM, 1989.

228. Klimt, *Danae,* ca. 1907. Galerie Wurthle, Vienna. The New York Public Library.

229. Schiele, *Reclining Girl,* 1910. Pencil. Landesmuseum Joanneum, Graz.

230. Schiele, *Self-Portrait with Nude Model in Front of a Mirror,* 1910. Pencil. Graphische Sammlung Albertina, Vienna.

231. Schiele, *Seated Young Girl,* 1910. Watercolor and gouache. Graphische Sammlung Albertina, Vienna.

232. Kokoschka, *Murder of a Woman,* 1908–9. Pencil, ink, and watercolor. Los Angeles County Museum of Art. The Robert Gore Rifkind Center for German Expressionist Studies. © ARS, New York/Cosmopress, 1989.

233. Gauguin, *Two Tahitian Women,* 1899. The Metropolitan Museum of Art, New York.

234. Gauguin, *Fatata Te Miti,* 1892. National Gallery of Art, Washington.

235. Picasso, *Picasso in a Top Hat,* 1901. Oil and ink. Private collection. Giraudon/Art Resource. © ARS, New York/SPADEM, 1989.

236. Picasso, study for *La Vie,* 1903. Pen and ink. Private collection. The New York Public Library. © ARS, New York/SPADEM, 1989.

237. Picasso, *La Toilette,* 1906. Albright Knox Art Gallery, Buffalo, New York. Art Resource. © ARS, New York/SPADEM, 1989.

238. Cézanne, *Les Grandes Baigneuses,* 1894–1905. National Gallery, London.

239. Rousseau, *The Dream,* 1910. The Museum of Modern Art, New York. Art Resource.

240. Picasso, *Young Nude Boy,* 1906. Musée Picasso, Paris. © ARS, New York/SPADEM, 1989.

241. Matisse, *La Joie de Vivre,* 1905–6. The Barnes Foundation, Merion Station, Pennsylvania. © Succession Matisse/ARS, New York, 1989.

242. Picasso, *Two Nudes,* 1906. The Museum of Modern Art, New York. Gift of G. David Thompson in honor of Alfred H. Barr, Jr. © ARS, New York/SPADEM, 1989.

243. Braque, *Large Nude,* 1907–8. Musée des arts décoratifs, Paris. Bildarchiv Foto Marburg/ Art Resource. © ARS, New York/ADAGP, 1989.

244. Picasso, *Standing Nude,* 1908. Museum of Fine Arts, Boston. Art Resource. © ARS, New York/SPADEM, 1989.

245. Picasso, *Nude Woman,* 1910. Charcoal. The Metropolitan Museum of Art, New York. The Alfred Stieglitz Collection. © ARS, New York/SPADEM, 1989.

246. Severini, *Dynamic Hieroglyphic of the Bal Tabarin,* 1912. The Museum of Modern Art, New York. Acquired through the Lillie P. Bliss Bequest. © ARS, New York/ADAGP, 1989.

247. Meidner, *Apocalyptic Vision,* 1912. Leicestershire Museums and Art Galleries.

248. Kirchner, *Artillerymen in the Shower,* 1915. The Museum of Modern Art, New York.

249. Dix, *Souvenir of the Mirrored Halls in Brussels,* 1920. Private collection. The New York Public Library.

250. Ernst, *The Virgin Spanking the Infant Jesus Before Three Witnesses,* 1928. Private collection. Art Resource. © ARS, New York/SPADEM, 1989.

251. Ernst, *The Robing of the Bride,* 1939. Collection Peggy Guggenheim, Venice. © ARS, New York/SPADEM, 1989.

252. Miró, *Oh! One of Those Men Who's Done All That,* 1925. Galerie Maeght, Paris. © ARS, New York/ADAGP, 1989.

253. Miró, *Standing Woman,* 1937, courtesy Pierre Matisse Gallery, New York. ARS, New York/ADAGP, 1989.

254. Magritte, *The Rape,* 1934. Courtesy of the Menil Collection, Houston. © Herscovici/ ARS, New York, 1989.

255. Magritte, *The Unattainable Woman,* 1928. Private collection. © Herscovici/ARS, New York, 1989.

256. Buñuel and Dali, still from film *Un Chien Andalou,* 1928. Photograph. The Museum of Modern Art, New York.

257. Dali, *The Great Masturbator,* 1929. Teatro-Museo Dali, Figueras. The New York Public Library. © DeMart Pro Arte/ARS, New York, 1989.

258. Picasso, *Family at the Edge of the Sea,* 1923. Musée Picasso, Paris. Art Resource. © ARS, New York/SPADEM, 1989.

259. Picasso, *The Three Dancers*, 1925. The Tate Gallery, London. © ARS, New York/ SPADEM, 1989.

260. Picasso, *Seated Bather,* 1929. The Museum of Modern Art, New York. Mrs. Simon Guggenheim Fund. © ARS, New York/SPADEM, 1989.

261. Picasso, *The Mirror,* 1932. Musée Picasso, Paris. Giraudon/Art Resource. © ARS, New York/SPADEM, 1989.

262. Balthus, *The Nude with a Cat,* 1949. National Gallery of Victoria, Melbourne. © ARS, New York/SPADEM, 1989

263. Balthus, *Toilette de Cathy,* 1933. Musée National d'Art Moderne, Centre Georges Pompidou, Paris. © ARS, New York/SPADEM, 1989.

264. Picasso, *Design for a Monument,* 1928. Pen and ink. Musée Picasso, Paris. © ARS, New York/SPADEM, 1989.

265. Dali, *Soft Construction with Boiled Beans; Premonition of Civil War,* 1936. Philadelphia Museum of Art: Louise and Walter Arensberg Collection. © DeMart Pro Arte/ARS, New York, 1989.

266. Bellmer, *The Doll,* 1934. Photograph. Galerie André-François Petit, Paris. © ARS, New York/ADAGP, 1989.

267. Konieczny, *New Arrivals at Buchenwald,* 1945. Watercolor. Buchenwald Museum.

CHAPTER 10:

268. Bernini, *Apollo and Daphne,* 1622–25. Marble. Gallery Borghese, Rome. Newsweek Books.

269. De Kooning, *Suburb in Havana*, 1958. Collection Mr. and Mrs. Lee V. Eastman. Bruce C. Jones/Fine Arts Photo.

270. Giacometti, *Standing Woman I*, 1960. Bronze. Foundation Maeght, St. Paul de Vence.

271. Giacometti, *The Glade,* 1950. Bronze. Foundation Maeght, St. Paul de Vence.

272. Giacometti, *Standing Woman,* 1959. Bronze. Sabine Weiss. ADAGP, 1989.

273. Giacometti, *Four Figurines on a Tall Stand,* 1950. Bronze. Collection M. et Mme. Adrien Maeght. Gallery Maeght, New York. ADAGP, 1989.

274. Giacometti, *Standing Woman,* 1957. Bronze. Sabine Weiss.

275. Moore, *Drawing of Seated Figure,* 1933. Pencil, chalk, and wash. Private collection. Reproduced by kind permission of the Henry Moore Foundation.

276. Moore, *Two-Piece Reclining Figure No. 1*, 1959. Bronze. Chelsea School of Art, London. Reproduced by kind permission of the Henry Moore Foundation.

277. Moore, *Two-Piece Reclining Figure No. 1*, 1959. Bronze. Chelsea School of Art, London. Reproduced by kind permission of the Henry Moore Foundation.

278. Moore, *Reclining Figure,* 1939. Elm wood. The Detroit Institute of Arts. Gift of the Dexter M. Ferry, Jr., Trustee Corporation.

279. Moore, *Reclining Figure,* 1939. Elm wood. The Detroit Institute of Arts. Gift of the Dexter M. Ferry, Jr., Trustee Corporation.

280. Moore, *Reclining Mother and Child,* 1960–61. Bronze. Minerals Separation, Ltd., London. Reproduced by kind permission of the Henry Moore Foundation.

281. Moore, *Reclining Mother and Child,* 1960–61. Bronze. Minerals Separation, Ltd., London. Reproduced by kind permission of the Henry Moore Foundation.

282. Neel, *The Pregnant Woman,* 1971. Robert Miller Gallery, New York.

283. Neel, *Self-Portrait,* 1980. Robert Miller Gallery, New York.

284. Kahlo, *What the Water Gave Me,* 1939. Collection Tomás Fernández Marquez, Mexico City. Photo by Raul Salinas.

285. Kahlo, *The Broken Column,* 1944. Collection Delores Olmedo, Mexico City. Photo by Raul Salinas.

286. Matta, *Composition,* 1945. Reproduced in *History of Surrealist Painting* (Weidenfeld & Nicholson, 1959).

287. Matta, *The Prophetor,* 1954. Reproduced in *History of Surrealist Painting* (Weidenfeld & Nicholson, 1959).

288. Matta, *The Glazer,* 1944. Destroyed; reproduced in *Érotique du Surréalisme* (Jean-Jacques Pauven, 1965).

289. Bourgeois, *Cumul I,* 1969. Marble. Musée National d'Art Moderne, Pompidou Center, Paris. Robert Miller Gallery, New York.

290. Bourgeois, *Torso Self-Portrait,* 1963–64. Bronze. Robert Miller Gallery, New York.

291. Bourgeois, *Fragile Goddess,* 1970. Bronze. Robert Miller Gallery, New York.

292. Bourgeois, *Filette,* 1968. Latex. Robert Miller Gallery, New York.

293. Bourgeois, *Trani Episode,* 1971–72. Hydrocal and latex. Robert Miller Gallery, New York.

294. Frink, *Seated Man,* 1984. Plaster. Courtesy of the artist.

295. Frink, *Falling Birdman,* ca. 1952. Ink and wash. Private collection, London.

296. Frank, *Woman with Outstretched Arms,* 1975. Ceramic. Courtesy of the artist and Zabriskie Gallery.

297. Frank, *Lovers,* 1974. Courtesy Zabriskie Gallery, New York.

298. Matisse, *The Dance,* 1909. Hermitage Museum, Leningrad. Iskusstvo Publishers, Moscow.

299. Matisse, *The Artist and His Model,* 1919. Oil on canvas, 25⅝ x 28¾ inches. Courtesy of Mr. and Mrs. Donald B. Marron.

300. Matisse, *The Swimming Pool,* 1952. Gouache on paper cutouts. The Museum of Modern Art, New York.

301. Matisse, *The Hair,* 1952. Paper cutout. Private collection. Verve Ed. Teriade, Paris. SPADEM.

302. Titian, *The Punishment of Marsyas,* 1570. National Museum, Kromeriz.

INDEX

Boldface indicates illustration

Abstract expressionism
 departures, 384–85
 philosophical basis, 379, 384
 reflected in film, 384–85
 techniques, 357, 384
Abu Simbel, 107, **108, 109**
Academic style, 287
Adam and Eve Getting the Forbidden Fruit, St. Botolph's Church, **172**
Adam and Eve Reproached by the Lord, Hildesheim Cathedral, **170**
Alberti, Leon Battista
 on the naked figure, 200–2
 on realism in art, 202, 204, 210, 213
 on Renaissance artists, 195–96
Altamira cave, 39, **40–41,** 60
Ammannati
 Fountain of Neptune, Nereid, and Triton, **195**
Animal games (neolithic wall painting), **93**
Apollinaire, Guillaume, 349
Apsaras, 135
Aretino, Pietro, 227, 232
Artaud, Antonin, 373
Artists
 artistic progress, 198–99, 219
 book publishing, 255
 in concentration camps, 377
 as craftsmen, 196–98
 frenzied, 294–95

later careers, 423, 424
 modern status, 277, 327
 as rebels, 287
 relationship with models, 27–28, 205, 313–14
 rising status, 232–33
 women, 264, 400, 411, 428
Atlas Mountains, North Africa, 67
Avenue of Priapus, **114**

Bacon, Francis, 161–62
 Three Studies for Figures at the Base of a Crucifixion, **160, 161,** 163
Baldung
 Death and the Woman, **180**
Balthus, 372–73
 Cathy Dressing, **374**
 The Guitar Lesson, **372**
 The Nude with a Cat, 372, **373**
 and Theatre of Cruelty, 373
Barbizet
 Ganymede, **272**
Baroque art, 279
Battle of Kadesh (stone relief), 109, **110**
Beauty
 convulsive, 363–64
 cult, 35
 Greek ideal, 27–28, 31–32
 ideal, 3, 20, 27–29, 31–32
 Judeo-Christian ideal, 3, 32
 proportion and, 3
 Surrealist, 363–64
Bellmer, Hans, 377

The Doll, **378**
Benjamin, Walter, 379
Bernini, Gianlorenzo
 Apollo and Daphne, **380,** 382–83
Bison (Paleolithic carving), **53**
Body proportions, 3, 20
Botticelli, Sandro, 214–15
 Birth of Venus, **190, 212,** 213–14, 218
 body portrayal by, 211–12
 Primavera, **214**
 special genius, 214
 techniques, 232
Boucher, François
 Miss Morphy, **281**
 The Setting of the Sun, **280**
 technique, 279, 281
Bourgeois, Louise, 407, 409–11
 Cumil I, **409**
 Filette, **411**
 Fragile Goddess, **411**
 Self-Portrait Torso, **410**
 Trani Episode, **412**
Braque, Georges, 346
 Large Nude, **347**
Breton, André, 356–57, 363–64, 377
Brunelleschi, Filippo, 196–97, 204
Bull cults, 93–94
Buñuel, Luis, 364
 Un Chien Andalou (film), **363**
Buxo Cave, Cantabria, 61

Cabanel, Alexandre, 301–2, 304
 The Birth of Venus, **302**

death, 214
Judith and Holofernes, **192,** 204–5, 207–8
personal characteristics, 204–5
place in history, 204, 214
sexual nuances in work, 205, 207–8
Donne, John, 279
Drever, James, 45
Dual sexuality
Dionysian, 117
modern works, 370, 397
primitive art, 63, 65
Duncan, Isadora, 315
Durer, Albrecht
graphic work, 255
personal characteristics, 235–36
Sea Monster Abducting a Woman, **256,** 257
Self-Portrait (naked), **234,** 235
studies of nature, 255
The Women's Bath, **254,** 255

Eakins, Thomas, 307–10
The Swimming Hole, **308**
Egyptian art
classes represented, 82
elegance, 104–5
formalization, 82
status of sexes in, 79, 101–2
Egyptian civilization
afterlife, 96–102, 106–7
Old and New Kingdoms, 107
organization, 80, 104–6
visual nature, 79
El Castillo caves, 1, 36, 43–45, 52–53
Éluard, Paul, 356, 365
Engels, Frederich, 90–91
Engravings, 255
Ernst, Max
The Robing of the Bride, **358**
techniques, 357
The Virgin Spanking the Infant Jesus Before Three Witnesses, **356**
youth, 354, 357–58

Eroticism
contraception and, 150
Greek drinking vessels, 129–30
nudes and, 27, 147, 262–63
technology and, 407
Etchings, 276–77
Eve, Autun Cathedral, **175**
Existentialism, 388
Expulsion from Paradise, Hildesheim Cathedral, **171**

Farnese Bull (Roman), **158**
Female exhibitionist (stone carving), **176**
Fertility
cave rituals, 61
cult of Dionysis, 118, 121
cult of Osiris, 96, 98–100
images, 65–66
Fertility figures
Egyptian, 85–86
Gothic, 175, **176**
Neolithic, 91, **92**
paleolithic, **62, 64**
uses, 63, 65
Fertility goddess (Neolithic, Anatolia), 5, 91, **92**
Figures in Complex Embrace (Indian temple carving), **136**
Film
early, 309–10
as modern art, 327, 363–64, 384–85
Nazi propaganda, 374
Fish, sexual symbolism, **50,** 51, 98, 150
Floating World, 144
Fountain of Neptune, Nereid, and Triton (Ammannati), **195**
Frank, Mary, 414–16
Lover, **417**
Woman with Outstretched Arms, **415**
Frink, Elisabeth, 412–14
Falling Birdman, **414**
Seated Man, **413**
Frottage, 357

Fuseli, Henry, 282
The Dane King Poisoned by His Brother, 282, **283**
Futurism
on lust, 350
tenets, 350–51
on violence, 350

Gauguin, Paul, 332–35, 341
Fatata Te Miti, **334**
Two Tahitian Women, **333**
Genitals, female
early representations, 45, **46, 50,** 51
Indian stylized form, 136
painting, 34
realistic painting of, 307, 328
Genitals, male
avoidance of depicting, 309
burial, 102
as center of sin, 168
circumcision, 102, **103**
at Delos, **114**
early representations, 45, **47,** 51
of foes, 98
painting, 32
in Roman art, 165
See also Phallic symbols
Gentileschi, Artemisia, 264–66
Judith Decapitating Holofernes, **265**
Susanna and the Elders, **263**
Géricault, Théodore, 304–5
death, 291
early work, 290
obsession, 291
The Raft of the Medusa, **286,** 288, **289,** 290–92
study of dissected limbs, **291**
Gérôme, Jean-Léon, 297, 304, 307
The Slave Market, 297, **298,** 301
Ghiberti, Lorenzo, 196–99
Abraham Sacrificing Isaac, **198**
The Creation of Eve, **199**
Giacometti, Alberto
existentialist skew, 388, 392
Femme Debout I, **386**

BOOK MARK

*The text of this book was
composed in the typefaces Granjon and Cochin by
Monotype Composition Company, Inc.,
Baltimore, Maryland.*

*Designed by Marysarah Quinn
assisted by
Debbie Jay and Laurie Jewell*